THE COOK'S GUIDE

Macmillan Publishing Co., Inc.
New York

Macmillan Publishing Co., Inc.
866 Third Avenue, New York, N.Y. 10022

Library of Congress Cataloging in Publication Data
Main entry under title:
The cook's guide

    1. Cookery.
TX651.S93   641.5   77-7138
ISBN 0-02-578780-2

First printing 1977

Printed in Great Britain

Introduction

To eat well is a pleasure; to cook well is an art – and one that is definitely
well worth learning for everyone.
THE COOK'S GUIDE is a comprehensive guide to the craft of cooking,
invaluable both to the complete beginner and the enthusiastic cook
who wishes to brush up on technique. It starts with the basics – a
well-planned kitchen, useful equipment and sensible storage arrangements
are essentials for any aspiring Julia Child – then covers the arts of freezing
and preserving, including pickling and chutney-making, jam- and
marmalade-making, and canning.
The necessary foundation for any good cook's repertoire is an
understanding of the properties and uses of such staples as flour, sugar,
eggs, milk, etc., and the heart of the book opens with an entire chapter on
this subject. Basic cooking techniques are not forgotten either; and how to
prepare and cook meat, fish, vegetables and fruits forms a comprehensive
chapter on its own, complete with easy-reference charts to give a see-at-a-
glance view of what to cook, how and for how long. The section concludes
with an entire chapter on what are considered to be the traditional
crowning glories of any cook – stocks, soups, breads, pastry and cakes.
The different methods are all explained with easy-to-follow basic recipes
and often, for further clarity, accompanied by step-by-step pictures.
THE COOK'S GUIDE is a 'must' addition to every bookshelf, an
invaluable reference volume for every cook.

Contents

Chapter One

Kitchen planning

For cooking to be a pleasure, your kitchen needs to have a pleasant atmosphere and to be well designed. So knowing some basic facts about design will be helpful whether you are planning a completely new kitchen, remodelling an old one or trying to make the best of what already exists.

A kitchen cannot be planned in a vacuum. It must be seen in relation to the rest of the house and the functions it will serve. Will it be used only for cooking? For cooking plus family dining? For meals with guests? Will it be the center of family activity, or will it be used by no more than one or two people at a time?

Naturally, the answers to these questions depend in part on the size of the room. Remember that everybody has a tendency to gravitate toward the kitchen so, if possible, arrange a place where people won't be in the way. Having decided how your kitchen will relate to the rest of the house, you will need to make decisions about large appliances and equipment. The two major ones will be split-level cooking versus a conventional stove and the size of the refrigerator (see below for pros and cons). In addition, you must decide whether you want various other items – dishwasher, freezer, waste disposal, microwave oven – now, or in the future. Will the washing machine and dryer be located in the kitchen? And the heating or hot-water supply? All these decisions must be made early since they will require electrical connections, water and waste pipes.

A well-planned working space is a prerequisite for any kitchen in order for it to function efficiently.

Fortunately, most ready-made kitchen units come in standard sizes. Therefore all you really need to know to start planning is (a) whether to consider standard-size units, and (b) the range and types of units available. If you design and build your own units, or have them built, they can be made to fit the space available.

Having made these basic decisions you are now ready to draw up your kitchen plan. On graph paper using a suitable scale – 1:10 or 1:12 for small and medium-sized kitchens; 1:20 for large – draw a carefully measured outline of your kitchen. Take accurate measurements of walls, windows, doorways, projections and recesses along the walls. Note at the side of the plan, ceiling and windowsill heights. Plot on the plan the locations of existing services: gas main, waste water pipe to external drain, water supply and hot water pipe. Note in the margin whether these can be moved and in what directions.

Next, make cutouts of major appliances, kitchen units, sink unit, table and chairs. Mark what they are in different colors (an edging of color will make them stand out on the plan). Now you are ready to try out any number of arrangements. If you are undecided about a split-level stove, or uncertain whether a standard or larger refrigerator/freezer is best, make cutouts for each size and try out both types. Remember, it may be wise to allow now for possible future additions (eg waste or garbage compactor). Don't be discouraged; only by examining all the alternatives will the best layout be attained.

The most important part of the kitchen is the work center where meals are prepared, cooked and cleared away. The three major units – sink, stove and refrigerator – should be grouped relatively close together with good countertop and storage space between each to minimize walking and crisscrossing the area. A line drawn correcting these three places forms the *work triangle*. The sum of the sides of the work triangle should be at least 12 feet (360 centimeters) but no more than 22 feet (660 centimeters). A triangle of less than 12 feet (360 centimeters) probably indicates less than adequate working space; more than 22 feet (660 centimeters) that you will have too much walking to do between appliances. A conveniently sized work center takes up no more than 100 square feet (9 square meters). If your kitchen is larger than this the extra space can be used for a dining area or snack bar for breakfast and family meals. Or it could be a children's play area or separate laundry section.

The shape and size of your kitchen largely determines the overall layout. These generally fall into four distinct types: galley, corridor, L-shaped and U-shaped.

The **Galley Kitchen** has all units along one wall. Provided the maximum distance between the furthest appliances is no more than 12-19 feet (360-540 centimeters), this plan works relatively well, though two or three people in the area simultaneously will cause congestion. Storage and countertops are less abundant than with other shapes. In small apartments or studios, the length of the unit can be reduced by means of a hot plate-refrigerator-sink unit, though work space is non-existent and storage scanty. Often these units are fitted with doors that incorporate more storage space as well as hiding the kitchen when it is not in use.

The **Corridor Kitchen** is a relatively narrow kitchen with a door at each end and enough width for units to run along the facing walls. It is best to have sink and

L-shaped kitchen

Corridor kitchen

U-shaped kitchen

Galley kitchen

8

stove on the same wall, because carrying hot saucepans across the area can conflict with other people walking through. Place the refrigerator on the opposite wall. The corridor should be at least wide enough to allow cabinet doors to open easily.

The **L-Shaped Kitchen** can have appliances and work surfaces along adjacent walls. This creates an efficient work triangle and leaves a large area of the kitchen free for other uses, such as an eating area or snack bar.

The **U-Shaped Kitchen** gives maximum storage and counter space and minimum walking distances, and is potentially the most efficient in terms of layout. Frequently one side of the **U** is a double-sided divider separating the cooking and dining areas.

Major Planning Points

Sinks
The sink will probably be the first item to be placed on the floor plan, since its location is likely to be restricted by the position of the existing plumbing. Drains are expensive, if not impossible, to move; so you should think twice and get expert advice before contemplating a major change. Usually the sink is placed under a window, which gives good light and often a pleasant view, but a window is not vital and an efficient plan should not be sacrificed just for the sake of having a view. Check that the sill height is a minimum of 33 inches (84 centimeters) to allow the sink to fit neatly under it. If possible do not place the sink in a corner where it will be difficult for a second person to help with washing the dishes.

Many types of sink are available: stainless steel or porcelain, single or double units, shallow or deep, with waste disposal unit or without, with single or double drainboard. If you have the room, a double sink with two drainboards or countertops and single swivel faucet allows for the most efficient dishwashing. Dirty dishes on the left if you are right-handed, are washed in the first basin, rinsed in the second and placed in a dish-rack on the right. Do not dismiss the deep sink because most kitchen units have shallow ones. It is especially convenient for washing large saucepans and for soaking (and hiding!) them during meals. On the other hand, you have to reach down further to get to things at the bottom.

Stoves
Stoves, especially gas types, are best placed away from windows and doors, because drafts increase fire risk and cause heat loss. Also a wall can be faced with a heat resistant and washable material which can be easily cleaned.

If you relocate the gas stove, make sure the gas pipe can be brought to the new location without major difficulty. Have the stove attached to the pipe with a flexible hose so that it can be moved out for cleaning.

Be sure there is room to open the oven door conveniently. Note where your chosen model is hinged (most are hinged at the bottom or on the left). A left-hinged oven, for instance, will be more convenient situated at the left end of your plan; if it is placed at the right end, you will always have to walk around the door to get back to your work area. For either a side-hinged or a bottom-hinged door you will need at least $3\frac{1}{2}$ feet (100 centimeters) of space in front of the oven to allow the cook to stand in front of the open door.

In addition to the stove's location, you will have to decide between gas and electricity, a subject on which many people have strong feelings. Gas cooking has the advantage of rapid regulation of heat, whereas, while electricity changes its heat output slowly, it provides a uniform constant heat. (If a pot boils over on gas you turn off the supply; on electricity you lift the pot off the heat.) Since gas tends to be cheaper than electricity in most areas, a gas stove will be cheaper to run, especially if you also use gas for heating. It is possible to have both gas and electricity for cooking, especially if you choose a split-level system, for instance gas top burners and an electric oven and broiler, or two electric elements and two gas top burners with either gas or electric ovens.

In choosing a stove you will first have to consider the space available – there are standard-size widths plus many non-standard sizes. Second, you will have to decide on the desirability of other features: the size, location, and number of ovens (and broilers), the self-cleaning oven; a rotisserie. The big decision may be between a split-level system and a conventional stove. A split-level system, currently fashionable, has the advantage of an eye level oven and below cooktop storage for pans. A disadvantage in small kitchens is the reduction of work space. Additionally, if top burners and oven are far apart, you may find yourself trying to watch something in the broiler while finishing off a sauce on a top burner.

Refrigerators
Since most refrigerator doors are hinged on the right (although you can order some models with left-side hinges), be sure to place yours so that you will not have to walk around the door. Often this means putting the refrigerator at the right end of a row. Ideally, the door should be able to open fully to the side so that shelves and trays can be easily removed for washing. In some models the door need not open this far for removing shelves.

As a general rule the refrigerator should not be placed beside the stove because radiant heat from the oven might heat the refrigerator's casing causing the motor to work overtime. New refrigerators are supposed to be well enough insulated to withstand the heat but, to be on the safe side, leave a 6 inch (15 centimeter) gap between the two. With a low refrigerator, continue the countertop to cover the gap and use the space for tray storage or hanging dish towels on a pull-out rack. Before you build in a refrigerator find out where and how much ventilation will be needed. Some need the circulation only at the top or bottom, others require the unit to be positioned at least several inches away from the wall.

Your biggest decisions will be the size of your refrigerator, and whether it should have a freezer section with a separate door. This may be at the top or side and is for longer term use than the small standard compartment in the unit. You will probably find a unit standing $5\frac{1}{2}$ feet (170 centimeters) to $6\frac{1}{4}$ feet (190 centimeters) with separate freezer best suited to your needs and less subject to over-stuffing and, therefore, inefficiency. It will allow you to shop weekly, or even less frequently. Single and career people especially will benefit from having a large freezer section.

Even if you plan to get a separate deep freezer, you will find a refrigerator-freezer handy. Since the refrigerator is located in the work triangle, things used regularly in small amounts in cooking (stock, parsley stems, other herbs, chopped onion), homemade baby foods, ice cream, fish sticks, other prepared foods, leftover meats and ice are all available. Also, this unit contains the freezer the family will open and frost up, saving you the even harder work of defrosting the larger deep freezer unit more frequently.

Study the layout of the refrigerator carefully before you buy. Is the vegetable compartment a good size for you? Is the egg tray large enough? Do other door shelves suit your needs? Where will you put the milk, taller bottles? Seriously consider getting a self-defrosting model – some have self-defrosting freezers which make life easier. Most refrigerators are electric, but you may find some gas models. The latter are silent, having no motors that make a noise.

Other large appliances

A deep freezer need not be located in either the work triangle or kitchen, since it is used for long-term storage rather than for frequently used items. Ideally, you will open it once a day or less to remove that day's or tomorrow's food. Your choice will be between front-opening and chest type models. The front-opening freezer is less economical to run because cold air escapes more easily when the door is opened, but it takes up less floor space and contents can be seen more easily. It should be placed in a cool area to keep running costs to a minimum. (See pages 26 to 29 for more detailed information).

A dishwasher is usually located near the sink because it requires both water and waste plumbing. Generally it is built-in, though some can be rolled up to the sink and attached, and others are countertop size. Look for ease of loading, flexibility of positioning glassware and cups, and the total capacity. The larger it is the more useful it will be – remember you do not run it until it is full, which may be once a day or every second or third day.

You will need to know whether your chosen model needs both hot and cold water connections or cold water only. If both, check that your hot water supply is adequate and a suitable type. If only cold water is used, the machine will heat it electrically and is, therefore, likely to be more expensive to run. All controls are on the front of the machine and are, usually, self-explanatory.

Ventilation is the next major problem area to be considered. It's one thing to cook a delicious, pungent-smelling meal but quite another to live with its lingering odor through the following hours or even days! Obviously the easiest form of ventilation is an open window, but many kitchens are now built without windows and sometimes (in the middle of winter, for instance) it is just not convenient or possible to open it even when you have one. The two most popular forms of artificial ventilation are exhaust fans, usually placed high up on an exterior wall and a ventilation hood which is fitted over the top of the stove.

Work surfaces and storage units

Most manufacturers' units are 36 inches (90 centimeters) high, which is considered a good all-purpose height for the average-sized woman. (Some units can be found to suit shorter or taller people). In actual fact various tasks require different work heights: 36 inches (90 centimeters) for the sink, 29-31 inches (75-80 centimeters) for mixing (lower for pastry rolling) and 31-36 inches (80-90 centimeters) for cooking, though the lower height becomes dangerous with small children around. But against these ideals must be balanced the desirability of a continuous work surface which is more flexible to use and easier to keep clean. In a corridor or U-shaped kitchen one area might be designed at a lower height to accommodate preparation tasks.

On your floor plan be sure to place work surfaces beside the stove (or stove top unit), sink and refrigerator. Note these minimum requirements: 18-24 inches (45-60 centimeters) on the handle side of the refrigerator; 24-36 inches (60-90 centimeters) on each side of the sink for washing and food preparation; and 24 inches (60 centimeters) on one side of the stove and 12 inches (30 centimeters) on the other if the stove is at the end of a row. In addition, try to fit in a 36-inch (90-centimeter) mixing area plus a similarly sized serving space near the stove.

Where a work space serves two uses, take the larger dimension and add 12 inches (30 centimeters). Thus, for example, a stove and sink on the same wall would be separated by 48 inches (120 centimeters) of counter space.

Most kitchen unit manufacturers supply work surfaces of any length required, so bridge over all storage areas, dishwashers, washing machines and dryers.

Most surfaces, being laminated plastic, will be spoiled by contact with pans straight from the oven. A built-in marble slab, wooden chooping board or a ceramic tile area will take care of this problem.

Storage units are of three basic sorts. Base cabinets are usually at least 24 inches (60 centimeters) deep. Wall-hung cabinets are shallower, often no more than 12-13 inches (30-32.5 centimeters) deep and should start no more than 5 feet (150 centimeters) above the floor, or 24 inches (60 centimeters) above the countertop. They should either reach the ceiling or have false fronts (or sliding doors if space is short) to fill in between top and ceiling. Exposed cabinet tops accumulate terrible amounts of greasy dust. Tall units are as deep as undercounter units and are used for general shelved storage, cleaning supplies and brooms. If your plan allows, at least one or two of these taller units would be most useful.

Heating

At the floor plan stage remember to consider the most efficient methods of heating and, especially, placement of any heating units. As a rule, the kitchen tends to be a warm – if not the warmest – room. In a large kitchen you will probably want more heat, preferably at the non-cooking end. Baseboard heating along one wall might be adequate or perhaps an extra-tall but narrow radiator. Try not to have table seating against a radiator, or you will have constant complaints.

Electricity

Once your floor plan is in order you are ready to design your electrical layout. This consists of two parts: electrical outlets and lighting. Be generous with both.

You will need one outlet for each built-in (present or potential) electrical appliance (stove, wall oven, refrigerator, waste disposal, dishwasher, ventilation hood over stove, washing machine and clothes dryer). In addition each work area should have a double outlet to take care of small appliances (mixer, coffee grinder and pot, blender, radio) which are likely to be used in several different locations. Be sure the rest of the kitchen is adequately supplied.

Make sure all outlets for large appliances are accessible – an outlet at baseboard level behind a dishwasher or washing machine is not reachable. It is advisable to have a separate special appliance outlet for each appliance wired to the main source, or a circuit breaker to prevent overloading.

Good lighting is essential even during the day. And except in small kitchens you will have at least two areas with different lighting requirements, namely the cooking/preparation section and the eating/living section. In the cooking/food preparation area, fluorescent lighting fittings provide a good level of illumination and can be attached neatly under wall-hung cabinets to light work surfaces where good illumination is most needed. Since these light sources are between you and your work rather than behind you, you will not be working in your own shadow. These should switch on independent of all other lights.

This part of the kitchen will also need an overhead light for general illumination so you can see into cabinets. This could be

either fluorescent or incandescent (tungsten), and should switch on and off independent of both undercounter and eating area lighting – in an eat-in kitchen there is great advantage in turning off the cooking-area lights when the meal is served!

Since fluorescent lighting is rather harsh for general illumination, you may decide on incandescent lighting for the eating area. But whatever your choice, put the lights for the two areas on separate On/Off switches and be sure a switch is beside each kitchen door. Remember a light can be controlled by two switches. Thus you may want a light switch by the back outside door and another by the door

A streamlined L-shaped kitchen combines efficiency with comfort—a compact work space and dining area.

to the hall or dining room. This will allow you to enter a dark kitchen, light it, walk through and switch off the light as you leave by the other door. Locate switches on the opening side of the door frame not behind the door on the hinge side.

Fluorescent lights are more economical than other types if you remember not to switch on and off frequently. This is because the starter (which also burns out before the tube) uses a lot of power. So 'save electricity, switch it off' does not

A pressure cooker can be an invaluable investment – with savings for the cook in time, energy and even fuel.

apply. Unless you will be out of the kitchen for more than an hour, don't bother to switch off.

Flooring

Floor finishes need to be abrasion resistant, since they have to stand up to heavy wear. Unglazed ceramic floor tiles are attractive, durable, easily kept clean and not hard on the feet. Be sure to select the nonslip type. They are best laid on a concrete floor. Wood floors can be sealed and polished or covered with sealed cork floor tiles, vinyl tiles or vinyl sheet flooring or linoleum. Also possible are heavy-duty, washable, stain-resistant carpet tiles or indoor/outdoor carpeting.

Finally, since you can't do everything yourself, you will have to deal with builders, plumbers and electricians. You will probably find that the workmen know their jobs and do them well. However, there is usually an intermediary – a contractor or architect – and your ideas and instructions may not always reach the workmen. Therefore, get to know them, respect their craftsmanship but be ready to ask lots of questions. Tell them what you want done and why – do not depend on others to have done this! Point out special features or oddities you want to save or emphasize, so they will treat them carefully. Stick to your original plan unless you have good reason to change it. Remember, changes will be expensive and you will be paying for them.

Before the builders arrive double-check

the plans (yours and the architect's or builder's), including all measurements. See that doors and windows are correctly positioned. Check the positioning of lights, light switches, outlets, water (cold, hot, waste) and gas pipes. If you want unusual or specific fittings (windows, doors, lights, cabinets) learn for yourself whether they are available from your local supplier. Too often you are told something is unavailable only at the crisis point (after the hole for the new window is made, for instance).

Before the plumbers leave, make sure the secondary cut-off valves are accessible and that taps for built-in appliances are reachable by a non-athlete. If you do not know, ask the plumber where the main water supply valve is (whether outside); this will be your best chance to learn. Also be sure plumbers install a back-up valve to prevent waste water from a sink, dishwasher or clotheswasher contaminating the water supply.

Small equipment, storage and maintenance

The choice of large appliances – stove, refrigerator, freezer – has already been discussed; now the decisions are smaller equipment, storage and maintenance.

Equipment

Having the right tool for the job makes any cook's task easier, quicker and more efficient. However, this does not mean that you should buy gadgets which you will seldom use. Your choice of utensils must depend on the life you lead and your style of eating. Start with a few well-designed tools and collect others when the need arises.

Cookware

The cookware you choose is important, because you will probably use it for many years. Check that saucepans and frying pans balance well both on the stove and in the hand – they should not be too heavy to lift when full. Handles should be well insulated, securely fixed and comfortable to hold. Lids should fit tightly.

Choose a heavy-bottomed pan, since it conducts heat better and prevents sticking and scorching. If you think you will do a lot of oven cooking, get pans with oven-proof handles which can double as casseroles. A non-stick surface is not essential for most uses and requires extra care to avoid scratching. Although matched sets look attractive, unmatched pans suited for different uses are far more practical. Saucepans present a hard choice because each type of metal has advantages and drawbacks.

Tin-lined copper with a heavy bottom is probably the best heat conductor and the quickest to respond to temperature changes, but it is expensive and needs constant attention to keep the copper gleaming. Excessively high heat will cause the tin to melt, and after some years of use, even with the best of care, the pans will have to be re-tinned.

Aluminum has good heat diffusion, but no matter how expensive, it will become scratched and pitted. Certain foods, especially acid ones and those containing egg (which becomes discolored), should not be cooked in aluminum pans.

Stainless steel is a poor heat conductor unless the bottom is made of a combination of metals. But it is long-lasting and durable.

Vitreous enamel on pressed steel or cast iron conducts heat well and the finish is easy to clean. Saucepans are heavy and expensive. Cheap soft enamel pans are unsatisfactory because they tend to be light and thin-bottomed, and they chip easily.

Corning-Ware® and other glass ceramic

saucepans with removable handles are attractive and easy to care for. They are good for boiling and stew-type dishes but sauces tend to burn in them because they retain heat too well. They should not be the only type of pan you own.

Basic needs

To start, a small saucepan with pouring lips on each side, two or three saucepans of different sizes, a 9-inch (23-centimeter) frying pan and one or two casseroles should be sufficient. Oval casseroles are practical because they can hold a chicken or whole fish as well as stews and soups. Casserole dishes should not be used on top of the stove if they are labelled *ovenproof* or *heatproof*, because they cannot stand direct heat. If they are called *flameproof*, however, they can be placed over direct heat.

A pressure cooker, although not essential, can be very useful for a busy cook. And, with the escalating cost of fuel, it also represents a considerable saving in cooking costs. In the interest of economy, when you buy a roasting pan, consider getting a large oval baking dish of heavy metal. In addition to poultry and roasts, you will find it useful for *gratins* and a variety of other dishes. A roasting pan should fit into oven and broiler easily with space for circulation all around. It should be of heavy enough metal to put on top of the stove for making gravy. A kettle, deep-frying pan and omelet pan are all nice to have but not essential. The kettle should have a comfortable insulated handle and good pouring spout. Choose a strong, deep-frying pan with draining

basket and lid. Two handles are useful, since they make it easier to lift when full. An omelet pan should not be too large (7-8 inches [18-20 centimeters] is easiest to handle). It should be of heavy metal and have sloping sides. Use it only for omelets and crêpes and sticking will never be a problem. Directions for seasoning and care come with the pan.

Baking equipment depends on what you are likely to make. Cake pans and baking sheets that nest well take up less storage space. A non-stick finish reduces the difficulty of getting a cake out after baking (as does a loose-bottomed pan), but care must be taken not to mar the finish; never cut pieces from a cake still in this type of pan. A pie plate can be used for both double and single crust pies and tarts. A flan ring and baking sheet are used for European free-standing pies.

Basic aids

A selection of good tools will help you to

work more efficiently in the kitchen. Most important are knives, for dull or poor ones are slow and frustrating to work with. Choose high-quality ones of stainless or carbon steel. Handles should be comfortable to hold and blades should be riveted to the shank of the handle, so they will not work loose in use.

For your first knives choose a large heavy chopping knife, a medium length filleting knife and a vegetable knife. These can be used for almost everything except bread and horizontal cake slicing, so a bread knife should also be given priority. In time a carving knife and fork are essential, but meantime a good kitchen knife makes an adequate substitute. Along with your knives be sure to get a knife sharpener or whetstone, because all kitchen knives need frequent sharpening.

A serrated-edge stainless-steel knife is useful for foods that are discolored by other metals. A blunt, wide-bladed knife is used for spreading icings and frostings

To sharpen a knife, stroke it across the steel from base to top, diagonally.

With the same motion, stroke the other side of the edge on the underside.

rather than for cutting but if you intend to do a lot of cake-making, it is a very useful investment. Its limber blade means it can double as a spatula and cake server.

A can opener, either hand-held, with a key that turns the cutting point, or wall-mounted, is an essential kitchen tool.

Get a good corkscrew of either the type wine waiters use or the kind with a round cap which fits the top of the bottle. The latter's advantage is that less muscle power is needed – you simply push down on the two handles and the cork comes up.

A small-size ladle, useful for getting all sorts of liquids out of saucepans, can double as a sauce spoon. A large whisk has more uses than a small one, especially if you do not have either a rotary beater or an electric mixer. A collection of spoons, both metal and wooden, is invaluable. Wooden ones should be made of smooth, close-grained hard wood. Some should be flat bottomed, others with a bowl. There is no substitute for a grater. The four-sided type with slicer and coarse, medium and fine graters serves all purposes. Kitchen scissors have many uses, including cutting raw meat, such as liver, and tender vegetables. The type with a C-shaped piece cut out of each blade slices easily through poultry bones.

Cooking cannot be done without a variety of implements. Strainers come in an assortment of sizes and are usually cup- or bowl-shaped. A bowl-shaped strainer of medium diameter and with a medium mesh is probably the most useful, since it can be used for sifting flours, making purées and straining liquids. Metal is best for most uses, but a nylon mesh prevents fruit and acid or white vegetables from discoloring. A colander is used to drain vegetables and other bulky items. Metal is preferable to plastic because it can also be used over boiling water as a steamer.

A slotted draining spoon is useful, but not essential.

Other, useful but not essential, aids include a vegetable peeler, rolling pin, lemon squeezer and garlic press.

Containers

Various-sized bowls aid kitchen efficiency; a nest of three covers most needs, but if you can only get one, make it large. The type with a lip makes pouring much easier. A deep bowl is needed for rotary and electric beaters; a wide, flat-bottomed shape is more suitable for a wire whisk. Ceramic, glass or metal bowls are superior to plastics, since they have a greater range of uses. Often plastic bowls cannot be used with boiling water, nor can they be kept 100 percent grease-free, and therefore they are unsuitable for whisking egg whites. Four to six small bowls or ramekins, preferably ovenproof so they can serve general cooking purposes, are useful for holding small prepared items, such as mashed garlic, chopped parsley, melted butter, and lemon peel and juice, until they are needed. Other miscellaneous items necessary for the practical kitchen are sets of 4 graduated measuring spoons and measuring cups. Measuring cups for liquids are usually made of heat-proof glass and come in 1-, 2- and 4-cup sizes. All show subdivisions in $\frac{1}{4}$ and $\frac{1}{3}$ units. Measuring cups for solids are of metal or plastic and come in 4-size nests. Also useful would be a kitchen scale.

A chopping board at least 8 by 12 inches (20 by 30 centimeters) and preferably a little bigger, is a must. A fine-grained hardwood will last for years. Some boards are made of formica or other plastics, but these become marked and rough with continuous use and can dull knife blades quickly. A wooden board, unlike formica, can be used as a resting place for hot

casseroles and pans as well as for chopping. Wire cake racks, used primarily to allow air to circulate freely around cakes and cookies, can also be a resting place for hot pots if they are not too heavy.

Several large, thick pot holders, which can be squares, gloves or the wrap-around two-handed type, are essential. If they have magnets in their handles they will stick to any metal surface, otherwise they should be hung on a hook beside the stove – they are of no use kept far from it!

Get thermometers – meat, deep-fat, candy – early in your cooking career when you will need them most. A meat thermometer is inserted into the thickest part of a roast to record the internal temperature, which is the best indicator of doneness. Deep-fat and candy thermometers measure the temperature of liquids.

A carving board with a juice well is not a great luxury because it makes the job so much easier. Make sure it is large enough to hold poultry and big roasts.

Electrical aids

In recent years an array of small electrical appliances has appeared on the market. No attempt can be made here to cover them all, and only the more basic and popular are covered, although others, of course, may be invaluable for your particular cooking needs. All electrical equipment should carry the UL (Underwriters' Laboratory) seal of approval.

The electric coffee pot is invaluable in any home, coming in sizes to suit every need from simple breakfasts to elaborate parties. The electric tea kettle is very new, but is both fast and economical, especially if you boil small amounts of water frequently.

Electric mixers are invaluable for creaming butter, whipping eggs, beating ghs and batters and mashing potatoes. ically there are two types, the table del and the hand-held or portable. h will do any work normally done by d with a wooden spoon or whisk. ers should have strong motors, yet in case of the hand models not be too vy. Varying speeds are an advantage coping with different jobs, such as ring, beating and whipping.

able models are fairly heavy and are t kept on the work surface near an let. They do not need to be held while operation, leaving you free to prepare er items.

ortable or hand mixers are not as erful as table models, but they have advantage of easy storage in a drawer cabinet. Some mixers come with one of beaters which are used for every- ag; other models come with several es of beaters for different jobs. Bladed ters are used for creaming and ting, wire ones for whisking and pping and, sometimes, spiral hooks for abining mixtures such as dough. Extra chments – blenders, mixers, shredders . juicers – can be bought for some table dels. If you think these attachments l be useful, then starting with an propriate model is a good idea.

lenders come either as independent e-standing units or as attachments for ae table-model mixers. Most have a up capacity, though other sizes can be found. Speeds range from Stir w) to Liquidize (extra fast) and are igned for a variety of jobs, including pping, grinding and puréeing.

Meat grinders can be free-standing and her manually or electrically operated; y can also be attachments on a table- del mixer. Grinders come with fine and rse blades and sometimes a sausage ffing cone. Some models also have

vegetable shredding and thin-slicing discs.

For many years, electric frying pans with high dome covers have been popular. Pan temperature, which ranges from Warm to 425°F (220°C), is easy to control and allows for a variety of cooking purposes including braising and stewing. In addition, most pans are attractive enough for table-side cooking Japanese style and for keeping buffet food hot. Most models are immersible in water when the control unit is removed.

In recent years, three other appliances have gained in popularity. Namely the electric casserole or crockpot, the infrared broiler, and the microwave oven. Electric casseroles, which usually have an earthen- ware pot set into an outer insulated unit with a heating element, cook very slowly at a very low temperature. They are economical to use and require no watching; they can be turned on in the morning and left to cook unattended all day.

Infrared broilers and microwave ovens cook rapidly. Ten minutes for a large roast is plenty in a microwave oven, and special browning dishes in newer models or putting the meat under the broiler will give it the rich cooked look we expect.

Electric trays keep food warm at the table although, despite some food ads, food cannot be kept warm for hours on end without reducing its quality. An electric coffee pot should make up to 12 cups, if you plan to use it mainly for guests. Most pots can be filled in advance and the electricity switched on shortly before the coffee is required; when finished it automatically switches to warm.

Dinnerware

Plates, serving dishes, glassware and cutlery all form a part of standard kitchen equipment. Dinnerware can be of

many different materials, among which earthenware, stoneware and china are the most popular. *Earthenware*, because of the type of clay used and the way it has been fired, is far less durable than *stoneware;* thus the latter is generally the better buy. *China* is a general term used for a hard, long-wearing, more or less translucent ceramic. It ranges from thick, heavy, glazed material to fine bone china, thin enough to see shadows. Cups, especially, break frequently, so it is wise to get extras when you buy a set.

Serving dishes can be in the same pattern as the dinnerware or quite different, ranging from oven-to-tableware to other sorts of cooking vessels. To decide how many serving pieces are needed, consider how many vegetables you customarily serve. In general, two oval meat platters, three serving dishes (preferably with lids), and a sauce boat will be adequate for the main course. Additional serving pieces such as a large flat plate suitable for either a cake or flan, a low, wide graceful bowl for puddings and fruits, another sauce boat and a sugar and creamer (at least 8 fluid ounces [250 milliliters] in size) will be useful.

Glassware, along with cups, seems to break more often than anything else. Thus try to get more than the minimum of any pattern you particularly like. Tumblers are needed for water, whisky (the traditional shape is short and squat) and tall drinks; mugs for beer and cider; medium-sized stem glasses for sherry; and large tulip-shaped glasses for wine. Choose your wine glasses carefully – larger sizes allow red wine to develop aroma and the shape holds that aroma in the glass.

Choose cutlery that balances well in the hand and does not seem too light in weight. It should be easy to wash, so investigate closely whether wood and

...ne (plastic) handles can be soaked in the ...hwater or go into the dishwasher. It ...ll be inconvenient if they cannot. ...addition to the standard cutlery, make ...re you have enough serving pieces, ...pecially serving spoons (including ...tted). Sauce ladles are also useful, as ...e a serving fork, and a cake or pie server.

...orage

...orage space in the modern kitchen must ...rve a variety of functions: in addition to ...ckaged food in jars, cans, bags and ...xes, it accommodates cooking equip- ...ent, dinnerware, cutlery and dish- ...ashing aids. Your storage units are likely ...consist of deep base cabinets, narrow ...all-hung ones, a walk-in or look-in floor ...near-ceiling type, and drawers. Some ...useholds have a wall area on which ...ings are hung, or open shelving. If you ...e thinking of these remember that ...posed objects get coated rather quickly ...th a film of cooking grease and dust. ...d, while sliding doors on cabinets ...e more economical in terms of space, ...ey do get dirtier, especially along the ...ding grooves.

Some of your storage areas will be ...armer than others. For instance, a ...binet adjacent to, or above, the stove ...ll be warmer than one farther away. ...leally, goods should be stored in well- ...ntilated-to-the-outside cabinets on a ...orth facing wall, since they keep better in ...cool place. Few of us, however, are likely ...range storage so that regular necessities ...e close to where they are likely to be ...ed, yet where they will not get over- ...eated.

Cooking equipment should be placed ...ar the stove if possible, with larger ...ts and pans in the base cabinets and ...naller items in drawers or in open ...ntainers at the rear of the counter. ...rawers for utensils are much easier to ...ep neat when they have vertical ...viders, since they enable you to ...parate knives from spoons, whisks from ...n and bottle openers. If possible, table ...utlery should be kept apart from cooking ...tensils. If no cabinet exists by the stove, ...se any area or drawer-space near the sink.

Dinnerware and glassware fit more ...asily on narrow shelves above counter ...vel or in a separate tall unit. In either ...ase their location should be convenient

...l selection of useful baking equipment.

to both the sink and dining area. If your shelves are too far apart, make or buy stacking units so that you don't have to pile different sizes of dishes on top of one another. Cups can hang on hooks attached to the underside of the shelf above.

One other non-food category needs drawer or cabinet space, namely wrapping materials. These include rolls of plastic bags, aluminum foil, wax paper, plastic wrap, and the like. Unfortunately, no two boxes seem to be the same length or width, and each has to be taken out for use. They should be located near the food preparation area.

Food storage can be divided into three categories: non-perishables; long-keeping perishables (lasting several weeks or more); and short-term perishables (lasting only a few days). Each type must be stored in a different way. However, if your kitchen is very warm or the climate is hot and humid, you find the refrigerator is the best place for both long- and short-term perishables.

Non-perishables (which go bad only if left unused for a long time) include cans, bottles, jars and dry goods like flour, sugar and salt. These often go in a wall-hung cabinet. They should be kept cool if possible and absolutely dry. Once open, dry goods keep better in airtight containers which have been clearly labelled.

Long-keeping perishables include open jars, various condiments, coffee and tea and certain fruits and vegetables – onions, garlic, potatoes, apples – if they can be stored in a cool dry place. Often, these keep better in the refrigerator than cabinets.

Short-term perishables include milk, meat, poultry, bread, green vegetables and opened canned goods. All need to be kept at below 50°F (10°C), preferably in the refrigerator.

A refrigerator must never be packed so full that air cannot circulate. Convection currents draw heat from the food and keep the temperature low. To keep this low temperature, it is not advisable to open the refrigerator door more than necessary, and *never* put hot food in a refrigerator – it may cool more quickly but it will also warm up the other food already stored there.

Correct containers

Foods tend to dry out during storage in a refrigerator, so they should always be wrapped or covered. This also prevents

smells and flavors of different foods cross-mingling. Do not pack goods in airtight containers, since anaerobic bacteria (those which survive without oxygen) may become active. The frozen-food compart-ment of your refrigerator allows for longer term storage of perishables. This will be further ensured by using freezer wrapping paper and not overstuffing the compartment itself, as this will cut down on efficiency and can, possibly, result in spoilage of the food. If the information on the packaging of frozen foods doesn't specify recommended storage times, con-tact your local Consumer Affairs Bureau; the Federal Government often publishes leaflets giving information about freezing.

Our mothers and grandmothers used to shop daily, buying in small amounts. But this method does not fit our modern life-style very well and we tend to buy ahead. To make the most of this, certain new habits should be formed. Put just-acquired items (both frozen and non-frozen) at the back of a shelf or at the bottom of a stack of similar items. (Also date them with a felt-tip pen.) In this way the oldest will always get used first.

Avoid buying dented cans, since they have a greater tendency to spoil, and never use a can that is bulging at the lid, because the risk of food poisoning is high. (The bulge can indicate an accumulation of gas, often caused by active bacteria.)

Make it a practice to empty airtight containers that hold flour, sugar and other items and to wash them throughly before filling with new supplies. This procedure prevents the new contents from being contaminated in any way by the old. Try to group similar items together, with those used most frequently in the front and nearest eye level. Thus unopened items should go at the back or on higher shelves.

The following arrangement is one of many possibilities. Arrange things in groups – soups, dry and canned veget-ables; fish and meat; fruits; jam; unopened flour; sugars – so that you can see all similar items at a glance. Do not pack things so closely together that some hide others. At least twice a year take everything out, clean the cabinets, and assess your supplies. Use whatever seems to be getting old. Group together items you use in cooking. Flour, sugar, herbs and spices, stock cubes, salt and pepper should all be easily reached from the cooking and preparation areas. Since herbs and spices come in small containers you may find it useful to improvise a small two-shelf unit on the side of the cabinet or on the door.

Baking aids (sugar, confectioner's sugar, cocoa, dried yeast, vanilla extract, food coloring, baking powder) form another natural grouping. Sauces should be stored together (Worcestershire, ketchup, prepared mustard).

Finally locate jams, marmalade, table salt and pepper where they are convenient to the table, since that is where they are used most often.

Maintenance

Whether we like it or not everything in the kitchen needs care, and care calls for some equipment. For washing dishes a basin, dish drainer, brush, sponges, dish-cloth and gentle nylon scouring pads are necessary. For the floor, a broom, dust-pan and brush and, if the floor area is large enough, a long-handled mop and bucket.

Dishwashing calls for a certain amount of organization, and if you are lucky or have planned well, you will have enough space to place the unwashed dishes on one side and the washed on the other. Glassware and cutlery washed in very hot water sparkle more and have fewer watermarks, so do these first, followed by dishes and saucepans. Both instant coffee and tea leave residues that discolor cups; this can be reduced by rinsing out the cups immediately after use. Soapy water and a hard scrub with a sponge will remove the deposits.

All pots and pans benefit from soaking before washing. So get into the habit of putting warm water and some dish-washing liquid into saucepans immediately after serving.

The exception is pans with fat. If you are saving the fat for drippings, pour it off while still liquid; if it is to be thrown away, let it solidify before cleaning it out with paper towels. Either way wipe the pan out well before washing it in hot soapy water. Grease poured down a drain can spell disaster in the form of a blocked up sink! A pan that sizzles as you put water in it is being damaged by the rapid change in temperature.

Dishwashing liquid has a variety of uses away from the sink. A little put on a damp sponge is excellent for cutting grease on the walls and other kitchen surfaces and for removing finger marks from paint anywhere in the house.

Cleaning the stove and refrigerator

Everyone dreads cleaning the stove and refrigerator, yet it has to be done. The instruction books that come with both appliances tell you what to do for your particular model. In general, after use wipe the stove top and oven with a damp soapy sponge. Never use abrasives, such as scouring powder, which can scratch the surface. A particularly difficult spot can be softened by leaving a wet sponge over it for several minutes, after which it usually wipes off easily. Remember to clean the drip pans (under the burners) regularly, not just after spills.

Oven cleaners often contain lye which can cause terrible burns if it gets on your skin. Since lye is known by several different names, you can't always tell when the product you buy contains it. Therefore be especially careful if the instructions tell you to wear gloves! If an oven is parti-cularly dirty, more than one application of oven cleaner will be needed. Roasting meat at a high temperature causes more spatter and grease than roasting at a low tempera-ture.

Defrosting the refrigerator and freezer

Although many refrigerators and freezers are self-defrosting, not all have this convenient though power-hungry feature. To keep the refrigerator and freezer operating at maximum efficiency, they should be defrosted when the ice builds up to a thickness of $\frac{1}{2}$ centimeter ($\frac{1}{4}$ inch). Even with self-defrosting models, you should empty out the contents and wash down all surfaces about once a month or at least four times a year.

Switch off the power unless your temperature dial has a defrost position. Remove all food from the refrigerator to a table or other convenient surface. Pack frozen foods tightly into one or more cartons with the slow-thawing items (roasts, poultry) around the perimeter and quicker thawing ones in the middle. Pile the boxes on top of one another and cover the top one with about 1 inch ($2\frac{1}{2}$ centi-meters) thickness of newspaper, which is an excellent insulator (in hot weather a layer can also be placed under the bottom box). Place a large pan under the freezer to catch as much water as possible (the chiller tray serves the same function on smaller refrigerators), leave the door open (unless there is a defrost setting), and go away for 15 to 30 minutes, returning at least once to empty the drip pan. (Note: One can buy small electrical appliances which go into the refrigerator/freezer and speed the defrosting process.) After 30 minutes the frost should either have melted entirely or look soft and mushy. In a chest-type freezer, you must get the ice out before it becomes water, since water is difficult to siphon or sponge out. Theoretically you should leave the mushy ice alone, but human nature being what it is, we all tend to help things along. Tease the ice off with your fingers or a dull spatula-like instru-ment. Never use sharp knives or other similar implements since these can punc-ture the lining. Have patience while the last bits melt off the piping, which should not be touched. While waiting for the last of the ice to melt, wash down the whole inside with a solution of 1 tablespoon of bicarbonate of soda dissolved in a gallon of water. Rinse and dry thoroughly. Turn the refrigerator or freezer back on. Wait 15 minutes before replacing the contents, so it has begun to get cold.

Refrigerator shelves sometimes need special attention. The solid shelf – plastic or tempered glass – above the vegetable compartment is frequently gridded to prevent slippage and spills can accumulate in these recessed areas, becoming gummy. This should be removed and washed and dried thoroughly. This also applies to the plastic front edge, under which spills accumulate. Other shelves (on doors, for instance) may also have decorative strips which should be removed and cleaned in the same way.

Self-defrosting refrigerators and freezers have a drainage hole at the bottom which carries water to the evaporator tray. Sometimes this hole becomes clogged, and the debris must be delicately extracted with a toothpick, skewer or knitting needle. Water leaking out from under the vegetable compartment is a sign the refrigerator needs attention. A build-up of ice at the bottom of the freezer signals a problem there. If you decide to switch off the refrigerator when going on vacation be sure to leave the door open (pull a shelf out so the door cannot close accidentally). A refrigerator or freezer left switched off and with the door closed develops a terrible musty odor that is hard to get rid of, as well as possible mildew.

Guide to Refrigerator Storage

Food	Storage Time	Special Points
Dairy Produce		
Milk	3—4 days	Keep in container or bottle (closed).
Cream	3—4 days	
Ice cream	Up to 3 months	Keep in original container or carton in freezing compartment.
Cheese, hard	2—3 weeks	Wrap in aluminum foil or plastic wrap, or store in a non-airtight container. Always remove cheese ½ hour before serving for maximum flavor.
Cheese, soft	Up to 1 week	Keep in covered container.
Butter	4—6 weeks	Keep in original wrapper or transfer to butter dish.
Fats and Oils		
Margarine (hard and soft)	6 weeks	As for butter.
Lard and cooking fat	Up to 4 months	As for butter.
Oils	Does not apply	Do not store in the refrigerator as they may solidify.
Eggs		
whole	2—3 weeks	Always keep some eggs out at room temperature for cooking purposes.
whites	4—5 days	Put in covered container.
yolks	2—3 days	Store in covered container with water.
hard-boiled	5—7 days	
Bread	Up to 1 week	Keep in its package or a plastic bag or wrap, closed tightly. Storing in the refrigerator reduces mold growth, but can hasten the staling process.
Meat and Poultry		
Raw meat—roasts and chops	3—5 days	Either leave in wrappings from butcher or supermarket or re-wrap loosely in aluminum foil or plastic wrap.
Raw poultry	2—3 days	Remove any tight wrappings (e.g. plastic wrappings used by supermarkets). Store giblets separately for 1—2 days. Either leave in wrapping paper from butcher or re-wrap in aluminum foil or plastic wrap.
Cooked meat or poultry	3—5 days	Wrap in aluminum foil or store in a covered container.
Purchased cooked meat	2—3 days	Wrap in aluminum foil or plastic wrap.
Ground meat and variety meats (offal)	1—2 days	Keep in original packaging or cover loosely. Alternatively place in a non-airtight container.
Bacon	7—10 days	Keep in original packaging, as tightly closed as possible.
Cooked made-up dishes	2—3 days	Cover with lid or aluminum foil or plastic wrap.
Fish		
fresh	1—2 days	Wrap all fish and shellfish loosely, but thoroughly, to prevent smell escaping.
shellfish	1 day	
cooked fish	1—2 days	
smoked fish	Indefinitely	

Food	Storage Time	Special Points
Fruits and Vegetables		
Vegetables		
root	Does not apply	Do not store in the refrigerator.
green	2—3 days	Put in plastic bags and store in vegetable compartment or at bottom of refrigerator.
Salad	3 days	Keep in closed plastic, lidded container or in vegetable compartment or salad crisper.
Fruit		
soft	2—3 days	Clean and prepare. Keep in lidded container or plastic bags.
hard	3—7 days	Wrap in plastic wrap or keep in plastic bags, if necessary.

Shelf position for refrigerated foods

Position	Temperature	Food
Freezer compartment	Varies: 0°F (−18°C) to 21°F (−6°C)	Ice, frozen food (packaged), ice cream, meat and poultry, fish.
Tray below freezing compartment	Very cold	Loose ice cubes, meat, fish.
Shelf immediately below tray	Very cold	Meat, fish, cold desserts.
Large (high) middle shelf	Cold	Cooked meat, made-up dishes, variety of goods in large bottles or jars, milk, cream.
Shelf above vegetable compartment or salad crisper	Cold	Variety of goods in small jars, fruits, vegetables.
Vegetable compartment or salad crisper	Least cold	Vegetables, salad greens, fruits.
Rack inside door	Least cold	Eggs, butter, cheese, fats (not oils), fruit juices, bottled soft drinks, salad dressings, some seasonings (in jars).

Ice cubes, ice cream, frozen foods

Loose ice cubes (for convenience), meat, fish

Meat, fish, cold desserts

Cooked meat, prepared dishes, milk & cream, large bottles & jars

Small jars (condiments), fruits, vegetables

Salad greens, fruits, vegetables

FREEZER

Butter, margarine, cheese

Eggs (keep fresh separated from older eggs)

Milk, tall bottles, cheese

Tall bottles (soda, juice, etc) and jars, bottled dressings

Chapter Two

Buying wisely

One person's bargain can be someone else's great mistake. An enormous jar of honey that would last a family of six for two weeks could mean months of honey with everything for a single person.

Wise buying is an individual affair. It depends on the number of people in a household, on the amount of time at your disposal and on your financial resources. The time saved by shopping locally can sometimes be of greater value than the monetary savings obtained at a more distant supermarket. The choice of where to shop is controlled by geographic factors. In a large town or city many options will be available, but a small village may offer only one general store and an inconvenient trip to the nearest town.

However, all of us share a considerable number of problems and when we deicde what to buy – which cut of meat or which plums – we do a constant mental juggling act, balancing quality and quantity against price. Generally the better the quality, the higher the price, and we reach our decisions by weighing these factors against one another.

Types of stores

Today, it is common to do all one's shopping—meat, produce and household supplies—in a supermarket or shopping center. Many people, especially in large cities, still shop at a variety of stores rather than always at one type. We may get staples at a supermarket or by buying in bulk; meat from a local butcher, some fresh vegetables, cheese and bread from a small grocer. We may also use open-air markets or roadside stands for a range of in-season produce.

Small is expensive. An independent local general store with room for limited stock cannot possibly buy on the same competitive terms as a large supermarket with rapid turnover. It, therefore, has few savings to pass on to the customer. In order to compete, the neighborhood store owner is often compelled to work late-night hours and remain open long after other stores have closed for the evening. Other attractions include friendly, personal service, which contrasts with the anonymity of the supermarket, and a sense of personal responsibility toward the 'regular' customer. Some local stores, particularly in rural areas, also offer credit. Sometimes small stores (especially those in rural areas) have small-scale suppliers (perhaps local farmers) of fresh vegetables or poultry and are able to sell these items at surprisingly competitive prices.

One way in which a small independently owned grocer can continue to trade successfully without sacrificing his independence is by joining a voluntary chain group. Voluntary chain members are able to buy from their wholesaler at advantageous terms and pass some of these savings on to their customers. They also have the advantage of being able to sell the group's own-brand goods at prices which will compete directly with similar own-brand goods offered in supermarkets.

It is easy to spot the good points about supermarkets. The size of their operation accounts for their competitive prices, and rapid turnover ensures a constant supply of fresh perishable foods. Many supermarkets operate their own date stamping system on perishable items. Although it may not be a Federal requirement many localities have enacted consumer legislation regulating the sale of goods. These regulations include unit-pricing which enables you to judge whether you are getting value for money and how much. Also, date-stamping and "last day of sale" notations allow you complete information and possible savings (ie sometimes marked-down in price if "last day").

Other advantages of supermarkets include the fact that you can do all your food shopping under one roof. Although fruits and vegetables are sometimes more expensive than they would be elsewhere, speed and convenience may outweigh monetary considerations. You can shop at leisure and choose from a wide range of goods which carry clearly marked prices. Frequently goods can be paid for by check, backed by a store identification or credit card. This is no small advantage in these days when we hesitate to carry cash in any quantity.

Supermarkets do, however, have disadvantages, too; and one at least can be so great as to completely counteract any potential savings: the temptation to buy things that you do not need because the goods are attractively packaged, and all you have to do is stretch out your hand and add them to your basket or wagon. Supermarkets are designed to encourage customers to spend money. Special offers are placed in an eye-catching position near the entrance, basic foods are found in the center of the shop so that rows and rows of tempting goods have to be passed en route, and small incidentals such as candy and magazines are positioned close to the check-out area where the customer will have to wait on the inevitable line. The only effective way to withstand all these temptations to impulse buy is to make a list before you leave home, remember to take it with you and stick to it! A sure recipe for overspending is deciding what to have for supper when you are actually in the supermarket. And keeping a rough total of what you are spending as you put goods into your basket can also act as a deterrent to your more expensive impulses.

Convenience foods, that is prepared foods in packages or cans, can prove expensive if bought frequently. There is obviously a place for the virtually instant meal in dehydrated, canned or frozen form as emergency food, but apart from this, they have little to recommend them on grounds of cost or flavor.

Another way in which the supermarket encourages you to buy more than you need is through prepackaging. Prepackaged items such as cheese, bacon and meat often contain larger quantities than you need, something that particularly discriminates against people living alone since most prepackaged goods are sold in quantities suitable for at least two people.

If you are lucky enough to live near a regular open-air market or near farm country, you should have access to a supply of cheap fresh fruits and vegetables. Be on the lookout for in-season produce and be flexible to allow for special bargains.

Shopping at open-air markets has to be done carefully. Make preliminary price comparisons between stalls before buying. Sometimes the reason why apples are 35 cents at one stall and 20 cents at another is obvious, but, as you get to know the market, you will notice that not only are prices consistently higher at some stalls than at others, but that goods at one end of the market are dearer than at the other.

If you find a stall where prices are generally low and quality high, it is worth using it regularly. When you get to know a stall owner, he is less likely to slip in the odd rotten onion or overripe plum than if you were a customer whom he did not expect to see again.

It is important to comparison shop, between stores and between brands. Always equate price with quality.

It is a good idea to buy bulky, unbruisable items like potatoes and onions first and the most perishable items like soft fruit last. In this way you will not have to rearrange your bag continually.

Buying in bulk

Bulk buying may sound like a good idea, but you need to estimate how long it will take to use up the bulk purchase. Buying seven pounds of confectioner's sugar just before Christmas would be a good buy if you are planning to frost lots of cakes, but silly if you seldom make icing of any sort. On the other hand, if you use three cans of baked beans a week, a case will last you about two months. And you will have reduced the weight of your weekly shopping bag considerably. Bulk buying is worth considering if you can combine with friends or relatives to share the goods. Quite often this happens when at least one person has access to an open-air market and a suitable car.

Before going to a bulk buying (or wholesale) center, make up a detailed shopping list that includes the prices of the items where you normally shop. For sometimes the bulk price is the same as, or higher than, the local price.

Many of these centers cater to freezer owners who want to stock up their freezer with larger packs than are available in supermarkets. Be cautious about buying unlabelled or unknown brands of frozen food. It is impossible to assess the quality simply by looking at it, so, however cheap, 24 hamburgers that taste like sawdust will be a saving that you will regret having made. Bulk meat packs consisting of half lambs or pigs are also available at these centers, but they may include cuts that you would normally not consider or want to purchase. Although more expensive, bulk packages containing a single cut such as chops may be more useful.

Many butchers also provide meat in bulk for the home freezer. Although their meat may be slightly more expensive than that at a wholesale buying center, the quality of the meat may be preferable.

Like canned or bottled food bought in bulk, frozen food has to be stored. You will not only need enough room in the freezer to store your purchases but you should also have enough space to maintain a balance among different types of food. A freezer containing a pig and an immense package of peas has not been well planned!

24

If, however, you manage to avoid the pitfalls of bulk buying, you will have the considerable advantage of saving money during a period of rapid inflation. You will also have cut down on time spent shopping and provided yourself with extensive supplies that will be particularly useful if you work, or if you find yourself cooking for twice as many as you had anticipated.

They're after your money

In a competitive field such as food retailing, traders employ numerous methods to attract customers. One such device is the giving of trading stamps. A stamp worth a small fraction of a cent is given for a specified amount spent. Double or triple stamps are offered at certain times to encourage the customer to shop when

business might otherwise be slack, or to make extra shopping hours financially worthwhile for the store.

Trading stamps appeal to the collecting urge in most people as well as to the idea of getting something for "nothing". If price and quality are the same as the nearest rival without stamps, something can be said for the one offering the stamps. Note that the offering of stamps or premiums often drives up the price of goods, so compare carefully when choosing between seemingly similar stores.

Other inducements used to lure us into shops and, once in, to spend, are special offers. A loss leader is the name given to goods, usually basic foods, which are offered at reduced prices. These goods are prominently displayed inside the shop and advertised on window posters.

nce inside the customer will almost
ainly buy other goods, and the
eased business will more than cover
store's slight loss on the product that
w the customer into the store in the
place.

ther methods include offering date-
ped food for sale close to the final
, allowing some minimum storage.
, you might see "blind" cans – ones
se labels are lost – offered for sale. This
be worth it if you are willing to take
ance.

lucing your spending
an your menus before you leave home
stick to them.
lways make a list and remember to
it with you.
sk yourself, do I really need it?
ulse buys are expensive. They can
be fattening, if you make a habit of
ng cookies or crackers and snacks to
etween meals.
eep in touch with the price of basic
ls such as butter, sugar, soap powder
the like. If you know what the current
is, you can determine for yourself
ther cut-price offers are really worth
ng.
Many local radio stations and news-
rs run up-to-the-minute announce-
ts on special bargains of the date or
, especially good buys in selected
t cuts, extra-low priced fruits and
tables, etc.
you travel around from store to store
arch of bargains, remember that you
ften spending money as well as time.
he time you have deducted bus fares or
from your savings you may not have
h left!

ra shopping hints
ways compare prices and quality.
heck date stamps on perishable goods.
ave your shopping bags and take a
cient supply with you when you go
ping.
henever possible, shop at off-peak
s. It will save time and temper.
f you are shopping in an outdoor
et, go first thing in the morning. The
s and vegetables will be at their best
o will you.

giene in food stores
t stores that deal in food and produce
required by law to maintain high

standards of quality and cleanliness. This
should reassure most consumers, especially those with very old people or babies in
the household. Any irregularity in standards should be reported immediately to the
local Board of Health or suitable alternative authority.

Bacteria that cause food poisoning can
be carried in a number of different ways.
Salmonella, one such bacteria, breeds
rapidly in undercooked meat and poultry.
Cooked chicken joints that are pink in the
middle are, therefore, to be avoided.
There is a danger of contamination by
salmonella through raw meat and one
should not cut raw and already cooked
meat with the same knife but, as a rule,
meat must be carefully checked by
inspectors from the Department of
Agriculture.

Botulism, found in canned goods with
bulging lids, can in extreme cases be fatal;
and staphylococci, another bacteria, can be
transmitted to food by handlers with colds
or with septic cuts on their fingers which
are not adequately covered by a waterproof
dressing.

Your rights as a consumer

Within recent years rapid inflation has
given rise to a fantastic growth in consumer awareness. A new word, consume-
ism, has entered the language. Government response to this public reaction has
taken many forms. The President, many
governors and mayors have on-staff
consumer advisors to investigate abuses of
the existing body of consumer-protection
laws as well as looking for new ways to
protect the consumer's rights. Many
localities have set up consumer advice or
protection bureaus.

The duties of these agencies range from
handling actual consumer complaints and
queries to sending out agents to look for
violations of the law. These violations may
relate to acts regulating Weights and
Measures, labelling and packaging of
foods, price and health standards or to
the Pure Food and Drug Act. These
agents can in some cases take unscrupu-
lous businessmen to court or, at the very
least, cite them making sure the public
has the option of not patronizing such
businesses.

Making a complaint
Achieving a satisfactory outcome to a

complaint about food is simpler than if you
are complaining about a pair of shoes or a
malfunctioning washing-machine. Legislation covering the selling of food is
comprehensive and there can be little
disagreement about the fitness of a
particular item of food. You can't argue
with 'a rotten egg'.

The first problem is in overcoming your
apathy once the initial fury at finding the
food inedible passes. Lethargy, plus the
dislike of making a fuss, deters many
people from making justifiable complaints.
However, in the case of a serious complaint, such as finding broken glass in a
container of yogurt, it is in everybody's
interest that you do tell the store of your
discovery. Any serious incident, which
endangers public health, should also be
reported to your local Board of Health.

Assuming that your complaint is a
minor one, you should return the offending
article to the shop from which you bought
it as soon as possible. Take the receipt, if
you have it, any packing materials and, if
practical, the article itself. Obviously you
can't return a bad egg, but you could take
the egg box with you. Ask politely but
firmly to see the manager. Explain your
complaint clearly – when you bought the
goods, and what the problem is. You gain
nothing by being rude and abusive. If you
lose your temper you will antagonize the
manager, and possibly forget the most
important point you were going to make.

If for some reason you cannot return to
the shop from which you bought the
unsatisfactory goods, you should write to
the manager. Keep a copy of all corres-
pondence and, if you have access to a
photocopying machine, you should enclose
a copy of your receipt. Do not send the
original. If you are unable to obtain any
satisfaction from the shop, contact your
local Better Business Bureau or Department of Consumer Affairs with the details.
A firm letter on official letterhead often
works wonders. If your complaint is more
serious and unlikely to be an isolated
incident but relates to the general cleanliness of a shop, or to foreign bodies found
in food, you should report the matter to
your local Board of Health or Department
of Consumer Affairs. Restaurants and
shops selling food are frequently cited
and/or closed by the local health authorities for running dirty premises. And many
of these cases have been brought to the
attention of the authorities in the first
instance by members of the public.

Chapter Three

Preserving is the art of keeping food beyond its natural span, and is almost as old as cooking itself. The traditional methods were salting (usually meat or fish), or drying (meat, fish, vegetables or fruit) – both rarely done at home now – and canning, pickle- and chutney-making and jam-making – these last concerned wholly with vegetables and fruit. In addition, the advent of the home freezer has added another, even easier, method of preserving nearly all food.

Home Freezing

An efficient food freezer should be capable of freezing a specified weight of food from 77°F (25°C) to 0°F (– 18°C) while at the same time maintaining the temperature of any frozen food already stored in the freezer at less than 0°F (– 18°C).

Freezers are available in a wide range of sizes, ranging from about 6 cubic feet (80 liters) to 30 or more cubic feet (800 liters). Approximately each cubic foot (28 liters) of space will hold about 20 pounds (9 kilograms) of frozen food. At least 2 cubic feet (55 liters) is the minimum requirement for each person in the family, though you should bear in mind the usual number of people to be allowed for: families that do a lot of home entertaining will probably require a much larger freezer.

Foods for freezing

With a few exceptions (listed below) almost all fresh and cooked food can be preserved by freezing, and following a few simple rules will ensure success.

1. Choose only really fresh food of prime quality – this especially applies to fish and seafood.
2. Cooked foods should be freshly prepared and allowed to cool before packing and freezing.

3. Food for freezing must be sealed in a container or wrapped to exclude air to avoid dehydration, loss of color, texture and flavor, and cross-flavoring during storage.
4. Pack foods in probable mealtime portions, interleaving chops, beef burgers, fish fillets, etc., with plastic, aluminum foil or freezer paper for easy separation.
5. Follow the freezer manufacturer's instructions when loading fresh food and *avoid placing fresh food in direct contact with food already frozen*. It is important to note that many freezers now come equipped with fast-freezing compartments that permit the rapid processing of unfrozen foods without raising the temperature of those already frozen. The thermostat setting for normal storage should keep frozen food at a temperature not warmer than 0°F (– 18°C).
6. The usual rules of hygiene in the preparation of food must be followed. In particular make sure that all packaging, kitchen tools and utensils, cutting boards and hands are thoroughly washed between handling fresh and cooked foods.
7. A few foods are not recommended for freezing: hard-boiled eggs, mayonnaise, baked egg custard pie and tarts, icings not made with confectioner's sugar and butter base frostings, light cream, soft meringues, boiled potatoes (except if new), stuffed poultry, bananas and vegetables intended for use in salads. Foods containing much gelatin do not freeze well.

Packaging food for freezing

The low temperature air in a food freezer is very dry, and any food not properly sealed will lose its natural moisture and may develop freezer burn. Inadequately packaged food is not unsafe but will be unpleasant to eat after storage.

Packaging materials must be free from taint and odors, and be both moisture- and vapor-proof to prevent loss of natural moisture and juices in the food. These

materials should also be resistant t cracking and breaking at freezer tempera tures and a suitable shape to ensur fast freezing.

Various packaging materials fill thes requirements. Plastic bags are availabl in many sizes for fruits, vegetables, fis meat, poultry, loaves of bread and bake foods. Plastic sheeting, freezer paper an heavy-duty aluminum foil are especiall useful for wrapping irregularly shape food and interleaving individual portion of meat, fish, poultry, hamburgers, an yeast or pastry dough.

Plastic containers and cartons wit tightly fittings lids hold soft fruit, sauce stews, casseroles and all liquids. Alu minum and waxed paper and cardboar trays using aluminum foil or plastic wra to cover, serve the same purpose. Plasti covered wire and freezer tape are use for sealing. Each package should b labelled and marked with the contents an the date of freezing. Different colors fo labels are helpful for later identification such as green for vegetables, red for mea blue for fish.

Meat

With all kinds of meat, prepare fo freezing by trimming off all excess fat an remove bones as far as practicable to sav space and packaging material. Bone which have been removed can be used fo stock, which can then be frozen afte skimming off all fat. The airtight wrappin of meat is especially important to preven dehydration. Protect the outer packagin by first covering any sharp projectin bones with waxed paper or clean chees cloth. Exclude as much air as possibl before sealing in foil or coated meat wrap Larger joints of meat should be cut int mealtime or family size portions befor freezing. Roasts of 2 pounds (1 kilogram and larger will probably require at leas 48 hours to freeze right through to th center of the meat.

Freezing cooked meat

Home or commercially frozen meat can be used for a recipe, then refrozen after being well cooked. Providing fat has been skimmed, the storage life of cooked stews and casseroles prepared in this way is up to two months. It is especially important for hygiene and cross-contamination to avoid handling fresh and cooked meat and poultry at the same time when preparing for freezing.

Fish

Fresh fish deteriorates quickly after being caught even if well chilled, so salt-water fish purchased inland is unlikely to be fresh enough for home freezing. All fresh fish suitable for freezing should be washed, cleaned, gutted and head, tail and fins removed and then washed again. Prepare the fish as for cooking, either whole, filleted or in steaks (see page 37). To increase storage life, whole round and flat fish, after freezing and temporary packing, can be glazed by dipping in an ice cold solution of salt and water, 2½ tablespoons (50 grams) salt to 2½ cups (600 milliliters) of water.

Game birds

Game birds after being hung for a time according to the taste and flavor preferred, should be prepared for home freezing in the same way as poultry (see chart, page 38). After preparation, pack in plastic bags, coated meat wrap or foil and seal.

Vegetables

As a general guide, all vegetables which are normally cooked before eating will freeze and store satisfactorily. Some, like tomatoes and onions, lose their original crispness and texture after freezing, but are useful for stews, casseroles and sauces. After washing and trimming, most vegetables must be blanched in boiling water for a short time before packaging and freezing. This retards the action of enzymes and prevents 'off' flavors. Any exceptions are given in the chart on pages 38-39. Blanching is most easily done by putting small quantities of vegetables in a wire basket and immersing this in a pan of boiling water, normally at a ratio of not more than 1 pound (450 grams) of vegetables to 3¾ quarts (3½ liters) of water. Blanching time begins when the water returns to a boil, and ends by plunging the vegetables into ice cold water. Most vegetables can be packed into plastic bags or rigid cartons,

28

and many can be frozen individually to produce a free flow pack (see under Fruit below).

Fruit

Fruit can be frozen whole, in halves or in slices, in a dry pack in dry sugar, in a sugar syrup or as a fruit purée. The sugar or sugar syrup helps to protect color and flavor. Light-colored fruits like apples, pears and peaches will darken after peeling and slicing. This discoloration can be almost eliminated by working quickly and placing the fruit in a solution of ascorbic acid and water, using 1 teaspoon ascorbic acid to 2½ cups (600 milliters) of water. Do not use iron or copper pans for this solution.

Freezing separately: After cleaning the fruit, with as little water as possible, dry it and spread it out in a single layer in a plastic bag laid on a flat aluminum baking sheet. Freeze the fruit in this position. Small fruit will freeze in a few hours and can then be shaken gently down into the bag. Fill the bag using fruit from other sheets. Although time-consuming, this method is best for small fruits like raspberries, strawberries and blackberries, producing a free flow pack. (The method applies to other kinds of food as well-diced vegetables and peas, for example).

Dry pack: This is suitable for fruits with a relatively tough skin. Gooseberries and currants, for example, need only to be washed and dried before freezing in closed bags.

Dry sugar pack: After cleaning and drying, sprinkle the fruit with sugar using ½ cup (100 grams) sugar to each pound (½kg) of fruit, shaking or stirring the fruit gently to ensure an even coating.

Sugar syrup: Prepare sugar syrup and allow it to cool before adding to fruit. Add sugar to boiling water and simmer only long anough for all the sugar to be dissolved. Sugar syrup can be used in one of three strengths:

1. Light sugar: 1 cup (225 grams) sugar to 2½ cups (600 milliliters) water.
2. Medium sugar syrup: 1½ cups (350 grams) to 2 cups (500 milliliters) water.

Two popular types of freezer commonly available: on the left, an upright refrigerator-freezer and on the right a chest-type model.

Heavy sugar syrup: 2 cups (450 grams)
ar to 2 cups (500 milliliters) water.
it should be required add 1 teaspoon
orbic acid to the solution when cold.
rées and juices: Fruit which has been
carded because of over-ripeness,
mishes or bruises can be frozen in
rée form after the blemishes or bruised
ts have been removed. Pass the fruit
ough a nylon strainer or food mill and
l sugar at the ratio of about ½ cup
o grams) of sugar to 1 pound (450
ms) fruit or according to taste. Apples
l tomatoes should be cooked before
aining.
rage life: With a few exceptions, most
it will freeze and store satisfactorily at
(−18°C) for up to nine months when
cked in dry sugar or in sugar syrup.
e storage life is normally reduced to
ut six months for fruits stored in
packs.

ke, breads and pastries

cakes, except those with icing, breads,
tries and cookies freeze well. Generally
es, breads and cookies have a better
ture if they are baked before freezing,
ereas pastry is crisper if it is frozen
ore baking. If the dough is to be used
pies with a cooked filling – steak and
ney, chicken or game – then this
uld be cooked before covering with
ugh.

Uncooked bread dough can be frozen,
t a better rise is ensured if the amount
yeast is increased by half. Pack the
risen dough in a greased plastic bag,
ve 1-2 inches (2½-5 centimeters) of
ice above the dough, and seal the bag.
o prepare for baking, remove the
tener and allow the dough to thaw out
d rise in the refrigerator overnight, or
2-5 hours at room temperature.)
vide large cakes into serving pieces
fore wrapping and freezing. It is easier
wrap soft and sponge cakes and those
th a buttercream filling and decoration
er they have hardened in the freezer.
kes that are to be filled when thawed
ould be packed with a piece of foil
tween each layer to prevent them from
cking together. Fresh white bread-
umbs will keep well in the freezer
cked in plastic bags.

Bought, sliced bread should be over-
rapped in foil or a plastic bag. Slices
quired for toast can be taken straight
m the freezer and toasted while still
ozen.

Dairy foods

Butter and cheese should be over-wrapped
in plastic or aluminum foil before freezing. Grated cheese, packed in usable
quantities in plastic bags, can be taken
straight from the freezer for use in sauces
and other savory dishes. Homogenized
milk can be frozen and stored for about
three months. Freeze in wax cartons,
leaving a headspace.

Eggs should not be frozen in their
shells as they expand and crack. The yolks
and whites should be lightly beaten
together with salt or sugar added – 1
tablespoon of sugar or 1 teaspoon salt to
every 6 eggs. Label the cartons with the
number of eggs and whether with sugar
or salt. Approximately 3 tablespoons of
the thawed egg mixture is the equivalent
of 1 egg.

Light cream is not suitable for freezing.
Heavy cream, with not less than 40
percent butterfat will, however, and if it
separates when thawing, stirring will
correct it.

Cooking home frozen foods

Small portions of fish, meat, poultry and
all vegetables can be cooked straight from
the freezer without thawing. Be sure,
however, that they are cooked right
through to the center before serving.
Vegetables which have been blanched
should be cooked in the minimum
quantity of boiling, salted water and
normally need less cooking time than
fresh vegetables.

It is important that large roasts, whole
fish and all whole birds should be thawed
completely before cooking. This is especially important with chickens, ducks,
geese and turkeys, bearing in mind that a
frozen bird of above 22 pounds (10 kilograms) will require three to four days in
the refrigerator to thaw to the center.

Home preserving

The long-term storage of fresh produce
usually requires some kind of treatment to
retard or prevent spoilage. The use of
the refrigerator has already been discussed in terms of purchased foods, but
a refrigerator can only provide a short-
term solution to the problem. To keep
most food for longer than a week requires
more sophisticated methods.

The old and still excellent ways of
preserving are by canning, jam-making

and pickling, to name only the broadest
categories. The objective is to make
seasonal foods available all year round.

Canning

Canning, one of the methods of preserving food by heat, will only be successful
if the processing is efficiently, carefully
and correctly carried out and the jars are
completely sealed for storage.

Home preserving of vegetables is not
recommended unless a pressure cooker
with a very accurate pressure control is
available. Vegetables, on the whole, are
low in acid and may contain bacteria
resistant to heat. They may also develop
a toxin during storage, which can cause
fatal food poisoning.

On the other hand, food that contains a
high percentage of acid – like fruit and
tomatoes – is ideal for canning, since the
acid inhibits the growth of bacteria and
prevents the formation of toxin.

Fruits vary, of course, in the amount of
acid they contain, and those with a lower
content need a longer processing. See the
chart (pages 40-41) for precise details.

Equipment

Two types of jars are specially made for
preserving; one with a spring-like clip and
the other with a screw band. These are
available in various sizes from hardware,
kitchen equipment and department stores.
Jam jars also can be used in most methods
but *not* in a pressure cooker. Whichever
type of jar is used, it must not be chipped
or cracked and should be scrupulously
clean. If glass lids are used these should
not be chipped. Metal lips should not be
scratched or damaged in any way.

If you are using jars with separate
rubber rings, make sure they are the
correct size. Always use new rings: they
stretch and will not form a satisfactory seal
if they are used a second time. Before
using rubber rings, soak them in warm
water for 10 minutes, then quickly dip
them into boiling water immediately
before using.

A large container for processing the jars
is another essential. If the processing is
done on top of the stove then the container
must have a false bottom – a wooden or
wire rack is ideal – so that the jars do not
come into direct contact with the container. If they do they will crack. The
container must also be deep enough to
hold sufficient water to cover the jars
completely. Special canning pans are

available, and one of these is a good investment if you do a lot of preserving each year. If you use the oven method (see page 31), a large asbestos mat is necessary to stand the jars on.

Other useful items of equipment are a thermometer, a long-handled spoon, a pair of tongs and a heatproof measuring cup.

Preparation of fruit

Fruit used for preserving must be fresh, firm and clean. Wash the fruit in cold water and leave to drain in a colander. Remove the peel and pits from citrus fruits, cut the segments away from the tissues and remove any pits. Pears and apples are best peeled, cored and cut into slices or quarters. Apricots, peaches and plums can be canned whole or halved with the pits removed.

Fruit may be preserved in fresh water or syrup although syrup is preferable, since it helps to preserve the color and flavor. The strength of the syrup depends on the sweetness of the fruit and also on how it is packed. The proportions are generally 1 cup (225 grams) of sugar to 2½ cups (600 milliliters) of water.

To make the syrup, dissolve the sugar in the water over moderate heat and when the sugar is dissolved, boil for one minute. If the syrup is cloudy, strain it through cheesecloth because clear syrup gives a better finish to the fruit. The sugar used for syrup may be granulated or lump or for a different flavor, clear honey or corn syrup could be used instead. The syrup is used either cold or very hot, depending on the processing method.

A brine solution is best for tomatoes. Make it with 1 tablespoon of salt to 4 cups (1 liter) water. If they are packed solidly no water is necessary, but 1 tea-

The canning of fruit is an enjoyable and rewarding task. Careful preparation and the right equipment are essential.

spoon of salt should be added to each 1 pound (450 grams) tomatoes.

Packing the jars

Rinse the clean jars in cold water, drain them but do not dry them – it is much simpler to pack the fruit into wet jars since it slips down more easily. Fill with the prepared fruit and press down with the handle of a wooden spoon. Make sure the fruit is tightly packed but be careful not to bruise it. Fill the jars to within ½ to 1 inch (1-2½ centimeters) of the rim, then pour the syrup or water over the fruit a little at a time. Twist the jar from side to side after each addition to remove any air bubbles.

Methods of processing

Processing the jars can be done on top of the stove or in the oven. There are several methods employed for both types; one example of each is detailed below. The advantages of the first are reliability

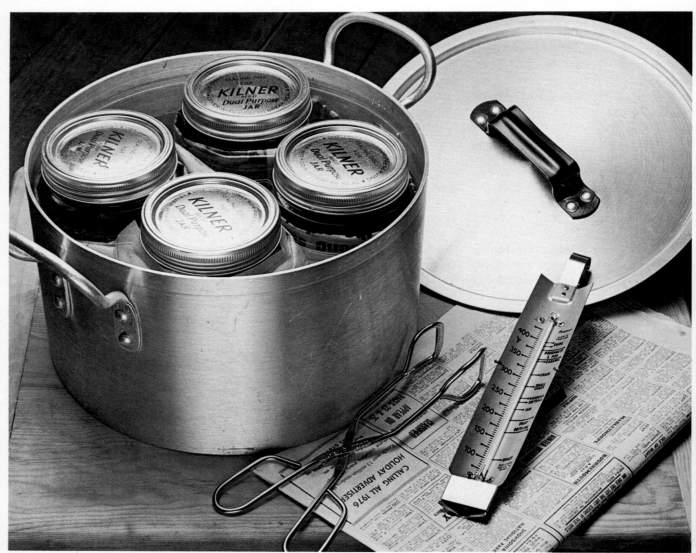

and economy of fuel, but it can only be done in a container large and deep enough to allow the jars to be completely immersed. It is more difficult to control the temperature with the oven method and the processing time is longer. See the chart on pages 40 to 41 for times and temperatures for different fruits.

Method 1: Slow water-bath
Pack the bottles with fruit and slowly pour in enough *cold* syrup (or brine) to come to the top of the jar. Place the lid on top and secure it with a spring clip or screw-band. Place the jars in a deep container, making sure they do not touch each other or the sides of the container. Completely cover them with cold water; cover the container with a lid. (If no lid is available, a pastry board is a good substitute.) Bring the water slowly to a boil. The temperature of the water should be raised gradually from cold to 130°F (55°C) in one hour and up to the required temperature (see chart pages 40 to 41) in up to another half hour. If the water is heated too quickly the fruit may rise in the jars and more time may be needed at the maximum temperature to enable heat to penetrate the fruit in the center of the jar.

When the processing time is finished, remove the jars from the container using a pair of tongs and place them on a wooden table or board. Tighten bands on the screw-topped jars and leave for 24 hours before testing that the seal is complete (see page 31).

Method 2: Pressure cooker
This is a quick method of preserving fruit because the temperature of the boiling point is raised when under pressure, so reducing the processing time and saving energy. The pressure to use should be 5 or 10 pounds (L or M). The basic principles are the same as other methods: the cooker must be deep enough to hold the jars and have a trivet or rack in the bottom. There should be 3¾ cups (900 milliliters) of water in the cooker before the trivet or rack and jars are put in, and it should be at boiling point before the jars are inserted.

The fruit is packed into warm jars and boiling syrup poured on top leaving 1 inch (2½ centimeters) headspace. Cover the jars and place them in the cooker making sure they do not touch each other or the sides. Cover the pan and bring up to L or 5 pounds pressure over moderate

Fill the jars, handling fruit gently.

The pressure-cooker method – quick and easy.

heat and process for the times given in the chart on page 40. Leave the jars in the cooker and allow pressure to reduce at room temperature. Remove the jars and finish as in the previous method.

Method 3: Moderate oven
This method can be used for all types of fruit and also for solid pack tomatoes. Preheat the oven to 300°F (150°C).

Pack warm jars with the fruit and pour in boiling syrup or brine leaving 1 inch (2½ centimeters) headspace. Place the lids on top but not the clips or screw-bands. Put the jars 2 inches (5 centimeters) apart on a baking sheet lined with newspaper and place in the center of the oven. After the processing time (see chart pages 40 to 41), secure the lids with clips or screwbands. Leave for 24 hours and test for seal.

Testing the seal
This is necessary to ensure that a complete vacuum has been formed during the processing and that no air remains in the jars.

After the jars have been left for 24

Pour the syrup into jars, covering the fruit.

Carefully test the firmness of each seal.

hours and are completely cool, remove the clips or screw-bands. Lift the jars carefully by the lids. If these are tight and secure the seal is complete. Wash the top of the jar carefully and refasten the clips. The screw-bands are replaced after being washed, dried and greased on the inside with a little oil – be careful not to screw them back on too tightly, or they may be difficult to remove after the jars have been stored. If the lids are loose the fruit should be reprocessed – the liquid should be poured off and reheated separately except when using Method 1 – or used within two days.

Label each jar with the name of the fruit or vegetable, date processed and whether with water, light or heavy syrup, or brine. They should be stored in a cool, dry dark place until required.

Canning vegetables
As already emphasized, the canning of vegetables should only be done in a reliable pressure cooker – if you are in any doubt it is wise to check with the manufacturer of the cooker. As the processing is rather lengthy, it is sensible to

preserve only the more expensive vegetables and those with a short season, such as asparagus and corn.

Vegetables should be young and very fresh, and processed as soon after gathering as possible. After preparation – corn kernels removed from the cob, and asparagus trimmed – they should be washed in cold running water. Vegetables need to be blanched before canning. This is done by plunging them into boiling water for two to five minutes, depending on the vegetables, then dropping them in cold water. Drain them well before packing into sterilized, warm jars. This helps to retain their color and causes them to shrink slightly, making it easier to pack them into the jars. Do not pack them tightly or press them down. Fill the jars with boiling brine made with 4 teaspoons (25 grams) of salt to 1 quart (1 liter) of water, leaving ½ inch (1 centimeter) headspace.

Cover the bottles in the same way as for fruit. Follow Method 2 for the processing *except* for the pressure and length of time. (See chart on pages 40 to 41 for this.) Place the covered cooker over medium heat and reduce it to low when steam starts to escape through the vent. Bring up to M or 10 pounds pressure and maintain this for the required time. Time

Chutney-making is a preserving method that is both easy and fun—and the tangy results are more than worth all the time and effort.

may vary according to the type of pressure cooker, so be sure to check in your instruction manual first.

When the jars have been sterilized the seal should be tested (see page 31). If it is not tight the jars may be re-sterilized, although there will be a loss of quality. Otherwise, use the contents at once.

Pickling and chutney making

Pickles and chutneys are condiments made with a mixture of fruits and/or vegetables, preserved by the addition of vinegar, salt and spices. They require similar equipment but differ in the length of cooking time required and the consistency of the end product. Chutney is a type of relish and is usually made from a combination of ingredients, while pickles refer to any food preserved in brine or vinegar and they often have only one basic ingredient.

Equipment

Pans should be large enough to contain all the ingredients. A preserving pan is ideal. Brass, copper or iron pans should *not* be used as they react with the vinegar and give a metallic flavor to the finished product.

A long-handled wooden spoon is required which should be reserved for chutney making and pickling only.

Heatproof jars of any type as well as standard canning jars with firm caps can

be used for the chutney. These should be clean, dry and warmed before pouring in the mixture.

A large ladle or heatproof jug is useful, especially when making a large quantity, to make it easier to fill the jars.

Chutney making

Vinegar is one of the most important ingredients in successful chutney-making, so it should be of good quality and have an acetic acid content of at least 5 percent. Do not use homemade vinegar because it most probably will not have the required acid content. Otherwise, you may use ordinary distilled white vinegar, which will best preserve the colors of the foods. Any well-known brand of cider vinegar is suitable – it darkens the food slightly, but adds a distinctive flavor and aroma. Wine vinegar will add yet another variation in taste. Note: avoid boiling the vinegar for too long, as this will will deplete the acetic acid that is so necessary for preservation.

You may substitute edible lactic acid for all or part of the amount of vinegar called for in both pickling and chutney recipes. As it is regularly available in 50 percent acid concentrations, use only 1/10 as much lactic acid as the amount of vinegar specified.

Both chutneys and pickles should be labelled with the name and date, then stored in a cool, dry, dark place. Most will keep for one to two years.

As vinegar has a slightly hardening

effect on some produce, particularly onions, carrots and other firm vegetables, it is advisable to cook them in water for a few minutes, then drain them, before adding to the other ingredients.

White sugar used may be cane or beet; brown sugar darkens the color and makes the flavor much stronger.

Ground spices are preferable to whole ones in chutney-making as they give a better flavor. If whole spices are used, double the amount given in the recipe, bruise them and tie them in a muslin bag before adding to the pan. The bag is then removed before the chutney is poured into the jars.

Pickle-making

Pickles may be made from a wide variety of fruits and vegetables. As with all methods of food preservation, the produce must be of good quality, fresh, firm and clean. Large vegetables – cauliflowers, cucumbers, cabbage and squash are best if they are separated or cut into pieces. Small vegetables such as onions (the small pickling variety), mushrooms and tomatoes can be left whole and only require to be peeled, halved or quartered and the seeds removed. Vegetables to be pickled should first be soaked in brine (see page 32) or dry salt for up to two days. Fruits that are usually pickled whole, such as damsons, plums and cherries, should be pickled before the preliminary cooking otherwise they will shrivel and dry up. Generally fruits that are most suitable for pickling are larger ones like apples, pears and peaches; berry fruits go mushy and are not pleasant to eat.

As well as fruits and vegetables, boiled eggs may be pickled and also some nuts, particularly walnuts.

Use only pickling or dairy salt, free from additives that may give a cloudy effect to the finished product.

Vinegar must be good quality, and have an acetic acid content of at least 5 percent. Brown malt vinegar is suitable for all pickles but if a light color is required, particularly for light-colored fruits and vegetables, then white distilled wine or cider vinegar may be used.

Spices are added to vinegar to give it a good flavor and they also help as a preservative. Whole spices should be used for spiced vinegar as the ground ones will make the vinegar cloudy. The spices used may be varied depending on the type of pickle and personal taste. A basic spiced

vinegar for pickling vegetables could be as follows: 2 inch (5 centimeter) piece cinnamon; 1 teaspoon cloves; 2 teaspoons whole allspice berries; 1 teaspoon black peppercorns; 1 teaspoon mustard seed; 2-3 bay leaves, 1 quart (1 liter) vinegar. Place the spices and vinegar in a saucepan, cover and bring just to a boil (do not allow the liquid to bubble). Remove the pan from the heat and set aside for 2½-3 hours. Strain the vinegar and if it is not going to be used immediately pour it into clean, dry bottles.

Spiced vinegar is used either hot or cold. Usually cold vinegar is best for the vegetables that should be kept crisp – onions, cauliflower and cabbage – while hot vinegar gives a better result to the softer fruit pickles.

Mango Chutney
Makes about 4 lb (1¾ kg)

3 lbs (1½ kg) green mangoes, peeled, halved and pitted
¼ cup (75 g) salt
8½ cups (2 liters) water
2 cups (450 g) sugar
2½ cups (600 ml) vinegar
3 oz (75 g) fresh root ginger, peeled and finely chopped
6 garlic cloves, crushed
2 teaspoons hot chili powder
2 in (5 cm) piece cinnamon stick
⅔ cup (125 g) dried dates, chopped

The finished product – spicy and piquant Pickled Beets.

Cut the mangoes into small pieces and place in a mixing bowl, sprinkle the salt over the top and pour in the water. Cover and set aside for 24 hours.

Drain the mango pieces and set aside. Place the sugar and vinegar in a preserving pan and bring to a boil. When the sugar is dissolved add the remaining ingredients and bring the mixture back to boiling, stirring occasionally.

Reduce the heat and simmer the chutney, stirring frequently, until it is thick; then discard the cinnamon stick.

Place in jars, seal and label.

Pickled Beets
Makes about 5 cups (1¼ liters)

6 medium-sized beets, uncooked and unpeeled
Cold water to cover
1½ cups (350 ml) wine vinegar
1½ tablespoons dry mustard
½ teaspoon salt
1 cup (275 g) sugar
2 onions, sliced
2 teaspoons dill seeds

Boil the beets until they are tender. Drain and set aside, reserving 1¼ cups (300 milliliters) of the liquid. When the beets are cool, slice off the tops and bottoms.

Then, using your fingers, gently slip off the skins. Slice the beets and set them aside.

In a medium-sized saucepan bring the vinegar and reserved cooking liquid to a boil over moderate heat. Add the mustard, salt and sugar. Stir to mix, and bring to a boil again. Remove the saucepan from the heat and set aside.

Arrange the beet slices and onions in layers in clean, screw-top jars. Add the dill seeds. Cover with the hot vinegar mixture. Tightly screw on the tops of the jars. Cool and place in the refrigerator. Allow the beets to stand for a few days before using. Serve very cold.

Note: Small, whole beets could be pickled in the same way.

Jams and marmalades

Jams and marmalades are probably the most popular and widely used forms of fruit preservation. They are the best way of using up surplus fruit and despite the excellence of some commercially produced jams nothing is better than really good homemade ones.

General information

Although different methods are used for jams and marmalades, the basic principles are the same. The fruit must be fresh, firm and under-ripe; over-ripe fruit will not make successful jam since it does not set. Fruit sets when boiled with sugar because it contains a natural pectin. The acid in fruit helps to extract the pectin thus ensuring a good set and a bright, clear color, which helps to prevent sugar from crystallizing when the jam is stored.

Equipment

A suitable preserving pan is the most essential requirement since jam is usually made in substantial quantities. The pan should only be half full when the sugar is added to the fruits, so that when the jam boils up quickly, during cooking, it will not rise over the side. Aluminum, stainless steel or unchipped enamel are the best. Jam made in a metal pan must not be left to stand in it longer than necessary. If the second stage (when the sugar is added) has to be delayed for some reason the fruit should be transferred to a plastic bowl and returned to the pan when the process is ready to be completed. A little glycerin or butter rubbed over the bottom of the pan will help to prevent sticking

34

and lessen the amount of scum.

Jam jars can be any type of jar, providing they are unchipped, clean and dry. They should be warmed slightly in the oven to prevent them from cracking when the jam is poured into them.

Commercial jam jars often have screw tops which provide an airtight seal. If the metal cover is lined with a thin piece of cardboard, this should be removed and the cover washed and dried. Lids must be put on while the jam is hot – if the jam is warm or actually cold, mold may form after a short period.

Use a heatproof measuring cup for pouring the jam into the jars, together with a long-handled wooden spoon for stirring, and a slotted one for removing foam.

A sugar or candy thermometer is a useful item if large quantities of jam are made, since it is the most accurate way to test that setting point has been reached.

Paraffin will be necessary to form an airtight, reliable seal.

Labels are essential to identify the type of jam and date on which it was made.

Fruits to use

Most fruits can be used for jam making but, as mentioned previously, they must be fresh, dry and slightly under-ripe. After preparation, the first stage for jam and marmalade is to soften the fruit. The fruit should be cooked slowly with a little water so that the skins soften and the pectin is released. The amount of water and cooking time depend on the ripeness of the fruit and also the quantity – the more fruit, the less water. Soft fruits such as blackberries, raspberries and strawberries do not require any water and the softening time will be much shorter. Fruits which are most easily made into jam are those which are high in pectin, although those low in pectin can be successfully made into jam with the addition of high pectin fruits or substitutes.

High pectin fruits include citrus fruits, cooking apples, cranberries, damsons, gooseberies, plums and quinces. Medium pectin fruits include apricots, blackberries, greengages and raspberries. Low pectin fruits include cherries, figs, grapes, pears, pineapple, rhubarb and strawberries.

To make successful jam from low pectin and acid fruit, extra pectin should be added and this can be done in one of the following ways:

1. Mix the low or medium pectin fruit with a high pectin one, for example, apple and blackberry or rhubarb and plum.
2. Add commercially-made pectin, which is generally available in powdered, or sometimes liquid, form.
3. Add lemon juice or citric acid. Commercial pectin must be well softened before it and sugar are added to the fruit. The amount of pectin needed varies according to the fruit used, but a general guide is $\frac{1}{2}$ cup (150 milliliters) pectin stock to 4 pounds (2 kilograms) fruit. Alternatively, $\frac{1}{4}$ to $\frac{1}{2}$ cup (50-125 milliliters) of commercial liquid pectin or 2 teaspoons dried pectin can be added to each 1 pound (450 grams) of fruit. If using lemon juice, 3 tablespoons to 4 pounds (2 kilograms) of fruit is generally considered sufficient.

Sugar

Granulated sugar can be used for jam and marmalade making. Brown sugar gives a dark color, so it is best used for chunky marmalade or black cherry jam.

The amount of sugar required to give a good set depends on the pectin quantity of the fruit and should represent 60 percent of the final weight of jam. Therefore, if a recipe uses 6 pounds ($2\frac{3}{4}$ kilograms) of sugar, the final yield should be about 10 pounds ($4\frac{1}{2}$ kilograms) jam. The following is an approximate guide to the quantity of sugar needed for the different types of fruit, depending on their pectin content:

High pectin fruits – $2\frac{1}{2}$ to 3 cups (575–675 grams) sugar to 2 cups (450 grams) fruit.

Medium pectin fruits – 2 cups (450 grams) sugar to 2 cups (450 grams) fruit.

Low pectin fruits – $1\frac{1}{2}$ cups (350 grams) sugar to 2 cups (450 grams) fruit.

If too much sugar is used, the jam may crystallize with storing; and if too little is used, it may ferment. However, when a less sweet jam is preferred, less sugar can be used – although it will not keep for so long, and the yield will be smaller. The jam will, however, have a much more fruity flavor.

Tests for setting

A test that setting point has been reached should be made after the jam or marmalade has been cooked for the suggested time in the recipe you are following. Care should be taken not to boil beyond the setting point, otherwise the color, texture

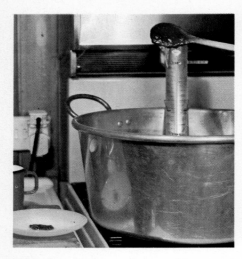

In jam-making, test for set with a candy thermometer or by the saucer method.

Once setting point is reached, carefully fill the jars with the hot jam.

and flavor will be spoiled. Thus the pan should always be removed from the heat during testing. Testing the setting point can be done as follows:

1. The simplest way is to put a teaspoon of the hot mixture on a saucer and leave it to cool. (This can be done in a few seconds in a freezer.) When cool, the surface should be set and the jam should wrinkle when pushed with a finger. If it is still runny, return the pan to the stove and continue boiling and testing until set.

2. A candy thermometer is the most accurate way of testing the set. Place the thermometer in a jar of hot water before and after testing. Stir the jam, then immerse the thermometer in it – be sure to use the kind of thermometer that comes equipped with a fastening clip and a bottom guard.

If the temperature is between 220°F (104°C) and 222°F (106°C) the jam is at setting point.

Finishing off

When the jam or marmalade is ready, remove any foam from the surface with a slotted spoon. If the jam contains whole fruit, such as strawberries, or peel, as in marmalade, leave it to cool until a thin skin forms on top (this prevents the fruit from rising to the top). Stir the jam gently and pour it into the warm jars. Fill to within $\frac{1}{8}$ inch of the top of the jar. Immediately place lid on and screw tightly closed. Wipe the rims of the jars with a damp cloth if they are sticky.

Label and store the jars in a cool, dark place.

If the jam is to be used within a few months and it will be stored in a cool, dry

36

place, paraffin may be used as a seal. Pour the jam as soon as ready into the warm jam jars to within $\frac{1}{2}$ inch ($\frac{1}{4}$ centimeters) of the top. Immediately pour a layer of paraffin about $\frac{1}{8}$ inch thick over the top, covering the jam. Turn the jar all around to be sure the paraffin touches the glass completely, making a good seal. Let the wax harden, pricking any bubbles that form on top. Place caps on the jars.

Jam making

Prepare and cook the fruit, with or without water, over low heat until it has softened and broken down. Add the sugar and pectin, if necessary, cook slowly stirring frequently until the sugar dissolves. Raise the heat and boil the jam rapidly without stirring. Take care that the jam does not rise to the top of the pan – if it does, give it a gentle stir to cool it down a fraction. If the initial cooking of the fruit has been sufficient, the jam should reach setting point within 5–25 minutes. Then pour the jam into the jars leaving a $\frac{1}{2}$ inch (1 centimeter) headspace, cover and label.

Strawberry Jam

5 lbs ($2\frac{1}{4}$ kg) strawberries, hulled and washed
$\frac{1}{2}$ cup (125 ml) lemon juice
8 cups (2 kg) sugar

Put the strawberries in a preserving pan and add the lemon juice. Simmer, stirring frequently, until the berries are soft.

Add the sugar and stir until it has dissolved. Bring to a boil and boil rapidly for 15-20 minutes. Test for setting. When

set, leave the jam for 10 minutes before pouring into the jars. Cover, seal and label.

Marmalade

Marmalade is traditionally made with citrus fruits, such as oranges, lemons, limes, grapefruits or tangerines, each imparting its own tangy flavor, but citrus fruit can also be mixed with other fruits to make a pleasant combination or flavored with ginger or other spices if wished.

The main difference between marmalade and jam making is that citrus fruit skin requires long slow cooking in a larger amount of water to soften it before adding the sugar. However, the cooking time can be shortened considerably by using a pressure cooker.

Preparation of fruit

The fruit must be fresh and just ripe. It should be washed and if necessary scrubbed with a clean brush. Remember that the pectin content is in the pulp, white pith and pits, *not* in the peel, so these must be added to the fruit while cooking.

In some recipes lemon juice or citric acid is added. This is because the acid content of the fruit may be lowered, owing to the high proportion of water and sugar used in making marmalade. Extra acid is unnecessary when marmalade is made with two or more fruits, or for lemon and lime marmalade.

To make the marmalade, scrub and scald the chosen fruit in boiling water (this makes it easier to remove the peel). Remove the peel as thinly as possible and cut into thick or thin shreds. Place the peel, acid (if used) and half the quantity of water in a preserving pan. Bring to a boil, then simmer for $1\frac{1}{2}$-2 hours or until the peel is soft.

Meanwhile, cut the fruit and pith into pieces and simmer in another pan for $1\frac{1}{2}$ hours. Strain the mixture through a colander placed over a bowl. Discard the pits, coarse tissue and pith and add the pulp to the peel. If a thicker marmalade is required the pulp should be pressed through a fine nylon strainer. Add the sugar and cook over low heat stirring frequently until it dissolves. Bring to a boil and cook rapidly until setting point is reached (see page 36). Remove any foam from the top, allow the marmalade to cool slightly and finish off as for jam making.

Freezing Chart

Food	Preparation	Storage life up to
Bread and cakes Bread, rolls, croissants, Danish pastries	Bake and cool before wrapping in plastic bags, seal and freeze. If sliced, individual slices can be toasted without thawing. Freeze breadcrumbs in convenient-sized plastic bags.	1 month
Cakes, scones, cookies	Bake and cool before wrapping in plastic bags or wrap. Preferably fill and decorate cakes during thawing. In recipes use egg yolks rather than whole eggs, high quality margarine instead of butter. Interleave layers of sandwich cakes with freezer paper or plastic wrap.	6 months
Unbaked yeast dough	Yeast does not remain stable very long when frozen. Pack the unrisen dough in greased plastic bags. Leave headspace and seal. Rising time may need to be increased: compensate by adding more yeast in doughs to be frozen.	2 months
Unbaked pastries and pies	Pastry is better frozen unbaked. Prepare in conveniently sized thin slabs. Wrap in foil or plastic sheet, roll out after thawing. Pies with a pastry base and/or covering should be prepared as for cooking. Cook and cool savory fillings before covering with pastry. Fruit does not require cooking. Foil dishes are ideal for packing: overwrap with foil before freezing.	6 months
Dairy Foods Whole eggs	Lightly beat yolks and whites together either with 1 tablespoon sugar or 1 teaspoon salt to every 6 eggs. Pack in waxed carton or tub leaving headspace. Seal well. Alternatively freeze in ice-cube tray and store frozen blocks in plastic bag. Seal well.	6 months
Egg yolks	Store better than whole egg. Gently mix yolks. Add a little sugar or salt. Freeze and pack as for whole eggs.	9 months
Egg whites	Pass through strainer, mix gently, add a little sugar or salt. Freeze and pack as for whole eggs.	9 months
Milk	Freeze only homogenized milk in waxed carton leaving headspace.	3 months
Cream	Freeze only heavy cream (not less than 40 percent butter fat). Preferably add sugar – one tablespoon to each 2 cups (600ml) cream. Pack in waxed cartons leaving headspace.	3 months
Ice cream	Store ice cream in original container. Homemade in wax cartons, leaving headspace.	3 months
Butter	Overwrap commercial packaging or tubs with plastic wrap or aluminum foil. Seal well.	salted up to 3 months; unsalted up to 6 months
Cheese	Hard cheese may become crumbly after freezing. Cream and cottage cheeses mixed with whipped cream make good sandwich fillings. Grated cheese freezes and stores well for use in recipes or for garnishing. Pack in tubs or cartons and grated cheese in plastic bags.	soft cheese up to 3 months; grated hard cheese up to 6 months
Fish White fish – cod, haddock, flounder, sole, whiting, etc	Small fish can be frozen whole after preparation. Glaze if preferred and pack in plastic bags or aluminum foil. Larger fish should be filleted or cut into steaks. Interleave individual fillets and steaks with aluminum foil, plastic wrap or freezer paper. Pack in flat wax or foil containers. Wrap in plastic or foil.	6 months
Oily fish – halibut, herring, mackerel, mullet, salmon, turbot, trout, etc	Prepare and freeze as for white fish. Storage life for oily fish is shorter than white fish.	3 months
Shellfish – crab, lobster	Only freeze shellfish if it is less than 24 hours since it was taken from the water. Cook crab and lobster, remove meat from shells and claws and pack in tubs, cartons or aluminum foil containers leaving headspace.	3 months
Oysters, scallops	Best frozen uncooked, remove from shells, retain natural juices. Wash fish in salt and water then pack in plastic tubs, cartons or aluminum foil containers with natural juices. Leave headspace before sealing.	3 months
Shrimp	Best frozen uncooked after washing in salt and water. Remove the heads and tails (if present) and pack in tubs, cartons or aluminum foil containers. The shells and veins should be removed during thawing.	3 months
Beef and lamb Large cuts	Remove bones and excess fat. Pad any projecting bones and seal as tightly as possible in aluminum foil or plastic bags. Seal well. Make stock from bones, freeze in ice-cube trays and pack in plastic bags.	9 months
Small cuts	Remove excess fat, wrap in aluminum foil or in plastic bag. Interleave chops, steaks, etc with aluminum foil, freezer paper or plastic wrap, draw out as much air as possible before sealing well in aluminum foil or plastic bags.	6 months

Freezing Chart

Food	Preparation		Storage life up to
Pork and Veal Large cuts Small cuts	Prepare and pack as for beef and lamb.		4 months 3 months
Ground meat and sausages	Prepare and pack as for small cuts. Freeze only freshly ground meat and bought sausages. Avoid salt in sausages as this reduces storage life.		1 month
Poultry and game	Remove head, tail and feathers. Clean and truss as for cooking, pad any projecting bones. Do *not* stuff poultry before freezing. Pack in plastic bags, excluding as much air as possible, and seal well. Make stock from giblets, skim all excess fat after cooling and freeze in tubs or cartons leaving headspace.		Chickens up to 9 months. Ducks, geese, turkeys and game up to 6 months.
Poultry pieces and quarters	Freeze and wrap individually in plastic bags or aluminum foil. Several portions can be frozen in one package providing pieces of poultry are interleaved with aluminum foil or plastic wrap.		Chicken up to 9 months. Duck, goose, turkey portions up to 6 months.
Variety meats (offal)	Prepare and pack as for small cuts. Maintain strict hygiene standards.		2 months.

Vegetables	Preparation	Blanching time in minutes	Storage life up to
Artichokes (globe)	Trim off coarse outer leaves, stalks, tops and stems. Add lemon juice to blanching water.	7	12 months
Asparagus	Wash, scrape stalks, trim to approx equal lengths. Divide up into thick, medium and thin stalks. Pack in rigid containers.	thin – 2 thick – 4	12 months
Beans (broad)	Pick young tender beans. Shell and discard any blemished beans.	3	12 months
Beans (French and runner)	Wash and trim ends, leave whole or slice thickly or cut into pieces about 1in (2½cm) long.	whole – 4 sliced – 3	12 months
Beets	Select young and small beets. Cook whole beets until tender, rub off skins and pack in rigid containers. Large beets should be sliced or diced after cooking.	none	6 months
Broccoli	Wash, and trim stalks cutting away any woody stalks. Divide up into thick, medium and thin stems. Pack in rigid containers, sprig to stalk. Separate layers with plastic wrap or freezer paper.	thick – 5 thin – 3	12 months
Brussels sprouts	Trim and remove discolored leaves. Cross-cut the stalks and wash in salted water. Can be frozen individually. Pack in rigid containers or plastic bags.	small – 3 large – 5	12 months
Cabbage	Trim coarse outer leaves. Wash in salted water. Cut or tear into shreds. Drain well and dry. Pack in rigid containers or plastic bags.	2	6 months
Carrots	Remove tops and tails. Scrape and wash. Leave small new carrots whole, but slice or dice larger carrots.	whole – 5 sliced – 3	8 months
Cauliflower	Select firm white heads. Remove most of coarse outer leaves. Separate into equal-sized sprigs. Wash in salted water, drain and pack in rigid containers. Add lemon juice to blanching water to retain color.	3	8 months
Celeriac	Wash, trim, scrape and slice, dry and pack into rigid containers or plastic bags.	6	9 months
Celery	Best suited after freezing for use as ingredient in recipes. Remove coarse outer stalks and strings. Cut into 2 to 3in (5–7½cm) lengths. Freeze hearts whole. Pack in containers or plastic bags.	hearts – 8 stalks – 4	12 months
Corn on the cob	Remove outer husks, trim ends and wash. Freeze separately and pack in plastic bags.	5 to 8 depending on size	12 months
Corn kernels	Remove outer husks, and scrape kernels off the cob. Wash, drain and pack in rigid containers or plastic bags. Can be added to other vegetables before freezing, eg peas.	5	12 months
Eggplant	Wash well and cut into about ½in (1cm) slices with stainless steel knife. Pack in rigid containers.	4	12 months

Vegetables	Preparation	Blanching time in minutes	Storage life up to
Leeks	Remove coarse outer leaves and trim root end. Wash well, leave whole or slice and pack into rigid containers or plastic bags. They freeze well in white sauce. Seal well to prevent cross-flavoring in storage.	whole – 4 sliced – 2	6 months
Mushrooms	Wash and peel field mushrooms. Trim stalks. Leave whole or slice. Add lemon juice to blanching water – or sauté in margarine – dry well and pack in rigid containers without blanching.	whole – 4 sliced – 2	12 months
Onions	Use only for cooking after freezing. Peel, slice into rings. Pack in small rigid containers and seal well to prevent cross-flavoring in storage. They freeze well in white sauce.	2	3 months
Parsnips	Choose young and small parsnips, scrape and wash. Cut into quarters or slices. Drain and pack into rigid containers or plastic bags.	3	12 months
Peas	Choose young sweet peas, shell and discard any blemished peas. Blanch in small quantities. Drain well and pack in containers or plastic bags.	1½	12 months
Peppers (red and green)	Wash, halve and remove seeds and stalk. Can then be sliced if preferred. Remove only tops and seeds if later to be stuffed. Freeze individually, whole or sliced. Drain and pack in plastic bags.	2	12 months
Spinach	Choose young tender leaves. Wash well in running water, drain and press out as much water as possible. Pack in rigid containers or plastic bags in portions or family mealtime quantities.	2	12 months
Turnips and rutabaga	Remove thick peel and cut into 1in (2½cm) cubes. Pack in rigid containers or plastic bags.	3	12 months
Zucchini	Wash and cut into 1in (2½cm) slices. Drain and pack into rigid containers interleaving layers with freezer paper or aluminum foil.	3	12 months
Herbs – mint, parsley, sage, thyme etc.	Wash, drain and dry. Chop finely and freeze in ice-cube tray. Wrap cubes in aluminum foil or plastic bags. After freezing and storage, color and flavor may be reduced.	1	3–6 months

Fruit	Preparation	Storage life up to
Apples	Peel, core and slice. Use ascorbic acid to prevent browning. Blanch for two or three minutes for dry pack. Alternatively pack in dry sugar or medium sugar syrup with ascorbic acid. Pack in plastic bags or tubs. Leave headspace in syrup pack.	9 months
Apple sauce	Peel, core and slice, cook until tender and strain. Add sugar and pack in tubs leaving headspace.	6 months
Apricots	Peel, remove pits and freeze in halves or slices in medium sugar syrup with ascorbic acid. Pack in tubs leaving headspace.	9 months
Avocados	Peel, remove pits and convert flesh to purée, adding 1 teaspoon of lemon juice to each 2 cups (600ml) of purée. Season with salt and pepper and pack in tubs leaving headspace.	2 months
Blueberries and blackberries	Pick firm berries, remove stalks, wash and dry. Freeze as dry pack, individually, or as dry sugar pack or in heavy syrup. Pack in tubs leaving headspace.	9 months
Blackcurrants	Strip firm currants off stem, wash and dry. Freeze as dry pack individually for jam making, or in dry sugar pack or in heavy sugar syrup. Pack in tubs leaving headspace.	9 months
Cherries	Pick fully ripe, firm fruit, wash and dry. Remove pits and freeze as dry pack for jam making or in light sugar syrup. Pack in tubs leaving headspace.	9 months
Citrus fruits: lemons, oranges, grapefruit	Peel and remove pith and pits. Separate into segments and pack in tubs with medium sugar syrup leaving headspace. Alternatively wash, dry and freeze whole, especially oranges for marmalade making.	9 months
Cranberries	Remove stalks, wash and dry. Freeze whole in dry sugar for sauce or strain for purée, then pack in tubs leaving headspace.	6–9 months
Damsons	Wash, halve and remove pits. Pack dry for jam making, in dry sugar pack for cooking and dessert varieties in heavy sugar syrup. Pack in tubs leaving headspace.	9 months

Freezing Chart

Fruit	Preparation	Storage life up to
Grapes	Seedless varieties of grapes can be frozen whole; otherwise halve, remove seeds and pack in a light sugar syrup leaving headspace.	9 months
Loganberries	Select firm berries, remove stalks, wash and dry and pack dry, individually or in dry sugar; pack in tubs leaving headspace.	9 months
Melon	Peel and halve the fruit to remove the seeds. Cut into slices, cubes or balls and immerse immediately into light sugar syrup. Alternatively sprinkle prepared melon pieces with lemon juice and pack in dry sugar. Leave headspace in cartons or tubs.	9 months
Peaches	Peel, remove pits and cut into slices. Immediately immerse in medium sugar syrup with ascorbic acid. If dry sugar pack is preferred, dip slices into ascorbic acid solution before sprinkling with sugar.	9 months
Pears	Peel, core and cut into quarters or slices. Immediately sprinkle with lemon juice to avoid discoloration. Then cook for about five minutes in light sugar syrup. Drain the fruit, cool and pack in tubs in medium sugar syrup with ascorbic acid leaving headspace. Freeze and store best as a purée.	6–9 months
Pineapple	Peel and core, then cut into slices, rings or cubes. Pack into light sugar syrup using any juice from the fruit. Leave headspace in tubs and cartons.	3 months
Plums	Wash, halve and remove pits. Pack dry or in dry sugar pack for jam making. For dessert use pack in heavy sugar syrup with ascorbic acid, leaving headspace in tubs.	9 months
Raspberries	Select firm berries and wash *only* if necessary. Freeze individually or in dry sugar pack.	9 months
Redcurrants	Strip currants off stems, wash and dry. Freeze individually or dry pack for jam making. Alternatively pack in tubs leaving headspace with heavy sugar syrup for desserts.	9 months
Rhubarb	Select only young and tender stalks. Cut into 1in (2½cm) pieces and lightly cook. Drain and cool and pack in dry sugar for pie fillings and jam making, or in heavy sugar syrup for dessert use, leaving headspace in tubs.	9 months
Strawberries	Remove hulls and wash *only* if necessary. Freeze individually or in dry sugar pack.	9 months
Tomatoes	Best frozen as a purée, otherwise wash, dry and freeze individually whole if to be used for cooking.	6–9 months

Canning Chart

Fruit	Preparation	Temp	Method 1 *Time maintained minutes	Method 2 Time maintained at L (5lb) pressure in minutes	Method 3 Time 1–4lb (450g–1.75kg) minutes	5–10lb (2.25kg–4.5kg) minutes
Apples (in syrup)	Peel, core and quarter or slice. Keep under salted water (1 teaspoon salt to 5 cups [1 liter] water). Drain and rinse before canning.	165°F (74°C)	10	1	30–40	45–60
Apples (solid pack)	Prepare as above. Blanch in boiling water for 2 to 3 minutes or steam over boiling water until just tender. Pack warm.	180°F (83°C)	15	3–4	50–60	65–80
Apricots	Remove stalks. Pack whole or cut in half and remove pits.	180°F (83°C)	15	1	40–50	55–70
Blackberries	Remove stalks and leaves.	165°F (74°C)	10	1	30–40	45–60
Cherries	Remove stalks.	180°F (83°C)	15	1	40–50	55–70
Citrus fruits (oranges, lemons, grapefruit, etc) (for marmalades)	Remove peel and white pith. Divide into segments and discard pits.	180°F (83°C)	15	1	40–50	55–70
	Wash and cut the fruit into pieces. No liquid is required for Method 2.	180°F (83°C)	15	15	50–60	65–80
Currants (black, red, white)	Remove stems and broken fruit.	180°F (83°C)	15	1	40–50	55–70

Fruit	Preparation	Temp	Method 1	Method 2	Method 3	
Damsons	Remove stems.	180°F (83°C)	15	1	40–50	55–70
Gooseberries (for cooking)	Remove tops and tails. If using syrup, nick the ends to prevent shrivelling.	165°F (74°C)	10	1	30–40	45–60
(for use uncooked)		180°F (83°C)	15	1	40–50	55–70
Greengages	Remove stalks. This fruit is often cloudy when canned.	180°F (83°C)	15	1	40–50	55–70
Loganberries and raspberries	Remove stalks. This fruit attracts maggots so pick carefully	165°F (74°C)	10	1	30–40	45–60
Peaches	Peel (see Tomatoes, below). Pack in halves or whole.	180°F (83°C)	15	3–4	50–60	65–80
Pears	Prepare as for apples in syrup. Pack and process as quickly as possible after preparing. Cooking pears should be stewed until tender.	190°F (88°C)	30	4	60–70	75–90
Pineapples	Remove peel and center core. Cut into rings or cubes.	180°F (83°C)	15	3	50–60	65–80
Plums	Remove stalks. Pack whole, or cut in half and remove pits. Replace a few kernels if desired.	180°F (83°C)	15	1	40–50	55–70
Rhubarb	Best canned when young so no need to peel. Wipe and cut stalks.	165°F (74°C)	10	1	30–40	45–60
Strawberries	Remove hulls. This fruit loses color and may rise when canned. A few drops of red food coloring may be added if desired.	165°F (74°C)	10	1	30–40	45–60
Tomatoes (whole)	Remove stems. Pack with or without skins. The skins can easily be peeled off if the tomatoes are put into boiling water for 5 to 15 seconds and then dipped in cold water.	190°F (88°C)	30	5	60–70	75–90
Tomatoes (solid pack)	Peel, cut in halves or quarters. Pack tightly in the jars, sprinkling salt on each layer – 2 teaspoons to every 2lbs (1kg) of tomatoes. A teaspoon of sugar added to each jar will improve the flavor. Press the tomatoes well down in the jars but do not add any liquid.	190°F (88°C)	40	7	70–80	85–100

*Increase process time for large jars when using Method 1
3–4lb (2kg) size by   5 minutes all packs except Tomatoes Solid Pack 10 minutes
5–6lb (3kg) size by 10 minutes all packs except Tomatoes Solid Pack 10 minutes
7–8lb (4kg) size by 15 minutes all packs except Tomatoes Solid Pack 30 minutes

Vegetables	Preparation	Blanching Times (minutes)	Time maintained at M (10lb) pressure
Asparagus	Peel or scrape the stalks and trim to equal lengths. Tie in bundles (about 6 in each). Pack into jars with stalks uppermost.	2–3	35
Beans, broad	Remove and discard pods. (Note: broad beans may turn brown during sterilization.)	3	40
Beans, French	Trim ends and remove string if necessary. Wash and pack whole.	3	35
Beans, runner	Wash, string and slice.	3	35
Corn	Remove and discard the husks and silk thread. Cut the kernels from the cob, making sure they are not damaged.	3	50
Peas	Remove and discard pods. Ideally select peas of even size for each.	2	45

Note: It is advisable to use jars of 1–2 pint (600ml to 1 liter) capacity to ensure the sterilizing process is complete. The above times are based on these sizes. If larger jars are used an extra 5–10 minutes should be added. Jars larger than 4-quart (8 liter) capacity must not be used for canning vegetables.

Chapter Four

The common ingredients of cooking – sugar, flour, milk, cheese, to name only a few – are so taken for granted that few people think seriously about how and why they work. Once you understand the ingredients, however, you will find them far easier to work with. You will be able to read and interpret recipes more easily and will notice how ingredients behave as you work with them.

Long-life foods

Sugar

Sugar is a crystalline substance used to sweeten foods and beverages and as a preservative – for example, in the preparation of jam. It is obtained from various plants but made commercially from sugar cane and sugar beet.

Sugar cane, the major source of sugar, is a bamboo-like grass which grows in tropical and sub-tropical climates. Sugar beet grows in mid-latitude climates. There is no noticeable difference, either in flavor or appearance between cane and beet sugar.

The first stage of the refining process is the formation of *massecuite*, which is a mixture of crude crystals and syrup. The crystals are separated from the syrup by a spinning process and the isolated syrup is then used for the preparation of golden syrup (like corn syrup) and molasses.

Golden syrup is a pale-colored syrup which is less sweet than sugar. It contains more water and glucose and a higher proportion of calories. Light corn syrup can be substituted for it in recipes.

Molasses is a dark, sweet syrup, which comes in two forms, sulphured and unsulphured. Sulphured molasses is the by-product of cane sugar making, which requires sulphur fumes. Unsulphured molasses is made from mature, sun-ripened canes and, if available, is preferable to the sulphured type.

Brown sugar, the partly refined sugar crystals, may be either dark or light and comes packed either plain or granulated, the latter having the advantage of not going hard when stored after exposure to air. Coarsely ground brown sugar is **raw sugar** in the United States and **demerara** in Great Britain.

White sugar is produced after further processes of refining. Granulated sugar is the coarsest and cheapest of the white sugars and is the most commonly used sugar in cooking. It is perfectly acceptable for sweetening liquids, preserving, making cakes and biscuits, and candies.

Superfine (or Castor) sugar is obtained by separating the finer from the coarser grains of granulated sugar or by grinding down granulated sugar. This sugar is less gritty than granulated and is therefore often used in baking. Ordinary sugar may be used instead.

Cube or **lump sugar** is made by compressing white sugar into lumps. This type of sugar is used to sweeten beverages or remove the sharpness from citrus fruits.

Confectioners' sugar is very finely milled white sugar which is mixed with a small amount of cornstarch to prevent lumps from forming.

Coffee sugar or **crystals,** used almost exclusively abroad, may be white, brown or multicolored and were originally developed for the benefit of coffee connoisseurs because they dissolve more slowly than other sugars.

Preserving sugar produces brighter and more translucent jams and jellies. Ordinary sugar is also suitable.

Sugar, whether it is brown or white, is an almost pure carbohydrate. Molasses contains calcium and iron, but in such small quantities as to be almost negligible. Sugar provides energy which is quickly assimilated into the body. However, research has disclosed the fact that the regular and large consumption of sugar contributes to tooth decay.

Sugar substitutes have been developed for the diabetic and weight conscious. These are suitable for sweetening liquids but are less satisfactory in cooking. They should be used in recipes specifically designed for them. The chief substitute, saccharine, is now under strict supervision and allowed to be used *only* by diabetics and those on a diet under doctor's supervision. It will soon not be allowed in products for general consumption.

In baking, sugar not only sweetens but improves texture. It gives cake a soft consistency when dissolved in a little liquid (including eggs). The resultant syrupy liquid also slightly softens the gluten in the flour. Creaming sugar and fat encloses air, thereby creating a much lighter mixture that will ultimately rise more.

Sugar boiling

Cooked sugar is the basis for most candy-making, some icings and the preservation and cooking of fruit. It is important when cooking with sugar to completely dissolve it before the mixture is brought to a boil. A heavy-based saucepan should be used if possible, so that an even temperature may

A representative selection of the sugar found in every well-stocked kitchen, including ordinary white granulated, brown sugars, lump sugar and confectioners' sugar

Sugar Boiling Chart

Temperature	Description	Use For
215°–234°F (102°–111°C)	Thread	Thin syrups or thick syrups
234°–240°F (111°–115°C)	Soft ball	Fondants and soft fudges
246°–252°F (119°–122°C)	Hard ball	Hard fudges
300°–310°F (149°–155°C)	Crack	Soft toffees
330°F (165°C)	Hard crack	Hard toffees and spun sugar
356°F (182°C)	Caramel	Coating fruit and cakes, also as a coloring agent for savory sauces

be maintained. For skilled candy-making a candy or sugar thermometer is required, but simple candies can be made without one, in which case the condition of the sugar solution when cooled rapidly is used as a guide to temperature.

To test a sugar solution, drip about ½ teaspoon into a cup half-filled with cold water. A *small thread* or *gloss* means that the cooled sugar will form a short thread when the thumb and forefinger are pulled apart. A *large thread* means the syrup is slightly tackier and a longer thread can be formed when the thumb and forefinger are pulled apart. A *small soft ball* means that the cooled sugar forms into a small lump which is very malleable. A *hard* or *large ball* means a firm, but still malleable lump is formed. A *small* or *soft crack* means that the cooled sugar sets into a brittle thread which will bend and break as soon as it enters the water. A *hard crack*, that the brittle thread formed snaps without bending. A *caramel* means the color of the sugar solution changes to light golden, then to deep brown and the cooled sugar is very brittle and breaks easily. (See the chart on page 44 for candy or sugar thermometer equivalents and uses).

While the sugar solution is boiling, it should not be stirred because this causes sugar crystals to form, which in excess cause grainy-textured candy. When a fine texture is required, as in fondant, a little acid such as lemon juice or tartaric acid is added.

Honey

Honey is natural liquid sugar made by bees. The bee converts the sucrose in the nectar of flowers into glucose and fructose by means of an enzyme it carries in its body.

Honey is an easily assimilated source of energy and the oldest-known method of sweetening food. It was used extensively in cooking and preserving before cane sugar became available. The flavor depends on the herbs and flowers from which the bees take the nectar; rosemary and heather are among the most prized and the honey of Mount Hymettus in Greece is particularly famous.

Honey can be substituted for sugar in many recipes, but more honey than sugar will be required and a reduction should be made in the liquid used. Only clear honey should be used in cooking.

Honey has hygroscopic properties, which means that it absorbs moisture. For this reason, bread and pastries made with honey remain moist for a long time and thus keep well.

Flour

Flour is finely ground cereal. Commercially, the cereal is always wheat except when otherwise qualified, and again if not qualified it means white wheat flour. Other flours are obtained from grains, fruits and vegetables such as oats, barley, buckwheat, corn, rye, beans, bananas, cassava, peanuts and potatoes and are always labelled accordingly.

Finely ground wheat flour consists basically of the starch and gluten of the grain, the bran having been milled out. When all the bran is included it is called wholewheat or graham. Abroad, forms of this are variously called wholemeal or wheatmeal flour.

The way you use flour depends on how much gluten and starch it contains. Gluten is the nitrogenous part of flour which absorbs water, and the higher the proportion of gluten the more water the flour will absorb, which means that the mixture will rise more and the yield will be greater. Flours with a high gluten content contain more hard wheat flours and are particularly suitable for making breads and other yeast doughs. The less gluten there is in flour, the higher the proportion of starch. Starch absorbs fat and so flours with low gluten content are the types most commonly used for making cakes and biscuits. Thus, cake flours consist mainly of soft wheat.

All-purpose flour is designed for a wide variety of recipes – bread, pastry, cookies, some cakes. It is a combination of hard and soft wheats. Substitute ⅞ of a cup for each cup of cake flour.

Most all-purpose flour is presifted.

Cake flour, a fine, soft-wheat flour, is used only in cake baking, where it gives a moist crumb and fine texture. Sift before and after measuring. If you have to use it for pastry or cookies, substitute 1⅛ cups for each cup of all-purpose.

Self-rising cake flour has leavening and salt added. Use only in recipes calling for baking powder. Self-rising flour has a shorter shelf life than cake flour because the raising agents lose potency.

All-purpose flour may be used.

Wholewheat flour makes excellent bread. So does rye, but oatmeal, cornmeal, rice flour and barley meal must all be mixed with wheat since they have little gluten.

In recipes where flour is called for, this means all-purpose flour, otherwise the type of flour (self-rising, etc.) is specified.

Flours differ from nation to nation: if you are using a foreign recipe, you will probably have to adjust the amount used.

Raising agents

Baked mixtures are induced to rise by air,

...am and carbon dioxide gas. Raising ...nts are the means by which air and gas ...introduced into a flour mixture.

...Air is incorporated by sifting flour and ...beating sugar, fats and eggs well. ...e creamed and beaten cakes, page 132.) ...am is given off by the liquid in the ...xture during cooking. This is why ...heating the oven is important. Carbon ...oxide gas is produced by chemical ...nge; when heated gases expand, the ...xture is stretched. Carbon dioxide gas ...roduced by yeast, bicarbonate of soda ...baking soda) and baking powder.

Yeast is a minute, single-celled fungus ...ich is used both as a raising agent and ...an agent of fermentation. Its properties ...utilized in the baking of bread and ...wing of alcohol.

...Yeast is activated into growth by the ...dition of carbohydrates – in the form of ...ar – liquid and warmth, in the correct proportions. An excess of sugar, cold, fat or salt will retard growth, while too much will kill the yeast altogether. The yeast is killed during the baking process but by then the yeast has done its work. As the yeast grows a ferment is produced which breaks down the carbohydrates and converts them into carbon dioxide which causes the dough to rise.

Fresh yeast is moist and crumbly in appearance and is preferred by some people to dried. Fresh yeast is obtainable from specialist food stores, and may be kept, well wrapped, in the refrigerator for two to three days, or in the freezer for several months. If you cannot find fresh yeast, dried yeast which is available in most food stores is a suitable alternative. Dried yeast comes in sealed, date-stamped packages containing 1 scant tablespoon ($\frac{1}{4}$ ounce). One package of dried yeast is the equivalent of 1 cake ($\frac{1}{2}$ ounce) of fresh yeast, since you use half as much dried yeast as fresh.

The alkaline **bicarbonate of soda or baking soda,** used alone or combined with an acid, releases a gas when heated with a liquid. Used alone it gives up only half its carbon dioxide, leaving a disagreeable taste and smell. When mixed with an acid, all the gas is released. Thus recipes calling for soda usually contain vinegar, sour milk, jam, marmalade, molasses, honey or spices. Without an acid ingredient, soda is usually combined with tartaric acid, calcium acid phosphate or sodium aluminum sulfate. The tartaric and phosphate combinations begin to work as soon as they come in contact with liquid in a dough and should be baked immediately to keep gas escape to a minimum. They are known as **single-acting baking powder.** The sulfate type also starts to work with liquid, but gets a second boost when coming into contact with heat; this type is called **double-acting baking powder.** Most modern recipes call for the double-acting type.

Thickening Agents

Thickening agents have the ability to absorb liquid and to increase viscosity. The major thickeners are flour, cornstarch, arrowroot and egg yolks (see page 58). In addition, semolina, tapioca, potato and other starches thicken well. Reduction, or boiling down, will concentrate a gravy or sauce, and small pieces of butter stirred into a sauce just before serving have a slight thickening power.

Béurre manié (made with 1 part butter and 2 parts flour kneaded together

– see page 45), whisked by small bits into a hot liquid, will thicken it. Simmer for 1-2 minutes to cook the flour; if you boil the sauce, however, the beurre manié loses its thickening power.

Cornstarch is made from the ground kernels of corn. It has twice as much thickening power as flour and makes a translucent sauce. It has a raw taste if not cooked enough, and cornstarch sauce should therefore be simmered or cooked over hot water for 5-10 minutes. Do not overbeat these sauces because that thins them. Overcooking over high heat also causes loss of thickening power.

Cornstarch thickens acid fruit fillings better than flour because it loses its thickening power less quickly in the presence of acid. A little cornstarch added to an egg custard mixture dispels the worry about scrambling through overheating, for eggs added to a cornstarch mixture can be boiled.

Cornstarch should be mixed with a little cold water or other liquid and stirred to a smooth paste before it is added to a hot liquid. If it is being used with sugar, sift the two together so the cornstarch is evenly distributed. This prevents lumps when the liquid is added.

Arrowroot is a pure starch obtained from the sun-dried roots of several different tropical plants. The roots are ground to a fine white powder that is nutritious, easily digested and need not be cooked. It makes clear, delicately textured sauces. Use only half as much arrowroot as flour to thicken sauces, soups and puddings; when substituting it for cornstarch use an equal amount.

Arrowroot should be blended with a cold liquid and then added to the hot liquid. Simmer it gently because, like cornstarch, it cannot stand high heat or boiling. After 3-5 minutes, the sauce should become clear and slightly thickened. Serve the sauce soon after making, as its thickening powers do not last.

A tablespoon of arrowroot or cornstarch will thicken $1\frac{1}{4}$ cups (300 milliliters) of liquid.

Gelatin

Gelatin is a colorless solid made from boiling bones, cartilage and tendons. Sometimes it is extracted from fish (isinglass) and seaweed (agar-agar and carrageen moss). In its pure form it is used in cooking to set desserts, mousses,

salads and savory dishes. Commercially, it is used in canned meat products, soups, candy and ice cream.

Gelatin is tasteless and odorless and its main characteristic is that when dissolved into a solution with a liquid it will 'gel' or set on cooling, and melt or liquefy on warming. Thus gelatin dishes must be refrigerated or kept in a cold place until ready to use. They cannot be frozen, however, unless the fat content is high, as with some ice creams.

In warm weather and without a refrigerator, use one-third more gelatin. Too much gelatin, however, results in an unpleasantly rubbery substance – it should wobble when shaken gently.

Unflavored gelatin comes in powdered form in 1 tablespoon ($\frac{1}{4}$ ounce) envelopes, though some stores carry gelatin sheets. Powdered gelatin should soak undisturbed for 3 to 5 minutes, then combined with liquid just at the boiling point. Sheet gelatin must be soaked for 2 to 3 hours and then dissolved in a little water over low heat. One envelope of gelatin will set 2 cups to a firm consistency for unmolding – 2 hours for a clear gelatin, 4 for one with fruits or vegetables. Three $4\frac{1}{2} \times 6$ in (11×15 cm) sheets will set 2 cups of liquid.

Generally speaking, and unless a recipe particularly specifies it, do not dissolve gelatin directly in milk or add it to hot milk, as this will cause the milk to curdle. Dissolve the gelatin first in water and, when it is cool and begins to set, add it slowly to cool but not cold milk.

Fold fruits or vegetables in when the jelly is at the point of setting, or else they will sink to the bottom of the mold and appear as a solid layer on top when unmolded.

Most fruit is suitable for making jellies, but those with attractive coloring and a strong flavor, such as blackcurrants, oranges, lemons and pineapple, are particularly successful. Pineapple contains and enzyme which breaks down the gelatin and destroys its setting properties, so it is necessary to boil fresh or frozen pineapple for 2-3 minutes to kill the enzyme.

Bavarian creams and some mousses are based on flavored egg custard made with gelatin. Stiffly beaten egg whites and whipped cream are folded into the custard when it has cooled and begun to set. If it has become too set, it should be put over warm water for a few minutes.

Simple aspic is made with gelatin and stock. To coat a mold, fish or other savory food successfully the object to be coated must be chilled and the aspic just beginning to set. Working quickly, cover the object with a thin layer of aspic. Let it set. Add any decorations, then cover with another layer of aspic. For special occasions, replace 2-4 tablespoons (25-30 milliliters) of the liquid with wine or liqueur. Dry white wine, vermouth and sherry go well with savories; sweeter wines, cognac and fruit-flavored liqueurs suit sweet jellies.

Fats and oils

Fats and oils come from both animal and vegetable sources. They are compounds of fatty acids and glycerol and consist of carbon, hydrogen and oxygen. Fats at normal temperatures are solids, whereas oils are liquid. The main animal fats are butter, lard, suet and drippings.

Butter is a natural food, made from cream (solidified milk fats). There are two main kinds of butter. The first, sweet cream butter, is made from fresh cream in the United States and also in New Zealand, Australia, and the British Isles. The second, lactic butter, comes mainly from continental Europe and is made from ripened cream, that is, cream to which special bacterial cultures have been added to enhance the butter flavor and develop a mild acidity.

Most American butter is lightly salted, which gives it a flavor most Americans prefer and also enhances its keeping properties. Sweet butter means **unsalted** butter. Without salt, its keeping properties are less good, but some prefer it for table use and it is recommended for cakes and delicately flavored buttercream frostings.

Whipped butter has been aerated to increase its volume, thereby reducing the fat content of each tablespoon used. Thus, you get 6 sticks to the pound rather than 4. Whipped butter, however, should not be substituted for ordinary butter in cooking, because the fat content of any given volume of whipped butter is less.

Lard is the white fat of a pig, melted down to produce cooking fat. The best lard is made from the fat inside the ribs, around the abdomen, and around the kidney. Most commercially made, lard, however, uses fat taken from all parts of the animal. Stored in a cool, dry place,

46

For salmon in aspic, first carefully skin the salmon.

Using a spatula, spread mayonnaise evenly over the surface of the fish.

Spoon aspic on the point of setting over the fish to cover completely.

Decorate with cucumber skin, radishes and olives as used here.

Spoon over another layer of aspic, then chill until set.

Arrange on a serving dish and garnish with leftover chilled chopped aspic.

lard will keep for several months. Pure lard is excellent for deep-frying because it can be heated to a high temperature before it burns. When used in cookies and pastry it creates a flaky texture, but it is not suitable for most types of cakes.

Suet is the fat which is found around the kidneys and loins of sheep and cattle. Commercially prepared suet, which has been ground and mixed with a little flour and preservative to keep the shreds separate, is not readily available. Fresh suet from butchers' shops is prepared by discarding the membranes and fibers and chopping or grinding it finely. Suet is used in making suetcrust pastry, dumplings, micemeat and steamed or baked puddings (eg steak and kidney).

Dripping is the fat which flows from meat when it is roasting. Clarified drippings can be used for frying and roasting. Beef drippings are regarded as best for this. Pork or chicken drippings are sometimes used in pastry making. Lamb and mutton drippings should be discarded because they give a tallowy taste.

To clarify drippings, melt in a saucepan over moderate heat. Strain into a mixing bowl through a strainer lined with cheesecloth. Pour boiling water (three times the volume of the fat) over the drippings and leave to cool. The clean fat rises to the surface and, when it is quite cold and solid, can be skimmed off the top. All sediment in the bottom of the fat should be scraped off with a knife or dabbed off with paper towels.

Vegetable fats are solids made by chemically processing oils from a variety of plants. **Vegetable oils** are made from the same raw materials, but are processed in a different way. Some of the major oils are corn, coconut, peanut, olive, safflower, sesame, soy and sunflower. Except for olive oil, which has a distinct flavor, these oils are refined after processing so they are not particularly distinguishable from one another in odor or flavor.

Some oils, however, are higher than others in polyunsaturated fats. Among the most beneficial in this way are corn and safflower oils. Most margarines and cooking oils are blends, and you must read the label to see how 'high in polyunsaturated fats' the product is.

Medical authorities believe that too much saturated fat causes a build-up of cholesterol in the bloodstream and of fatty deposits on the walls of the arteries, which

can cause strokes and contribute to heart attacks. Polyunsaturated fats do not create deposits and they help to break down those caused by saturated fats. Since the typical western diet is high in hidden saturated fats (in meat, eggs, cheese and chocolate), using polyunsaturated fats daily helps maintain a balance.

Margarine is a commercially manufactured substitute for butter. It is now made with vegetable oils, though animal fats could also be used. It is deliberately constituted to have the same proportion of fat and water as butter, and is colored and flavored to resemble it. For most purposes it can be used interchangeably with butter.

Margarine is not recommended for frying or for greasing cake tins, since when it is melted a sediment is deposited which causes food to stick to the pan. It gives a light texture to pastry, cakes and cookies.

Soft or table margarines are increasing in popularity. They are made from a special blend of oils which remain soft at low temperatures. Like regular margarines they can easily be substituted for butter in any recipe.

White vegetable fats are sold under a variety of brand names. They are essentially flavorless and are designed to be used as a vegetable-oil substitute for lard. They contain no water and can therefore be used for frying.

Cooking

Connoisseurs state that nothing can surpass butter for all cooking purposes except deep-frying; health authorities feel butter (and all other saturated fats) should not be part of the normal diet; the rest of us have our budgets to consider and margarines are, on the whole, certainly cheaper. Thus, many people use both, employing margarine in strongly flavored foods, perhaps combining it with butter in more delicate cakes, and using butter alone for sauces and as a spread.

Fats for frying

The best fats for deep-frying contain no water or solids. The best for this purpose are lard (which has a distinct flavor), white cooking fat and vegetable oils except peanut, which has a low smoking point. These three types can all be heated to above the temperature required for frying. Dripping is extremely variable, depending on how well it has been

clarified, and it is better for shallow-frying. Butter and margarine both contain water and solids, which make them unsuitable for deep-frying. They also burn at low temperatures. Butter, but not margarine, is suitable for sautéing, as is cooking oil.

When butter begins to melt in a pan, the liquids in it begin to evaporate causing the butter to foam. When the foam subsides, the butter is still not very hot, but it is time to add the food to be sautéed. Butter mixed with an equal amount of cooking oil can be heated to a higher temperature before burning. Add the oil first, let it heat a few seconds and then place the butter in the oil. This combination foams in the same way as butter alone. Therefore, as the foam begins to subside, add the eggs, meat, fish or vegetables to the pan.

Butter can be heated to a higher temperature if the water, salt and solids are removed. This is known as clarifying. To clarify, melt the butter in a saucepan over moderate heat and cook gently without browning until all bubbling has stopped. This shows that the water has evaporated. Let the pan sit off the heat for 2-3 minutes while the milk solids and salt settle to the bottom. Strain the butter through cheesecloth into a bowl, leaving a milky residue behind. Clarified butter is used for making black butters (really a medium brown in color) for brains, fish and other dishes. It is known as *ghee* in India and is widely used for cooking in that country.

Deep-frying fat should be strained after use to remove food particles and to ensure nothing remains to cause 'off' flavors. Add a little fresh fat each time you fry to prolong the life of your fat. When the fat becomes thick and dark, it should be discarded because the smoking point will have dropped below normal frying temperature and the flavor will be unpleasant.

Fats for baking

Butter, margarine, lard, white cooking fat and oil can all be used in pastry making. The last three, which are water-free, make the shortest crust, that is, the most crumbly, but they are all lacking in flavor so butter or margarine, the least short of all the fats, are sometimes added.

The differences in shortening power are explained by what happens when fat is rubbed into flour. The fat encloses flour particles giving them a waterproof coating. Thus only the loose flour particles absorb the water added after the rubbing-in. The pure fats do a better job of enclosing than those with moisture.

During baking the fat melts and the flour cooks as separate particles bound together by fat. The air caught inside the fat along with the flour expands, assisting in making the layers inside good pastry.

Fats are incorporated into cakes by creaming and melting, the latter mainly in Europe. The first requires a fat that creams easily, that is, can be beaten to a smooth fluffy mass which has absorbed a lot of air. The fat should also have either good flavor or no flavor. Butter has excellent flavor, but creams only moderately well. Margarine, especially the soft type, has fairly good flavor and creams easily. White cooking fats are easy to cream, but other ingredients must supply the flavor. Lard's distinctive flavor makes it unsuitable for most cakes.

Fats for creaming should be at about 70°F (21°C). A fat taken from a cold place should not be warmed by heating, however, because the outside is likely to melt before the inside has warmed. If you cannot wait, use the following method for creaming with a wooden spoon. Warm the bowl, cut the fat into small pieces and mash each with a spoon. Continue hitting and beating until the fat has softened and become a creamy mass, then add the sugar and beat until light and fluffy. With electric beaters, the fat should be cut into pieces and whipped until the butter begins to fall away from the beaters. Then add the sugar.

Melted fats are added to dry ingredients in some European recipes. Plain cakes require a good-flavor fat, but highly spiced cakes can be made with any fat including drippings.

Vinegar

Vinegars can be made from a variety of raw materials. Natural vinegar results from a bacteria working on an alcoholic liquid to produce acetic acid. It can also be distilled chemically like distilled white vinegar.

Malt vinegar is based on malted barley, others are made commercially from cider and red or white wine. Other bases can be used though those are found only in specialty shops or homemade. Herb and spiced vinegars use a common vinegar as a base and are flavored by adding fresh herbs (tarragon, thyme or a mixture) or spices (ginger, clove, allspice, alone or in combination).

Try various brands of the same type of vinegar, say cider; for you will find some harsh, others sharp, mild or mellow. A good flavor makes all the difference in food preparation, especially in salad dressings (French, mayonnaise) and other sauces. Vinegars for pickling should contain 5 percent acetic acid to have adequate preserving powers.

Vinegar is also essential in the preparation of dishes such as pickled herring, and is also used in cakes with bicarbonate of soda, for the two blended together act as a raising agent.

Remember that all vinegars are corrosive and should be kept away from copper, zinc, aluminum and iron. Use them in glass, ceramic, enamel and stainless steel containers.

Chocolate and cocoa

Chocolate and cocoa both come from the beans of the *cacao* tree, a shrub native to Central and South America, but now grown throughout the tropics. The difference between chocolate and cocoa is that chocolate contains cocoa butter, or another fat as a substitute, whereas cocoa

A homemade herb vinegar (such as marjoram, below) makes a pleasant change.

has had 75-90 percent of the cocoa butter removed.

Cocoa butter is a pure fat, shiny yellow-white in color and with a faintly sweet chocolate flavor. It is used as a suntan oil and in many pharmaceutical preparations as well as in candy and as a butter substitute in some diets. It is high in saturated fats. Under normal storage conditions, it will keep for years without going rancid.

There are two main types of chocolate. Candy and fillings are made from a particularly refined chocolate with a higher proportion of cocoa butter. Although chocolate bars can be used in cooking, they do less well than cooking chocolate.

Cooking chocolate is packed in 1-ounce quantities which are either solid cubes or

a semi-liquid in a sealed envelope. Chocolate is either *unsweetened* or *semisweet*. If no designation is given in a recipe the unsweetened type is called for. Semi-sweet chocolate is about 40 percent sugar. German chocolate is another type of sweetened cooking chocolate. If your chocolate has the word "flavor" in its name, it is modified rather than pure.

Chocolate scorches easily and therefore it should never be melted over direct heat. The best methods are to place the chocolate in a double boiler or in a heatproof bowl set over hot but not boiling water. (The steam rising from boiling water can enter the chocolate and make it cloudy.)

When the chocolate has just melted, remove the bowl from the heat, stir it to

melt any solids, and cool it to tepid but still liquid before adding it to cakes, puddings or cookies. Sometimes a liquid – coffee, brandy, orange liqueur, rum – is added before the chocolate is melted.

Cocoa comes in two forms; an unsweetened powder used in cooking and a sweetened powder which is diluted with water or milk to form a drink. The cocoa specified in recipes is always the unsweetened type.

Cocoa often becomes lumpy when combined with liquids. To avoid this, either sift it with other dry ingredients or add a very little water to the cocoa and stir to form a thick, smooth paste. To make plain cake or cookies chocolate flavored, replace 3–5½ tablespoons of flour with cocoa.

Rice

Rice is one of the most important food grains in the world, and is the staple food of millions of people. There are about 7,000 varieties of rice and almost as many colors – rice can be red, brown, blue, purple, black or ivory. Long, short and round grain rice are the three most commonly used varieties in western cooking.

Because it keeps well, cooks more quickly and has a better appearance, most rice is milled before it is marketed. Milling removes the bran skin which lies under the husk, therefore some of the protein, minerals and vitamins are lost. Brown rice which has only the husk removed is more nutritious than other

varieties and is often used in vegetarian dishes.

Rice can be bought in several forms, among them are parboiled, precooked (which only requires reconstituting in hot water) and frozen boil-in-bags. Rice is also ground and used for puddings, or very finely ground to make rice flour for use in cakes and cookies.

Rice which is to be served as an accompaniment for a curry or used to make a pilaff or biryani should be a long-grain variety. Risottos are best made with absorbent Italian rice such as avorio or crystalo. Round-grain rice is the most suitable to use for rice-based cereals and desserts.

Rice absorbs liquids in varying amounts. Each variety, and sometimes

Rice is found throughout the world in many forms. Above, a selection of some common types: (left to right) brown, avorio (Italian-type) Basmati (long-grain), wild, round-grain (for rice pudding desserts), rice flour and natural.

different crops of the same variety, have unequal powers of absorption. The amount of liquid given in any recipe. therefore, can only be approximate. When cooking rice, check halfway through the cooking time and add more liquid if necessary.

Rice, when cooked, increases two and a half to three times in bulk, so 1 cup of uncooked rice will yield between 2½-3 cups of cooked rice. Servings vary with individual appetite and type of meal. For

51

rice-based meals such as Chinese and Indian, allow $\frac{1}{4}$ to $\frac{1}{3}$ cup (25-40 grams) of uncooked rice per person. If rice is to be used as a potato substitute in a western-style meal, $\frac{1}{4}$ to $\frac{1}{3}$ cup (25-40 grams) should be enough for two people.

Boiled rice

Plain boiled rice should be made with a long-grain variety. Many techniques can be used in cooking rice, and sometimes one works better than another for a particular brand or package. One method of cooking is to have the rice absorb all the liquid by the time it is done. This retains all the nutrients, but requires planning ahead and may not work well for some brands.

Measure the rice then wash thoroughly in cold running water. When the water runs clear, leave the rice to soak for 30 minutes, then drain. Put the rice in a saucepan and pour over twice as much water and add 1 teaspoon of salt. Place the pan over high heat and bring the water to a boil. Cover the pan, reduce the heat to low and simmer for 15-20 minutes or until the rice is tender and all the liquid has been absorbed. Remove from the heat and serve hot.

A second method is to boil the rice in a large quantity of water, drain and put in a colander to steam. Nutrients are said to be lost when the cooking water is drained off, but the end product is dry and fluffy. Rinse the rice and add it slowly to 4 to 5 times as much of rapidly boiling water. Let the rice boil rapidly, uncovered, for the time suggested on the package, stirring once with the back of a fork to loosen any grains stuck to the bottom. Bite a rice grain in half; it should have no hard core nor should it be limp. Cook 30 seconds more and test again if too hard. Drain the rice into a colander and rinse under running water. Now shake the colander well to remove as much water as possible. Refill the saucepan with 1 to 2 inches (2.5 to 5 cm) of water, place the colander, covered, on top and return to the stove to steam for 10 minutes or longer. (Don't let the saucepan boil dry.) Alternatively, place colander on an oven-proof plate and stand in a low oven 250°F (120°C) for 8 minutes to dry out. Do not leave it in the oven any longer than this or it will become too dry.

Boiled rice can be reheated most easily by steaming it in a colander placed over boiling water.

52

Italian rice

Italian rice is cooked in a completely different way from long grain. It is a thick, short grain, highly absorbent rice and requires slow cooking. The liquid is added a little at a time, the first amount being absorbed before more is added. Cooking times vary between about 20 and 30 minutes. The end result is creamier and more moist than long grain.

Basic rice pudding

Rice pudding is made with short or round grain rice. This absorbs liquid to form a soft, smooth mass. (Ordinary rice may also be used.) Preheat the oven to cool 300°F (150°C). Grease a 5-6 cup (1$\frac{1}{4}$ liter) baking dish with butter. Place $\frac{1}{4}$ cup (40 grams) of round grain rice, 2 table-spoons sugar, 3$\frac{3}{4}$ cups (900 milliliters) milk and 1 teaspoon vanilla extract or a pinch of grated nutmeg in the dish. Place the dish in the oven and bake the pudding for 3 hours. For a richer pudding, beat in 2 egg yolks 30 minutes before the end of the cooking time. For a more attractive appearance, remove the dish from the oven, sprinkle the top of the pudding with 1 tablespoon of sugar and place the dish under a hot broiler for 1 minute to glaze.

Pasta

Pasta is a name that is almost synonymous with Italian cuisine, and is a farinaceous product made from flour, water and sometimes eggs. The flour used is durum wheat flour with a high gluten content, which gives the dough its slightly brittle consistency.

Pasta is usually made commercially, although some types – most particularly egg noodles, ravioli and gnocchi – are still made at home. Spinach is sometimes added to the basic pasta dough.

Some Italian specialty shops sell freshly made pasta which is soft and pliable because it has not been fully dried. This should be cooked on the same day it is purchased. It is finer in flavor and texture than ordinary commercial pasta.

All pasta should be cooked in a large saucepan with at least three times as much water as pasta – 2 quarts (2 liters) of water for each $\frac{1}{2}$ pound (225 grams) of pasta. Bring the salted water to a rolling boil and add the pasta slowly so that the water never stops boiling. Long pasta should be pushed in gradually as it softens. Keep the

water at a rolling boil. Stir gently once with a fork to separate any clumps. Sticking or clumping can be prevented by the addition of a few drops of oil to the boiling water.

Never overcook pasta. It is ready to serve when 'al dente', which in Italian means the pasta still offers some resistance to the teeth. Cooking time varies greatly with the size and age of the pasta. Home-made varieties may be ready in 5 minutes, whereas thick or long-stored pasta can take as long as 15 minutes. Always test just before the minimum cooking time is up. Drain well in a large colander and serve immediately. It does not reheat well. Unsauced leftovers should be dropped briefly into boiling water to heat through. Those with sauce should be reheated over low heat, stirring gently and often.

Pasta is always served with a sauce of some kind – even though it may be as simple as melted butter and grated cheese. In Italy, pasta is served as the course before the main, usually meat, course, of the meal, although in other parts of Europe and the United States, pasta is more often served as a main course. The lighter, smaller pasta, such as vermicelli, are often used in soups.

Short keeping foods

Milk

Milk, which is produced by all mammals, is the most complete form of food. However, each species has unique requirements, and the milk differs in the amount of fat, protein and minerals in it. Thus, cow's milk, although good, is not ideal for humans. While most milk in the West comes from cows, goats and sheep are also suppliers, though today their milk is mainly used in cheese-making and sometimes ice cream.

Cow's milk in all its forms (butter, cheese, yogurt) is used extensively as a food and in cooking. Soups, sauces, custards and desserts all require milk. As befits a food with so many uses, milk is processed in a variety of ways. Bottled or cartoned milk is most commonly used in the home. This milk is perishable and should be kept at 40°F (5°C). It also needs to be protected from sunlight, which destroys the B vitamins.

Milk is available in numerous forms. Untreated or raw milk has had no pro-

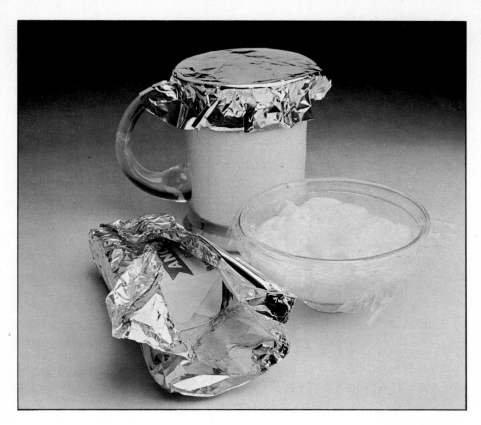

Milk and other dairy foods will keep better if they are properly wrapped.

cessing before bottling. In many counties and states it can no longer be sold commercially. Almost all of the milk now marketed is **pasteurized** to destroy disease-carrying bacteria. The milk is heated to 161°F (72°C) for 15 seconds, then rapidly cooled to 50°F (10°C), placed in sterile bottles and sealed. The cream separates from the milk and rises to the top of the bottle.

Homogenized milk has been pasteurized and then forced under high pressure through a tiny valve to break up the clusters of milk fat globules to a uniform size. This distributes the globules evenly throughout the milk and no cream rises to the top of the container. Almost all milk now sold is homogenized. In cooking it gives a different texture – sauces are thicker and fat separation is greater; gravy, cooked cereal and custards all tend to curdle more easily.

Skim milk has the same protein and mineral value as whole milk, but the fat content has been reduced to less than 1 percent, thus reducing its caloric value by half. This type of milk is recommended for people on low fat diets, and those who need to watch their cholesterol levels.

Milk is also processed to improve its keeping qualities. This type, not widely available, comes in different forms: **ultra-heat treated (U.H.T.)** and **sterilized** milk are both whole milks that need no refrigeration until they have been opened. The ultra-heat treatment process is similar to pasteurization except the milk is heated to 270°F (132°C) for 1 second. It is then packed into cartons under sterile conditions and will keep without refrigeration for several months. Its flavor is similar to pasteurized homogenized milk.

Sterilized milk has been homogenized before being poured into bottles which are closed with a hermetic seal. The bottles are then heated to 230°F (110°C). Because of the high heat the milk appears thicker and creamier than pasteurized milk and often has a slightly 'cooked' flavor. It will keep almost indefinitely, unopened, without refrigeration.

Canned milk with a reduced water content is sold as **evaporated** and sweetened **condensed** milk. Evaporated milk is either unsweetened full-cream or skimmed milk. The milk is reduced by evaporation (hence the name) to about one-third of its original volume. It is then sterilized and canned while still hot. Evaporated milk, when reconstituted to its original volume with water, has the same nutritional value as fresh pasteurized milk.

Evaporated milk is often used in cooking, as a substitute for cream in desserts, for example. Some varieties can be whipped and will thicken slightly. It can be stored for a long time in cabinets.

Condensed milk has also been reduced by evaporation until the water content has been reduced by as much as 60 percent. This means that 1 pint (400 milliliters) is the equivalent of 1¾ pints (750 milliliters) of ordinary milk. Condensed milk contains a large amount of sugar – as much as 4 ounces (125 grams) in a 16 fluid ounce (400 milliliters) can. This high proportion of sugar linked with the low proportion of water helps to prevent the condensed milk from deteriorating once the can has been opened. Because condensed milk tends to settle, the can should be turned over every two weeks. Condensed milk can be used in place of fresh milk for fudge, puddings and ice cream.

Milk can also be kept a relatively long time when dried. **Dried** milk is prepared from whole, partly skimmed or skimmed milk. The skim milk powder keeps better than the full cream type after opening, since the removal of the fat prevents the milk from becoming rancid. They should be stored in a lightproof container in a cool place.

Dry milk is frequently used to enrich foods such as bread, cooked cereal and desserts. Dieters sometimes replace cream in soups with skim milk enriched with 3 or 4 tablespoons of dried for each cup (300 milliliters) of skim milk. It can also be reconstituted with water. For drinking, always make up the milk several hours in advance and serve it well chilled. Its somewhat unpleasant odor and flavor will then have disappeared. A quart of dry reconstituted with one quart whole milk not only tastes like fresh, but also stretches milk. The powder blends smoothly if you first mix it with only a small amount of liquid to form a paste. Stir as you add the rest of the water. In cooking, dried milk should be sifted with the other dry ingredients. Reconstituted dried milk scorches more easily than whole milk, so take extra care. Use a double boiler over low heat and never use more than 3 tablespoons of powder to 1 cup (300 milliliters) of water.

Milk is also fermented to form cheese (see below), yogurt, buttermilk and sour milk.

Yogurt: Yogurt is a semisolid dairy product produced by fermenting milk with a culture of bacteria. During fermentation the lactose (milk sugar) is

53

converted to lactic acid causing the milk to clot.

Yogurt has the same food value as milk, though the sugar level is sometimes lower. It is a good source of protein and calcium, but despite the obvious dietary benefits of yogurt and the fact it is easily digestible, there is no evidence to support claims that it aids longevity or has any therapeutic value which cannot be obtained from an equivalent amount of milk or cheese. Because yogurt continues to mature even in cold storage, most commercial yogurts are marked with a date stamp and have a storage life of about two weeks. This does not mean that the yogurt is unfit for consumption after the date stamp has expired, but it will become considerably more acidic.

Diet conscious people sometimes substitute yogurt for sour cream in sauces, soups and salad dressings. Once it is added to cooked dishes they should not be heated above a simmer or the yogurt will curdle.

Buttermilk: Buttermilk is the liquid left after churning butter. It is about 90 percent water, 5 percent sugar, 3 percent casein, mineral salts and lactic acid, which gives it a sour taste. It is now also made from pasteurized skim milk to which a bacterial culture is added to develop flavor and a thicker consistency. It is good for both drinking and baking.

Buttermilk is used with baking soda as a raising agent, in the proportion of $1\frac{1}{4}$ cup (300 milliliters) of buttermilk to $\frac{1}{2}$ teaspoon of soda. Although buttermilk is available commercially in cartons, you can make a substitute for cooking using ordinary milk. Place 1 tablespoon of lemon juice or vinegar in a measuring cup and add $1\frac{1}{4}$ cup (300 milliliters) of fresh, evaporated or reconstituted dried milk at room temperature. Stir, then let the milk stand for 10 minutes to clabber, that is, thicken to approximately the consistency of yogurt.

Sour milk: Sour milk can only be made from unpasteurized whole or skimmed milk that has been allowed to ferment (sour) naturally. It is, therefore, virtually unobtainable today. Pasteurized and scalded milk will spoil rather than sour if left at room temperature or in the refrigerator for too long. In recipes that call for sour milk either use buttermilk, or sour fresh milk by using 1 tablespoon of lemon juice or vinegar to 1 cup (300 milliliters) of fresh milk and letting it

54

clabber. Like buttermilk, sour milk combines with baking soda to act as a raising agent. The presence of lactic acid in both produces a tender crumb in baking, while in sauces it gives an attractive, slightly acid flavor. Sour milk and buttermilk should never be allowed to boil.

The term 'scalding' is frequently used in conjunction with milk. It means to heat the milk to the point at which bubbles appear at the edge of the pan 180°F (80°C). Before pasteurization this was done to kill harmful bacteria, but now scalding is used exclusively to hasten or improve a food process. Scalding is most frequently called for in bread and baked custard.

Cream

Cream is the part of milk which contains all the fat. If fresh milk is left undisturbed, the cream will rise to the top and can be easily skimmed off.

Cream comes in several thicknesses, each of which has a different set of uses. Half-and-half, as its name suggests, is half-cream, half-milk and contains 12 percent butterfat. It is used with coffee, cereal, cold cream soups and berries by those who feel heavier cream is too self-indulgent or rich. Light cream, with about 32 percent butterfat, is used in the same way as half-and-half by those who are less diet conscious. Heavy cream, with 40 percent or more butterfat, is the only kind that will whip.

Sour cream comes in cartons or jars and is used especially in Eastern European cooking. Like yogurt, it must not be boiled or it will curdle.

Clotted cream – a British specialty – comes from Devon or Cornwall in England where the milk has a particularly high fat content. Clotted cream is made by leaving fresh milk to stand for 12 hours or more. It is then gently heated in a large shallow pan and the cream is skimmed off in layers, the last layer forming a crust.

To whip cream, use a wire whisk, a rotary beater, an electric beater or, if you have none of these, a plain fork. Put the cream in a cool mixing bowl and whip slowly. When the cream begins to thicken, whip it faster until it is as thick as you require. Do not over-whip as the cream will turn to butter. The volume of whipped cream may be increased by folding a stiffly beaten egg white into $2\frac{1}{2}$ cups

(600 milliliters) of cream. Add sugar to sweetened toward the end of the beating process. Partly whipped sweetened cream freezes better than unwhipped cream.

Milk can be substituted for cream in recipes that call for a lot of cheese, such as *quiche lorraine*.

Sour cream is cream which has been fermented by adding a bacterial culture. It has a tangy flavor and a smooth, semi-solid texture. Like the fermented milks (see above) it should not be heated above simmering point or it will curdle.

Sour cream can be made at home by vigorously shaking together $1\frac{1}{4}$ cups (300 milliliters) of light cream and 2 tablespoons of commercial buttermilk. Stir in another $1\frac{1}{4}$ cups (300 milliliters) of cream and let the mixture stand for 24 hours at a temperature between 70-80°F (24-27°C). It is now ready to use, though another 24 hours in the refrigerator makes a smoother product. A thicker sour cream can be made by replacing some of the light cream with heavy cream.

Cheese

What cheese is

Cheese was originally a method of solidifying and preserving milk, but it has become a favorite food for its own sake. It is versatile and nourishing, containing a high proportion of protein and fat. Since a pound of cheese is made from 10 pints of milk, its nutrients come in a concentrated form.

The milk used in cheese-making in Europe and America usually comes from cows, goats or ewes. The processes used in the cheese-making and the climate and vegetation under which the milk was produced vary so greatly that many cheeses cannot be reproduced outside their original districts. Others are more easily made, however, and are produced commercially in large quantities.

Cheese is made by curdling milk, which can be full cream, partly skimmed or skimmed and pasteurized, or raw. This curdling can be achieved by the natural souring of unpasteurized milk, by the addition of rennet or of a bacterial starter culture, or by a combination of these methods. All help to form the cheese curd. This is cut into pieces, heated, stirred, salted and put to drain. After draining, the curds are put into molds of a variety of shapes and sizes.

Soft cheeses are cured without pressure

being applied. They retain between 45 and 85 percent of their moisture, are highly perishable and need to be kept under refrigeration. They can be un-ripened (cottage), mold-ripened (Brie) or bacteria-ripened (Limburger). All are mild in flavor. Of the soft cheeses, only cottage, cream cheese and ricotta are generally used in cooking, and they must be heated very gently.

Semihard cheeses have been cured

A selection of cheeses that is ideal for a wine-and-cheese party or guaranteed to make a fitting end to any meal.

under some pressure to press out a greater amount of moisture, retaining only 40 to 45 percent. If they are aged for more than 60 days they need not be made from pasteurized milk, which gives them a superior flavor. They can be mold-ripened (Stilton) or bacteria-ripened (Bel Paese). Most are poor for cooking.

Hard cheeses retain 30 percent or less moisture and are excellent for cooking. All are bacteria-ripened; some for a few months, others for more than a year (Cheshire).

Processed cheeses are pasteurized mix-tures of young cheeses, aged cheeses,

emulsifiers and milk or water. They have good keeping qualities but little real flavor or texture. They should not be confused with the real thing!

Types of cheese for cooking

Although cheese is used regularly in cooking, it does not take kindly to excessive heat or overcooking. Thus it is important to choose the right type of cheese and to cook it properly. First, try to employ the cheeses that heat well. These are mainly hard types: Cheddar, Edam, Swiss, Romano, Monterey Jack, Cheshire, Parmesan, Leicester, Mozza-

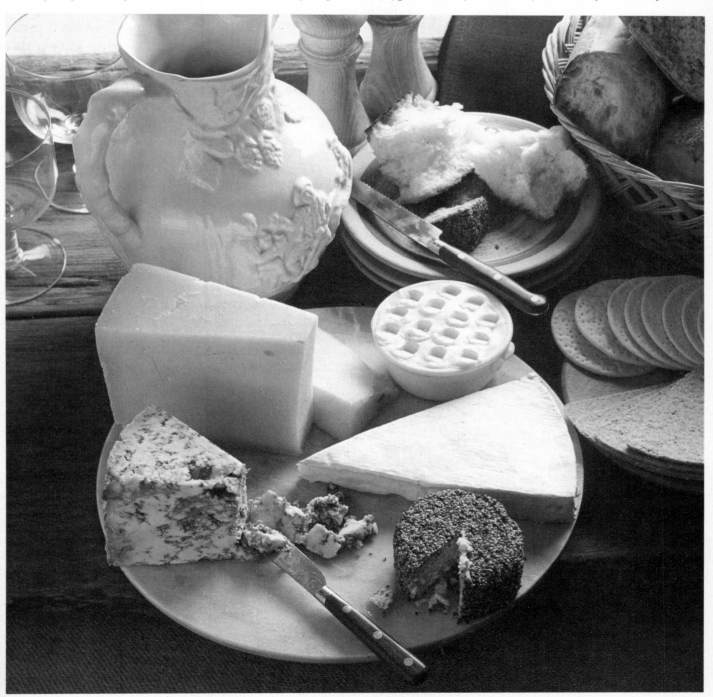

rella. Second, have the other ingredients hot before adding cheese, except when cold ingredients are mixed together before baking, as for quiches. Third, heat the cheese for the minimum time needed in a moderately hot oven or under the broiler. Fourth, never keep a cheese dish hot; serve it within a few minutes of being cooked.

If cheese is heated for too long or at too high a temperature, the fat and protein separate, causing the protein to become tough and stringy. If cheese is melted over low heat as in a cheese sauce, the fat is less likely to separate out. For *gratin* dishes, mix the grated cheese with half its volume of dried breadcrumbs. The breadcrumbs will absorb the fat and a crisp, brown surface will be achieved more easily.

Dessert cheese

Hostesses at dinner parties often produce a cheese board either before or after the dessert. Generally a selection of two to four cheeses of different textures and flavors are presented, accompanied by butter, biscuits or crusty bread, and sometimes dessert fruits such as apples. cherries, grapes and pears.

All types of cheese should be served at room temperature. If soft runny types of cheese are provided, be sure to remove them from the refrigerator and unwrap them onto the board three to six hours in advance. This will allow them to ripen and spread out before serving.

Storing cheese

Once cut, cheese deteriorates fairly rapidly and it is advisable to buy only enough for a few days or a week at most. Store it in the refrigerator or a cold place. It should be covered loosely, but not so as to make it airtight.

If it is airtight it may become moldy, while if it is entirely exposed to the air it will become hard and dry. Cheese can be stored in the refrigerator for about one week but should be wrapped in waxed paper or aluminum foil, otherwise it will dry too rapidly.

Cheese can be hardened and dried by hanging it in a cheesecloth bag where the air can circulate around it. Dried, grated cheese can be stored in a screw-top jar for several weeks. If you have a home freezer, freshly grated cheese, packed in plastic bags, is a useful standby to have to add to sauces, soups and savory dishes.

56

Eggs

Eggs have always been symbols of birth, rebirth, fertility, fortune and even witchcraft. The Easter egg, for instance, inherited from a pagan past, is a symbol of spring and rebirth.

Nowadays, however, the egg is chiefly regarded as a basic and versatile food, which can be prepared by itself or used in cooking. It is high in protein and fat as well as in calcium, iron and some vitamins. The fat, however, is saturated and eggs, particularly the yolks, should be avoided by those on low fat diets.

Hen's eggs are most commonly used in cooking, but duck and goose eggs are also suitable.

Hen's eggs have either brown or white shells, but color is of no significance since the food value of all eggs is the same. The flavor of eggs, however, is somewhat dependent on the hen's diet, and you may find that eggs from one source, say farmyard hens, are more tasty than those from another. It is pointless, though, to use the more expensive eggs in combination cooked dishes because the subtle flavor difference will be unnoticed.

Eggs served by themselves should be as fresh as possible, but when used in cooking they need to be at least three days old. If you hard-boil eggs fresher than that they will be difficult to peel and turn slightly greenish; when you beat them they will not retain air well and will fail to reach proper volume.

You can tell if an egg is fresh by placing it in cold water. Lay it horizontally in the bowl and if it stays that way it is fresh, but if it stands vertically it is too stale to eat. In practice, however, few eggs are likely to be bad unless they have been in the house for too long, and this is only likely to happen if you mix new and old eggs together. Make it a practice to put cartons of new eggs behind or under the older ones.

Eggs keep best under refrigeration at a temperature below 45°F (7°C) and preferably below 40°F (5°C). At these temperatures they will keep for as long as two months. Since they pick up odors, keep them away from strong-smelling foods. Store eggs round end up (notice this is the way they are packed in egg cartons) because this keeps the yolk suspended in the right place, surrounded by the white. This positioning retards spoilage since the less perishable white part envelops and protects the yolk. An egg left lying on its side will lose this protection as the yolk comes into contact with the shell. No matter how dirty, never wash an egg before storing it, just wipe it off with a damp cloth. Washing will remove the protective film over the shell which keeps air out.

Grading: Before eggs are boxed they are graded first for freshness and quality by candling. This means each egg is held in front of a light and inspected. A newly laid egg has a transparent, unclouded white, a small air space at the rounded end, and a pinkish yolk with no dark spots. Those that don't meet these criteria are labelled 'seconds' and are graded no further.

Quality eggs are then graded by size. The terms may vary according to the locality, but are basically *medium*, *large*, and *extra-large* or *jumbo*. If a recipe calls for a specific size it will say so, otherwise assume you should always use large- or extra-large size eggs.

Breaking eggs: Not everyone has mastered the art of breaking eggs. If you hit them too hard or on the wrong surface, they shatter leaving a mess of egg and shell in some inconvenient place. Your aim is to crack the shell halfway between the round and pointed ends, so that when the egg comes apart you will have two equal-sized 'egg cups'.

1. Tap the egg sharply but not hard on an edge or rim. In most kitchens the edge of the counter is the best place because it forms a sharp right-angle corner. The edge of a cup or bowl is less satisfactory because it tends to be round and wide or too thin. Additionally both move too easily on impact. The tap should crack but not shatter the eggshell; no liquid should run out. Nonetheless do the cracking adjacent to the bowl into which you are putting the egg.

2. Hold the cracked egg over a bowl. Put your two thumbs up to the crack so they touch. Gently force the shell apart, allowing the contents to fall into the bowl.

3. If you are separating the white and yolk, have three bowls handy: one for the white, one for the yolk and one to break the egg into. Never try to save time by separating the white directly into the egg white bowl. It is far too easy to have a yolk break and get into the white, which is disaster.

Crack the egg, open it with your thumbs as described in steps 1 and 2. Open it only wide enough to let the white

but not the yolk spill out, which in practice means to hold the egg almost vertical as you pull it apart. To get all the white out, slowly and gently transfer the yolk from one half of the shell to the other, letting the white slide into the cup below. Should the egg yolk fall into the cup, scoop it out with the egg shell.

If the yolk looks as if it will break, STOP. Empty the white from the cup into the larger bowl and then try to get the rest of the white out. A little white with the yolks won't hurt.

If the yolk does break and get into the white in the cup it can sometimes be removed by scooping it off with a corner of paper towel. If things are too bad, put the egg in a jar, beat it lightly, film it with water and save it for another use within four days.

Although eggs should be stored at low temperature, both the yolks and whites work better in cooking if they are at 70-75°F (21-24°C). But eggs at room temperature are difficult to separate because the yolks break easily. Therefore separate the eggs as soon as you take them from the refrigerator and let them warm up after.

Egg yolks

Egg yolks generally behave like whole eggs. When beaten with sugar they will turn almost white and form a ribbon. In sauces, custards and other uses, they cannot be cooked at a temperature above 170°F (78°C) without scrambling; on the other hand, if they are cooked with other ingredients at just below this temperature they will thicken to a mayonnaise consistency. Cooked at the same low temperature, they are able to thicken sauces.

Egg yolks can be stored in a lidded jar in the refrigerator for up to three days, covered with a little water to prevent a hard skin from forming. They can also be frozen if they are stabilized to prevent them from becoming pasty on thawing. Stir the raw yolks with a fork, then add $\frac{1}{4}$ teaspoon of salt or a teaspoon of sugar or clear honey to each 2 ounces (50 grams) of yolk, depending on the future use. Freeze in small quantities, making sure you label what stabilizer you have added and the number of yolks in a package.

Egg whites

Egg whites have the unique characteristic of being able to increase seven times in volume when beaten. To achieve this result some care must be taken. First, the egg whites and utensils must be completely free of fat and contain no speck of yolk. Second, for best results the utensils should be chosen with some care. Last, a specific method of beating should be followed.

If you are beating by hand, an unlined copper bowl and a large thin-wired whisk half the diameter of the bowl give the best result. A pinch of salt is added to the egg whites which creates a slightly acid condition which stabilizes the beaten whites. But copper is expensive and hand beating somewhat hard, so you may prefer the alternative in excellence, a stainless steel bowl and electric beaters. In this case, measure the diameter of your beaters and get a deep bowl about twice that width in diameter. In this case, cream of tartar is added to stabilize the whites.

A pottery, glass or china bowl, however, works well enough if it is shaped to suit the whisking utensil. Use a scant $\frac{1}{4}$ teaspoon of cream of tartar for each 4 egg whites. Aluminum bowls turn whites grayish and plastic bowls cannot be kept absolutely fat-free, so neither of these is recommended.

Cream of tartar should not be added in one type of recipe – the small group of desserts that are supposed to separate into a sponge top with a sauce below. With cream of tartar they fail to separate.

Whatever type of bowl you use, wash it with detergent and hot water along with the beaters. As extra insurance they can also be rubbed with a piece of lemon. Have the oven heated before you begin beating. The beaten egg whites should go into the oven the moment they are ready.

Begin beating slowly until the whites begin to froth. Add the salt or cream of tartar and quicken the speed of beating gradually until you are beating vigorously. Try to keep the entire mass in motion continuously. When the mixture forms soft rounded peaks add slowly, by the spoonful, any sugar the recipe calls for. Continue beating until the whites stand in stiff pointed peaks when you lift up the beater. The traditional method of being able to turn the bowl over without the whites falling out means the eggs are a trifle overbeaten and too dry. Although the whites then have maximum volume the cells break down somewhat when cooked.

To incorporate beaten egg whites into other ingredients, slide the whites on top, and, using a large metal spoon, lightly cut and fold them together. Be careful not to over-mix (see page 132 for folding).

Leftover egg whites can be stored for three or four days in a screw-top jar in the refrigerator. They can also be frozen without any further preparation. Either freeze each egg white separately in individual ice-cube trays or keep adding whites to a single jar, keeping note of how many you have in it. Either way they are good for meringues, yolkless soufflés and Angel Cake. Be sure that thawed whites have returned to a warm room temperature before you try to whisk them.

Meringues: Meringues are basically a confection or cake-topping made from egg whites and sugar. Depending on the type of meringue you wish to make, there are several basic methods of preparation.

To make meringue shells, beat 3 egg whites together in a large bowl with a whisk, beater or electric mixer until they form stiff peaks. Beat in 3 tablespoons of sugar and continue beating for 1 minute or until the peaks are stiff and glossy. Fold in $\frac{2}{3}$ cup (150 grams) more sugar with a metal spoon. Spoon the mixture into an icing bag with a plain nozzle and pipe the mixture, spaced apart, onto a baking sheet greased and lightly floured or lined with non-stick silicone paper. Bake in an oven preheated to a very cool 250°F (130°C) for 1$\frac{1}{2}$ hours, or until the meringues are crisp on the outside and pale beige in color. If they brown too quickly, open the door of the oven. Remove from the oven and turn the meringues over with a long spatula. Gently press the undersides to form a small pocket and return to the oven. Bake for a further 30 minutes. Cool completely before filling with cream, fruit purée, etc.

Meringue topping is discussed fully under cakes, page 139.

Eggs in cooking

The four major uses of eggs in cooking are emulsifying, thickening and binding, coating and raising. The yolk is used as an emulsifying agent in such oil-based sauces as mayonnaise (see page 119).

Beaten eggs are used to thicken and bind sauces and custards. Croquettes, fritters and fish or meat cakes are coated in beaten egg before frying to prevent them from disintegrating.

Eggs are used as a raising agent in such foods as beaten sponge cakes. The whites

58

To make a meringue shell, draw a 9 in (23 cm) circle on non-stick silicone paper.

Spread a third of stiff meringue mixture over the circle, about ¼ in (½ cm) thick.

Pipe the remaining mixture around the sides, to make a shell

When the shell is baked and cooled, transfer it to a serving plate.

may be beaten separately to 'lighten' a dish such as a soufflé.

In cooking, the two most significant properties of eggs are their ability to hold air when beaten and their extremely low cooking temperature. Their air-holding ability has been discussed in connection with other ingredients, and here only the art of beating is discussed.

Eggs can be beaten with a fork, a wire whisk, a rotary beater or an electric beater. Whole eggs and yolks should be beaten vigorously, unless the recipe says otherwise, until they are light in color and texture. If sugar is added they become almost white and so thick they will run off the beater in a long stream or ribbon rather than falling off in globules. This can take 5 minutes or more with an electric mixer. Sponge cakes are made in this manner. (Beating egg whites is discussed on page 58 under that heading.)

Beaten whole eggs begin to cook when their temperature is as low as 150°F (70°C). When milk is added the setting temperature rises slightly. If eggs are heated to a higher temperature they begin

to scramble. If you catch this happening in time, put the base of the saucepan in cold water and stir hard; a spoonful of cream sometimes also helps.

When eggs are added to hot ingredients, you must first add about a quarter of the hot mixture, by spoonfuls, to the eggs in order to warm them gently. Once the eggs are warmed they can be poured into the rest of the hot mixture. Unless the mixture contains cornstarch the eggs should not be heated above 170°F (78°C).

When egg mixtures such as custards are overcooked or overbaked they become watery, develop small holes and are rather tough. These signs indicate that the egg part of the mixture has shrunk, squeezing out the liquid's moisture.

The basic methods of cooking eggs are boiling (hard or soft), scrambling, frying poaching and baking. They are also made into omelets and soufflés or eaten raw – as in steak tartare or eggnog.

Boiled eggs: Boiled eggs should not, in fact, be boiled but simmered gently to prevent them from cracking. There are two chief ways of soft-boiling an egg.

1. Lower the egg into a pan of boiling water. Boil for 1 minute. Turn off the heat, cover the pan and leave for 5 minutes. (This is also known as coddling.)

2. Place the egg in a pan of boiling water and simmer for 3-4 minutes according to the size of the egg and its temperature. At the end of this time the egg white will be lightly set and the yolk runny.

For hard-boiled eggs, put the eggs in a pan of boiling water and bring the water back to the boil. Simmer over moderate heat for 10 minutes. With a slotted spoon, remove the eggs from the pan and place them at once under cold running water to prevent the yolks from discoloring.

Scrambled eggs. In a small bowl, beat 2 eggs together with seasoning to taste and, if desired, 2 tablespoons of milk, cream or water, until the mixture is frothy. Melt 1 tablespoon of butter in a frying pan and pour the egg mixture into the pan. Cook for 3-4 minutes, stirring constantly with a wooden spoon, until it thickens.

Fried eggs: Heat 1 tablespoon of olive or cooking oil or butter in a frying pan. When the oil or fat is sizzling, break an egg carefully into the pan. Reduce the heat to low and cook gently, being careful

A fluffy omelet is beautiful and delicious, yet so very simple to make well.

not to break the egg yolk, until the white is set and the yolk firm. Remove from the pan with a slotted spatula.

Poached eggs: Poached eggs may either be cooked in boiling water or steamed in a poaching pan. For the first method, half fill a saucepan with water. Add ½ teaspoon of salt and 1 teaspoon of vinegar. Place the pan over moderate heat and bring the water to a boil. Break an egg into a cup. When the water is boiling, carefully tip the egg into the center of the bubbling water. Reduce the heat to moderately low and simmer gently for 3 minutes. Remove with a slotted spoon.

To use an egg-poaching pan, half fill the bottom of the pan with water. Place ¼ teaspoon of butter in the center of each cup, unless you are using a non-stick pan. Place the pan, with the cups in place, over the heat. When the water boils break the eggs into the cups. Cover and simmer for 3-5 minutes or until the eggs are lightly set. Loosen with a knife and slide them onto a plate.

Baked eggs: Baked eggs are usually prepared in individual cocotte dishes, although several may be baked together in a small ovenproof dish. Place the dish or dishes on a baking sheet. Put ¼ teaspoon of butter in each dish and place the baking sheet in the oven preheated to fairly hot 400°F (200°C) for 2 minutes. Then, break an egg into each dish, season to taste and return the dishes to the oven. Bake for 4 to 5 minutes, or until the eggs are lightly set.

Omelet: To make perfect omelets every time you will require a special omelet pan – to be used for nothing else. However, few of us can aspire to this happy state of affairs, especially if we are just beginning to equip a kitchen. Any medium-sized, heavy-based frying pan can be substituted; use a 7-inch (18-centimeter) pan for a 2-4—egg omelet, a 9-inch (23-centimeter) size for a 6-egg one. You should not attempt to make a larger-size omelet than this.

Omelets must never be overcooked; the perfect one will still have a soft, creamy semiliquid center. To make an omelet for three people, break 6 eggs into a bowl. Season to taste and add 2 tablespoons of cold water. Beat well to mix with either a fork or wire whisk. Heat the pan over moderate heat for 30 seconds, or until it is quite hot. Add ½ tablespoon of butter and, when the foam subsides, pour in the beaten eggs. Stir the eggs, then leave them

for a few seconds until the bottom sets. Reduce the heat to low. Using a wide spatula, lift the edge of the omelet and at the same time tilt the pan away from you so that the liquid egg escapes from the top and runs into the pan. Put the pan down flat again over the heat and leave until the omelet begins to set. Tilt the pan away from you again and, with the help of the spatula, flip one-half of the omelet over to make a semicircle. Slide the omelet onto a plate.

Soufflé: To make a cheese soufflé for four, first generously grease a medium-sized soufflé dish with butter. Sprinkle about 4 tablespoons of grated cheese (preferably a hard cheese, such as Cheddar) around the inside of the dish.

In a large saucepan, melt 4 tablespoons (50 grams) of butter. Stir in 4 tablespoons of flour with a wooden spoon to make a smooth paste and cook, stirring constantly, for 1 minute. Remove the pan from the heat and gradually stir in 1¼ cups (300 milliliters) of milk. Return to the heat and cook, stirring constantly, for 1 minute, or until the sauce is thick and smooth. Add spices and seasoning to taste and remove from the heat. Beat in 5 egg yolks, one by one and set aside to allow the mixture to cool slightly. Meanwhile, beat 6 egg whites until they form stiff peaks.

Stir about 1 cup (125 grams) of the grated cheese used to line the dish into the egg yolk mixture until it has blended. Quickly fold in the egg whites and pour the mixture into the prepared soufflé dish. Cook in the oven preheated to 400°F (200°C) for 25-30 minutes, or until the soufflé is well risen and golden brown.

Breadcrumbs

Three types of breadcrumbs that can be made at home are used in cooking: fresh white breadcrumbs, dried white breadcrumbs and browned breadcrumbbs.

Fresh white breadcrumbs: Fresh white breadcrumbs are used for panades, for stuffings and for some desserts and cakes. Prepare them from bread which is at least one day old. Remove the crusts and reserve for browned breadcrumbs. Blend, grate or rub the rest through a wire strainer.

Dried white breadcrumbs: Place the fresh white breadcrumbs on a baking sheet and bake in a very slow oven, so that the crumbs do not brown. Dried white breadcrumbs are used for coating foods for frying (see frying instructions on page 74).

Browned breadcrumbs: Place the bread crusts on a baking sheet and bake in a very slow oven until dry. Crush finely with a pestle and mortar, with a rolling pin or in a blender. Browned breadcrumbs can be used for coating in frying, but they are more often used for *gratins* and may be used for covering the surface of a ham before baking. They are also served hot, on their own, with game.

Storage

White breadcrumbs soon become moldy but they will keep for up to two days stored in a screw-top jar. To store longer, freeze in a plastic bag. Dried white breadcrumbs will keep for several weeks in a screw-top jar. They, too, can be frozen. Browned breadcrumbs keep indefinitely in a screw-top jar or other suitable container in a cool, dry place.

The onion family provides us with a most indispensable group of seasonings for all types of cooking. It includes leeks, scallions and garlic.

Herbs and Spices

Seasonings

Seasoning is both an art and a term that covers a whole range of things we add to our food to enhance its flavor. Seasoning can be delicate and subtle to bring out natural flavor, or emphatic, though it should never overpower the food's basic flavor. Failure to season results in dull, uninteresting food.

The art of seasoning is something you have to learn by trial and error. You have to try seasonings alone and in combination; tables showing what goes together are a help (see pages 66 to 71). In general add seasonings towards the end of cooking in small quantities and let them cook for a short time to bring out maximum flavor.

In many recipes the last instruction is "correct the seasoning" or "season to taste". This means you should taste in all parts of the mouth, not just on the tongue, and add more seasoning if needed. In practice this means more salt and perhaps pepper. Often when a dish tastes flat or uninteresting it is undersalted. Add salt in small amounts, stir and taste. Remember

that as the salt dissolves it will become somewhat stronger.

The foremost seasoning is without a doubt salt, followed by pepper, the onion family, herbs and spices.

Salt and Pepper

You may have assumed that all salt is the same, but since it is obtained in several ways and undergoes preparation, it is available in several forms. Salt is obtained from sea water and brine wells by evaporation and purification.

Rock salt is mined, then purified, crushed and graded.

Sea salt, as its name implies, comes from sea water. Usually the individual grains are quite large. This is the salt to use in grinders. It is often sprinkled on meats and other foods just before serving and because it dissolves relatively slowly, it is also sprinkled on breads and pretzels that come with a salted surface. Kosher salt is an extremely coarse form of sea salt. Along with ordinary sea salt its availability varies widely depending on local demand. However, it is called for more and more, in recipes both for its distinctive flavor and cooking properties. Kosher salt is readily available.

Ordinary salt, usually evaporated from brine pumped from deep wells, is used both for table and cooking purposes. It comes either **plain** or **iodized,** that is, a small amount of sodium iodide or potassium iodide has been added, important in areas where there is little iodine in the diet. Some authorities say salt can be sprinkled on meat before broiling or roasting, but others say if it is used it toughens the meat; others simply say do not salt before cooking because it toughens the meat.

Pepper, in all of its various forms is discussed later, on page 64.

The onion family
The onion or *allium* family is important in seasoning. In addition to the onion, other members include chives, garlic, shallots, leeks and scallions. Some of these are used only as seasoning, others are also vegetables in their own right.

Onions used as seasoning in cooked dishes are usually sliced or diced (see page 91 for technique). They are then sautéed in a little hot fat or butter. For a mild flavor cook them until they are translucent; for a strong flavor brown them slowly. But remember that high heat and long frying create strong odors and an unpleasant taste; scorching causes bitterness.

Garlic, an essential for many recipes, can make or destroy a dish but, correctly used it imparts an exquisite flavor to meats, casseroles and sauces. It can be used peeled or unpeeled, the latter giving the milder flavor with no aftertaste. Garlic is stronger if cut lengthwise and even more so if crushed in a garlic press or with salt using a round-ended knife. When it is used whole in stews and braising, remove it before serving. Never brown garlic because it gives a bad taste. Add it after the other vegetables and cook for only a few minutes. Garlic is bought by the bulb or head. This separates into many smaller pieces when you remove the outer skin. Each of these little pieces, also encased in a skin, is called a **clove.** Fresh garlic will keep well in any cool place where you keep root vegetables, but often it is more conveniently stored in the refrigerator. As long as you do not pierce the skin around the cloves, garlic will give off no offensive odor.

Shallots have a delicate flavor somewhere between onion and garlic and are especially used in wine cookery and delicate dishes. They are not particularly easy to find in many areas, but since they keep well in a cool place, a pound, if you find them, should last at least half a year. Often the bulb part of scallions is substituted, but the flavor is not identical.

Chives and **scallions** are most frequently used raw in salads and as a garnish. Chives can be minced easily by cutting with scissors (a trick that can be used with other herbs as well). Since they are best very fresh and are also hard to find commercially, keep a potted plant on a sunny windowsill. Both the green stem and white bulb of scallions are used in salads. Thinly slice or dice, discarding only the coarse upper part of the green stem.

The onion family's characteristic smell can be removed from hands, knife and cutting board by rubbing on salt, lemon juice or vinegar and washing under cold water (beware of open cuts which will sting). Eat raw parsley to remove onion and garlic odors from your breath.

Herbs and spices

Herbs are mainly the leaves and seeds of herbaceous plants that grow in mid-latitude countries. Some are annuals resown each year, others are perennial. Most can be grown in your garden or window box, doing best in a sunny location with poor, even dry, soil. The flavors of herbs are best when freshly picked. When you have to use dried herbs, buy them in small amounts and store them airtight in a cool, dry, dark place, which generally means not on a pretty spice rack next to the stove. Replace herbs regularly, at least once a year, because they lose flavor and become musty. When you substitute dry herbs for fresh, use half the quantity, that is 1 teaspoon of fresh herbs equals $\frac{1}{2}$ teaspoon of dry.

The terms *fines herbes* (fine herbs) and *'bouquet garni'* appear frequently. **Fines herbes** is a French term for a finely chopped fresh herb mixture, usually parsley, tarragon, chives and chervil. The term can also mean parsley alone. *Fines herbes* are used in soups, sauces and omelets.

A **bouquet garni** is a mixture of thyme, parsley and bay leaf. See the illustrations below for how to make your own bouquet garni. It is used primarily to flavor stews and casserole dishes.

A chart relating specific herbs to food is given on pages 66 to 71.

Spice is the collective name given to various aromatic substances which are used to season and flavor sweet and savory foods. Most, but not all of them, come from tropical lands. They are mostly hard and can be crushed and grated to form a powder - nutmeg, allspice, pepper, cinnamon. Unlike herbs they are often used in sweet cookery.

Spices, like herbs, are more pungent when freshly bought - you have only to compare the smell and taste of new and old spices to recognize the great difference. Like herbs, spices also should be bought in small amounts and kept tightly covered in a cool, dry, dark place. Keep ground spices no more than a year; after this they rapidly lose their pungency. If spices are being used in a savory dish like a curry, add them to the fat and fry over low heat for a minute without scorching. This process will enhance their aroma and flavor.

Spiced foods lose flavor when frozen for any length of time. Therefore, use

64

them within two or three weeks of freezing. When doubling a recipe do not automatically double the spices; let taste be your guide.

Peppers and other specialty flavorings

Pepper is undoubtedly the most widely used spice. **Peppercorns** are the dried fruits of a climbing vine native to India. They are sold green and soft (unripe fruit), black (sun dried) and white (ripe fruit with outer hulls removed before drying). Generally black pepper is used in cooking, since it is the most flavorful. White pepper is for white sauce and other dishes where black flecks would be undesirable, though black can be used.

Peppercorns bought whole and ground coarsely in a peppermill taste fresher and have more flavor than the pre-ground commercial powder sold as pepper. A single layer of peppercorns can be cracked easily in a garlic press (remove with point of knife).

Chili powder is a blended pepper made from sweet paprika, cayenne, turmeric, cumin, coriander, oregano and cloves. Fresh red or green chillies should not be substituted for chili powder. To substitute dried chillies for fresh, drop 6 chillies in $1\frac{1}{4}$ cups (300 milliliters) of water and simmer for 20 minutes or until tender. Working carefully wearing rubber gloves, split and seed the chillies. Then scrape off the soft red pith to add to your recipe; the cooking liquid can also be used. The problem with this method is that you have no way of comparing the strength of the chili pith with that of fresh chillies, so be prudent and use a small quantity at first; taste, add a little more. Repeat this several times if necessary.

Anchovies, though neither herb nor spice, add a piquant taste that is not easily identifiable, though pleasant, to sauces, meat and gravy. But you must use them sparingly: no more than $\frac{1}{8}$ teaspoon of mashed fillet or paste to $1\frac{1}{4}$ cups (300 milliliters) of sauce (the paste is weaker in flavor and saltier). For a sauce soak the fillet in warm water to 5-10 minutes, then drain. For a salad or antipasto soak in cold milk or water for up to 1 hour; drain and dry before using. Anchovies keep well as long as they are completely covered with either brine or oil, depending on which they were originally packed in. Worcestershire sauce is made with an anchovy base.

Herb chart

Herbs	Cheese	Eggs	Meats
Basil	Rarebit Cream cheese Cheese spreads	Devilled Scrambled Egg salad Soufflé	Beef, lamb and veal roasts and stews Meat pies Ground beef Lamb chops
Bay leaf			Beef, lamb and veal stews and pot roasts Tongue Bacon Pâté

Chervil	Cottage cheese
	Cream cheese
		Omelet (with parsley
		  and chives)
		Scrambled
			Beef, lamb and veal
			  stews and pot roasts
			Pork chops

Chives	Cheese spreads	Omelet Scrambled	
Coriander, crushed seed		Omelet Curried Scrambled Egg salad	All meat curries Pork sausages Meatballs Marinated meats
Dill, seed or weed	Cottage cheese Cream cheese Canapés	Devilled Egg salad	Pork and lamb chops, roasts and stews Meatballs Curries
Marjoram (M), (including Oregano)	Cheese spreads	Devilled (O) Omelet Egg salad (O) Scrambled (M) Soufflé (M)	Beef and lamb roasts, stews and pot roasts Pork dishes (M)
Mint	Cream cheese spreads		Lamb stews and roasts Mint sauce for lamb
Parsley	Cottage cheese Cream cheese Soufflé	Devilled Omelet Scrambled	Beef, lamb and veal stews Meat pies

Poultry	Seafood	Soups	Vegetables	Other
Fried chicken	Fish Shrimp Crabmeat Lobster	Minestrone Pea Potato Spinach Tomato Vegetable	Asparagus, beans, broccoli, cabbage, carrots, celery, cucumbers, eggplant, peas, tomatoes, turnip, spinach, onions, zucchini	Goes especially well with tomato in all forms. Gives a Mediterranean flavor to salads.
Chicken stew and fricassée Venison Rabbit	Shellfish Fish Marinated fish	Consommé Chicken Vegetable Stocks	Artichoke, cabbage, carrots, tomatoes	A leaf is used in a *bouquet garni*. Tomato sauces.
Chicken fricassée Chicken and turkey pie Stuffing	Shellfish	Cream of potato Cream of spinach Tomato	Celery, cucumbers, eggplant, lettuce, peas, potatoes, spinach, tomatoes	Good in all salads.
		As a garnish	As a garnish on new potatoes, carrots, turnips, tomatoes, peas, beans, cauliflower, mushrooms	Chopped as a garnish for salads, especially tomato, lettuce and potato.
Chicken curry Stuffing		Pea Stocks	Cauliflower, onions, spinach, tomatoes	Leaves also known as Chinese parsley, and *cilantro*; can be chopped and used like parsley in Chinese-style meat and poultry dishes. Good with cooked fruit.
Chicken and duck curries Stuffing	Shrimp Lobster Halibut Herring Curries Salmon	Cabbage, borscht, dried bean, cucumber, tomato, zucchini	Beets, beans, broccoli, Brussels sprouts, cabbage, potatoes, cucumber, French beans, turnips	Dill leaves, known as weed, can be chopped and sprinkled on salads and on rice.
Fried chicken (M) Chicken fricassée (M) Roast duck and turkey (M) Stuffing (M)	Broiled fish Shrimp Crabmeat (M) Stuffing	Creamed celery (M) Cream of chicken (M) Onion (M) Potato (M) Spinach (M) Bean (O) Minestrone (O) Tomato (O)	Broccoli (O) Asparagus (M) Eggplant (O) Brussels sprouts (M) Cabbage (O) Squash Zucchini Lentils (O) Dried beans (O) Mushrooms Tomatoes (O) Celery (M) Peas (M) Potatoes (M)	Oregano gives an Italian or Mediterranean flavor to many dishes. Do not cook more than 10-15 minutes for best flavor.
		Cream of pea Potato Cucumber	Carrots, peas, new potatoes, spinach	Fruit salad Fruit juice Melon balls Yogurt and cucumber salad.
Chicken fricassée Chicken and turkey pie Stuffing	Fish and shellfish Stuffing	Vegetable soups *Court-bouillon* Poultry and meat stocks	Cabbage, cauliflower, celery, onions, potatoes, tomatoes, turnip, eggplant	Chopped as garnish for most savory dishes. Stems in *bouquet garni*.

Herbs	Cheese	Eggs	Meats
Rosemary		Omelet Scrambled Soufflé	Lamb roasts and stews Kebabs Pot roasts
Sage, rubbed or ground	Cheddar cheese spread Cheese omelet Fondue		Pork Veal Sausage Stuffing Marinades
Savory, Winter or Summer		Devilled Omelet Scrambled	Roasts of beef, lamb, pork or veal Meat pies Ground beef
Tarragon		All egg dishes	Lamb dishes Veal dishes Lamb and pork Grilled steaks and chops
Thyme	Cottage cheese Cheese spread	Devilled Scrambled Baked	All roasts and stews

Spice chart

Spice	Cheese	Eggs	Meats
Allspice, ground or whole			Beef, lamb and veal pot roasts, stews
Anise	Cottage cheese Mild-flavored cheese spreads		Beef and veal stews
Caraway seed	Cheese spreads Cottage cheese	Omelet Egg salad	Beef roasts and stews Pork goulash Sauerbraten
Cardamom seed			Curried meats
Cayenne pepper	Cheese biscuits or crackers Macaroni cheese Soufflé Welsh rarebit	Omelet Soufflé Devilled	Pork sausage Paprikash Curried meats

Poultry	Seafood	Soups	Vegetables	Other
Any chicken or turkey dish Stuffing	Fish casseroles Scallops Stuffing	Chicken Lamb broth Tomato Fish chowder Pea	Cauliflower, potatoes, turnip, carrots, eggplant, mushrooms, peas, spinach	
Chicken, duck, turkey casseroles, Fried chicken Stuffing		Chicken Turkey Tomato	Beets, Brussels sprouts, celery, onions, squash, zucchini and tomatoes	
Chicken and turkey dishes	Grilled fish Fish casseroles Stuffing	Chicken Cucumber Potato Tomato Vegetable Split-pea	Asparagus, beans, Brussels sprouts, cucumbers, potatoes, tomatoes, carrots, squash, zucchini	Traditionally cooked with all bean dishes. Part of *fines herbes*.
Chicken Turkey	Fish Shrimp	Chicken Mushroom Pea Tomato	Beets, artichoke, beans, carrots, squash, zucchini, French beans, mushrooms, onions, new potatoes	Salads Wine vinegar.
All chicken and turkey casseroles and pies Fried chicken Roast duck Stuffing	Tuna Scallops Crabmeat Fish Lobster Shrimp	Fish chowder Chicken and mushroom Tomato Vegetable	Carrots, beans, onions, potatoes, mushrooms, squash and zucchini, spinach, turnips	Spray part of *bouquet garni*.

Poultry	Seafood	Soup	Vegetables	Other
Chicken and turkey fricassée and pies Braised chicken Duck stew	Poached fish	Chicken Consommé Potato Tomato Vegetable	Parsnips, turnips, spinach	Often used as an alternative to pepper in Middle Eastern cookery. Good in fruit salad, gingerbread, pumpkin pie, mince pie and fruit cakes.
Braised chicken Roast duck Chicken and duck pilafs				Used mostly in candy; cakes, biscuits, apple pie, fruit salad, stewed fruit, baked apple, also sweet rolls and fruit breads.
Roast goose	Broiled fish Crab and Lobster Poached fish Stuffed fish	Borscht Potato	Potatoes, cabbage, carrots, celery, cucumbers, onions, sauerkraut	Used in breads: rye, onion, pumpernickel. Used in cakes, biscuits, apple pie.
Curried poultry	Curried seafood		Carrots, pumpkin	Ground, on all melons except watermelon. Danish pastry, sweet yeast breads, apple pie, stewed fruits and baked apple.
Broiled chicken Paprikash Curried chicken	Broiled shrimp Crab and lobster	Vegetable	Cabbage, spring greens, turnip greens	Use sparingly since it can be very hot.

Spice	Cheese	Eggs	Meats
Celery seed	Cheese biscuits or crackers Cheese spreads	Omelet Scrambled Soufflé	Pot roasts and stews
Chili powder	Cottage cheese Cheese spreads Fondue	Devilled Omelet Scrambled Egg salad	Tamale pie Chili con carne Beef stew Meatballs
Cinnamon, ground or stick			Beef stew (stick) Sauerbraten
Clove, ground or whole			Ham Pork Tongue
Cumin seed	Cheese canapés Cheese spreads	Curried Stuffed	Curried meat Meatballs
Fennel seed			Italian sausage Beef Lamb Pork
Ginger, fresh, ground, preserved			All meats
Mace, ground	Welsh rarebit		Veal chops
Mustard, seed or ground	All cheese dishes	Devilled Egg salad	Coating for lamb roast Ham, pork
Nutmeg, whole or ground		Custard	Swedish meatballs Meat pie
Paprika	As a garnish	As a garnish	Beef and veal paprikash Garnish
Pepper, (black or white), whole or ground	All cheese dishes	All egg dishes	All meat dishes
Sesame seed	Fondue Omelet Cheese spreads	Scrambled	
Turmeric		Egg salad Devilled	Meat curries

Poultry	Seafood	Soups	Vegetables	Other
Chicken fricassée			Beets, braised lettuce, cabbage, cucumbers	
Broiled chicken Poultry casseroles Fried chicken	Shrimp Fish	Black bean Pea Tomato	Eggplant, broad beans, onions, corn, tomatoes	Used as a substitute for fresh chillies in Indian and Mexican cooking.
			Carrots, onions, pumpkin, rice	Used in desserts and breads: sweet rolls, fruit bread and cake, all apple desserts, chocolate desserts, rice pudding, gingerbread, stewed fruits, applesauce.
Braised chicken		Onion	Carrots, onions, pumpkin, mushrooms	Used in desserts and breads: sweet rolls, fruit bread (banana, for example), fruit compote, chocolate desserts, gingerbread, apple purée.
Curried poultry Stuffing	Shrimp Lobster			Used in cakes and biscuits.
Chicken and duck pilafs	Seafood Pilaff Baked and poached fish	Potato	Cabbage, onion, potato	Gives an Italian flavor to foods. Can be used in apple desserts, cakes, biscuits.
Fried and roast chicken Baked duck Chicken and duck casseroles			Carrots, pumpkin	Gives an Oriental flavor to meat and poultry dishes. Used on fruit desserts, gingerbread cookies in fruit cake.
Chicken fricassée		Vegetable	Beans, onions, corn, tomatoes, eggplant	Used in sweet and other breads; chocolate, lemon, lime and orange desserts.
				Spice cake, gingerbread, molasses cookies.
		Black bean Pea Tomato Potato	Eggplant, beans, onions, corn, tomatoes, spinach, mushrooms	Fruit breads, sweet rolls, banana bread, puddings, apple dessert and pies, applesauce.
Chicken paprikash Garnish	As a garnish	Pea	Cauliflower, spinach, corn	Comes in several strengths. Much used in Hungarian cooking, frequently instead of pepper.
All poultry dishes	All seafood dishes	All soup dishes	All vegetable dishes	Used in some spiced breads and cakes (gingerbread).
Fried, broiled and roast chicken Roast duck	Broiled fish Crabmeat Shrimp		Corn	Used on breads and rolls and in cakes, pies and crackers.
Chicken, duck and turkey curries	Seafood Pilafs		Rice Vegetable curries	Gives a rich yellow color to all it touches.

Chapter Five

Once you understand what you are doing and why, cooking becomes much easier. While the number of recipes is infinite, the preparation techniques are limited. So an experienced cook can read a recipe and mentally reduce its apparent complexities to a series of well-known techniques. *Sole Bonne Femme*, for instance, is identified as oven-poached fish with a white sauce made with the poaching liquid.

Before you get down to cooking you must figure out the timing and order of events. Again, some experienced cooks can do this in their heads, but many prefer to write everything down. Preparing a meal for either the family or guests requires the cook to ask and answer a series of questions.

What will the main course be? What will go well with it? What vegetables, fruits, are in season? What have we not had to eat recently? What is needed for balanced nutrition? For good color contrast? How much work will it require and when will I do it? Will it fit my budget?

Decisions based on these questions will result in menus for the week or day.

Next the cook asks: What can be prepared in advance? What needs to be done early because it will be needed in another step of the recipe (a pie crust baked before the filling is made, for instance)? What needs long cooking? What can be partly prepared in advance? What must be done at the last minute? The answers to these questions may lead to modifications in the menu to even out the workload.

Many people find it helpful to write out the menu then make a time chart listing when to do things. A time chart should show when to prepare things for cooking, when they should start and finish cooking. For a dinner party, especially, include such details as washing the salad greens, making the salad dressing, setting the table and clearing up. Above all *begin early* and don't have lots of last minute details.

Reading a recipe

At the time you are menu planning and before you go shopping *read through the recipe*. Check that all ingredients are available. Be sure you understand the entire process described.

Before you begin work on a recipe, clear off the work surface and get out all the ingredients you will need. Start with those in the refrigerator to give them the maximum time to warm up. Gather up bowls, pans, utensils and measuring equipment. Now you are ready to begin making the recipe. Clean up and wash up as you go.

How to measure

The three types of measurements used in European cookery are: scales for solids, a measuring cup for liquids and spoons for small amounts. In the United States, however, everything is done by volume, using a standard measuring cup that holds 8 ounces (225 grams).

Measuring dry ingredients: although the same standard measuring cup is used for both dry and liquid ingredients, different types of containers are recommended for each. Dry ingredients are measured most accurately and easily with a set of 4 cups – $\frac{1}{4}$, $\frac{1}{2}$, $\frac{3}{4}$, 1-cup sizes – which are filled to the brim and smoothed off with the flat edge of a knife.

Flour and confectioner's sugar are measured after sifting, and the cup should not be tapped or shaken to level the contents. Granulated sugars are also put in without pressing down, whereas brown sugar is always packed down hard to get the maximum amount into the cup. Only items that would have large air pockets without pressure – cooked meat and vegetables, shredded coconut, coarsely chopped nuts – should be gently pressed down. Shortening can be measured in the same way as dry ingredients or by the water displacement method. To measure $\frac{1}{2}$ cup of shortening, pour $\frac{1}{2}$ cup of *cold* water into the 1-cup measure. Add pieces of shortening and push them under the water. When the water reaches the brim, you have $\frac{1}{2}$ cup of shortening. For $\frac{2}{3}$ cup of shortening, fill the 1-cup measure with $\frac{1}{3}$ cup of water. Drain well before using. Always try to measure fats last, since the cups won't be fit for dry ingredients afterwards.

Liquid measuring cups, usually made of heatproof glass, have a $\frac{1}{4}$-inch (5 cm) gap between the top measure and the pouring lip. Be sure the cup is at eye level when you fill it, otherwise you can be off by quite a lot.

Measuring spoons are carefully calibrated and should not be confused with ordinary spoons of the same name. The standard tablespoon holds one thirty-second of a pint. Thus 4 *tablespoons* equal $\frac{1}{4}$ cup. Three *teaspoons* equal one tablespoon, and a *dessert spoon* holds 2-2$\frac{1}{4}$ teaspoons.

When a recipe in an American cookbook calls for a teaspoon or tablespoon, it means a *level* spoon, that is, even with the rim of the bowl. Use the dry-ingredient knife method for leveling. Not all foreign cookbooks, however, use a level spoon; some mean the contents of the spoon are rounded, that is, as much above the bowl as in it. A rounded spoon is equivalent to two level spoons. With luck the introduction to your book will tell you which system is being used.

Types of heat

At least half the food we eat is heated in some way. Heat can be either moist or dry. Moist heat means the food is in contact with a hot liquid or steam. Dry heat means no water (or water-based liquid) comes in contact with the substance being cooked.

Moist-heat cooking

Boiling: The term 'to boil' means water has reached the temperature of 212°F or 100°C and has many large bubbles breaking above the surface. By regulating the heat, water can be kept at a fast boil (lots of large bubbles breaking well above the surface) or a slow boil (fewer large bubbles).

When the heat is reduced further only tiny bubbles form and rise to the surface, just breaking it. This is called *simmering*. When the surface quivers but no bubbles come to the surface is termed *poaching*. It is important to know and remember the differences between these three terms. Water alone never boils over, but as soon as another substance is added to water the mixture can boil over.

Strangely, common terminology is often in conflict with the process used. Thus the term 'boiling' is often applied to foods which are, in fact, simmered. Boiled beef, for instance, would be a tough, tasteless disaster if cooked above a simmer. True boiling is too fierce a heat for meats, poultry, fish and some vegetables and fruits. True boiling is the method used for cooking some suet puddings and vegetables such as cabbage, that need to be cooked quickly. It is used in jam and marmalade making to evaporate the water and concentrate the fruit and sugar solution. Liquids that need to be reduced in volume, and so made more concentrated, are boiled rapidly without a lid to drive off the excess water. This is the case for syrups, purées, and savory glazes.

Some starchy foods such as rice, macaroni and pasta are best cooked by boiling, because the rapid bubbling keeps the grains moving and prevents them sticking together.

Simmering: Simmering occurs at a temperature just below the boiling point, when a slow stream of bubbles reaches the surface without breaking. It is much more gentle than boiling, and does not toughen meats and poultry. Salt beef, ham roasts, poultry, stocks and soups are all cooked by this method.

Unfortunately, on many gas and electric stoves it is hard to maintain a simmer and, without constant watching, the liquid keeps coming to a boil. If something needs to be simmered for a long time and your stove is a problem one, it is best to do it in a cool oven 275°–325°F (140°–160°C). Bring to a boil on the top, then transfer to the preheated oven. Check it after a while and reduce the heat if necessary.

On top of the stove keep the saucepan partly covered to reduce evaporation. Ideally the pan should have a tight-fitting lid, but on most stoves this guarantees a boil. Cover tightly for oven simmering.

Stewing is a type of simmering – the term is applied to the mixture of meat and vegetables cooked in liquid which forms a rich gravy. Certain fruits such as apples, apricots and rhubarb are stewed in a sugar syrup. The liquid and solid parts mingle and are served together.

Poaching: To poach means to cook in a liquid which is just below simmering point. Water, stock, milk, wine and cider can all be used as the liquid. Poaching is mainly used for foods with a delicate structure that need gentle, low temperatures, such as fruit, fish and eggs. It can be done on top of the stove in a shallow open pan or in the oven. Often a lid or poaching paper covers the food lightly to make the process self-basting. Generally, fruit, eggs, gnocchi and small pieces of fish are poached on top of the stove, and larger pieces of fish are cooked in the oven. Kippers or other smoked fish can be poached in a special way called the jug method. The kippers are placed in a jug or deep bowl and covered with boiling water. They are left for 5-15 minutes (depending on the type and thickness of the fish used), then drained and served.

Steaming: Food is cooked in the steam from boiling water. It is slow but uses fuel economically and produces light, easily digested foods with little loss of nutrients.

Sometimes foods, especially vegetables, are placed on a perforated surface above the water. They can be loose or set in open dishes. At other times a covered bowl is set in or over the water.

For either method, a tightly fitted lid is necessary to keep the steam in. If a lid needs to be removed, this must be done quickly with a cloth to prevent the condensed steam from dripping onto the food or onto the arm or hand.

Roasting bags and/or aluminum foil placed over a roast or turkey both entrap steam. Thus the meat is cooked in moist heat rather than roasted, which is a dry heat method.

Pressure cooking: This is another form of steaming that on average reduces cooking times to a quarter, greatly saving on fuel and time. Busy people find pressure cookers invaluable, since most things take less than a half hour to cook. During the cooking period, however, the cookers cannot be left unattended because the pressure must be watched closely. All types of food can be cooked in them.

Dry-heat cooking

Baking: Baking is cooking in an oven by heat which is radiated from the lining of the oven, circulated by convection currents, and passed to the food by conduction through its container. A wide range of temperatures can be achieved in an ordinary oven which makes this method one of the most versatile. Baked food should not be in contact with liquid, and should have a brown, crisp surface as is the case with pastry, bread and cakes.

Roasting really means cooking on a rotating spit over an open fire, so today oven roasting is, in fact, baking. The term roasting, however, continues to be applied to meats and potatoes cooked in dry heat. Meat to be roasted should be put on a wire rack raised a little above the roasting pan, to allow air to circulate all around the roast. It should never be covered. Basting with pan juices during roasting keeps the exterior moist.

Rotisserie cooking: Rotisseries can be fitted into some stoves or bought as a separate unit. The food is secured on the spit, which is turned electrically, and cooks under direct heat. Because of the continuous rotation it does not usually need basting.

Broiling: Broiled food is cooked by intense direct heat under or over gas, electricity or charcoal. This method is suitable only for tender foods which do not need prolonged cooking: steaks, chops, fish, liver, kidneys. These should not be much over 1 inch (2½ centimeters) thick.

Meat should be subjected to a fierce heat to 'seal' the surface, after which the heat is reduced until the meat is cooked. Poultry and fish need a moderate heat throughout. Whole round fish, such as herring or mackerel should be scored three or four times before broiling to allow the heat to penetrate quickly.

All foods should be turned once during cooking. This is best done with tongs or two spoons; never pierce the surface with a fork because this allows juices to escape. Broiling is also sometimes used to brown the top of dishes described as *au gratin*.

Infrared broilers use rays of shorter wavelength than ordinary broilers. They greatly reduce cooking time, since the heat penetrates the food more quickly.

Frying: Frying is considered a dry heat method of cooking because of the high temperatures involved and the absence of a water-based liquid. When the food comes into contact with hot fat, moisture evaporates rapidly from the surface, causing shrinking, and the outside is quickly sealed. There are various ways of frying: pan broiling, sautéing, shallow frying and deep-fat frying. Each uses a different amount of fat. Many consider the first two methods far better for health, though little fat is absorbed if deep-fat frying is done at the correct temperature.

Pan broiling or dry frying is suitable for beefsteaks, hamburgers, lamb chops, sausages and bacon. Pork chops are usually too dry. A heavy frying pan is preheated and rubbed with a small amount of fat so that the bottom is covered with a film of fat but there is no excess. Sear the meat until blood rises to the surface, then turn it without piercing and brown the other side. Reduce the heat and continue to cook until the meat is done to taste. Pour off fat as it accumulates or the meat will be fried rather than broiled in quality. Never cover the pan.

Sautéing uses high heat and a small amount of fat, usually clarified butter or equal parts of vegetable oil and butter. The heat must be kept high throughout cooking in order not to draw juices. The food must be small and uniform in sizes and the surface dry. The pan must not be crowded. Shake the pan gently to keep the contents moving.

Sautéing is suitable for thin meats and some vegetables. Often the cooking is finished with moist heat by reducing the temperature, adding a liquid, covering and simmering for a short time. In other cases, the food is ready to serve with no further cooking. A good pan gravy can be made by deglazing the pan with stock and wine.

Shallow frying is less commonly used in the United States. Enough fat (vegetable oil, drippings, lard) is heated in a wide, shallow frying pan to come halfway up the side of the food to be cooked. The fat must be hot before the food is placed in the pan, otherwise too much fat is absorbed and the food becomes greasy. If the fat is *too* hot the outside will cook too quickly and the inside will be undercooked. A good test is to see if a cube of bread will brown in 1 minute before adding the food to be fried. At one time a guide to the correct temperatures was when a blue haze rose from the fat. This is no longer recommended, since modern cooking fats smoke at much higher temperatures than that needed for cooking.

All foods should be lowered gently, one at a time, into the pan to prevent splashing. Never fill the pan too full. Always drain fried foods on crumpled paper towels before serving.

Deep-fat frying is best done in a special deep frying pan with wire-basket and lid, or in a strong deep saucepan with well-fixed handles to make it easy and safe to lift. A wire draining spoon is useful to have for removing single pieces of food or crumbs which may become burned and give a bitter taste to the fat or oil. Suitable fats are clarified drippings, lard and vegetable or corn oil. Safflower oil is recommended for those on a low-cholesterol diet. The pan must not be more than half full with fat or oil because the fat bubbles up when food is immersed. Flames should not be allowed to come up the side of the pan, and it should never be left unattended during cooking. Do not allow water from a kettle or nearby saucepan to splash into the fat, because the fat will spurt out, burning whatever it hits. In case the fat catches fire, have the pan's metal lid handy to drop over the burning fat. Salt will also smother flames. Under no circumstances should you try to move the pan. And *never use water* which will only spread the fire

The fat or oil should be heated gradually to the desired temperature so that any moisture has time to evaporate. The temperatures for deep-fat frying are harder to judge than those for shallow-frying, so a deep-fat thermometer is recommended. Frying temperatures vary from 330°-390°F (170°-200°C), and individual recipes should be consulted for specific temperatures.

Meat, Poultry and Fish

Meat, poultry and fish form an important part of most people's diets. Not only are they rich in protein, vitamins and fats, but they also taste delicious when well-prepared and served with a sauce. They require careful cooking and repay attention to detail.

Learn to look at meat as it cooks, so that with experience you will be able to tell when it is finished, whether it is cooking too quickly or too slowly, and whether it needs basting. The appearance of fish, especially fillets, tells a lot more about doneness than time cooked.

Listen to meat and poultry cooking. Chickens being braised or roasted make gentle crackling noises. If they are too loud or too frequent, the temperature is too high. Not enough noise warns you the temperature is too low. Sound also warns you that the simmer has come too close to a boil.

Overcooking is the worst thing you can do to meat, poultry and fish. The result is dry, uninteresting and even tough and stringy. This happens most easily to fish, some poultry, and meat that lacks fat. None of these should be cooked in advance and kept waiting; rather, let the diners wait for them.

Interestingly, some cuts of meat that are tender when slightly underdone become tough when well cooked, then tender again after further slow cooking. Liver is a prime example; also flank steak when used in Chinese stir-fry cooking.

Meat

The term 'meat' encompasses beef (from ox, bull and sometimes cow), veal (calf), lamb and mutton (sheep), pork, ham and bacon (pig). It forms a basic part of most diets and is one of the largest expenditures in any family budget. Each carcass consists of meat cuts of various qualities. Some are tender, others tough. Tender cuts are naturally more expensive than the others; though cheaper cuts, cooked with care, can become tender and have good flavor.

Meat is cooked by all the methods described in pages 96-98. Dry heat should be used only for tender cuts; moist is best for all the others. Cooking meat not only destroys bacteria but also causes changes to take place in meat that makes it more tender. Fat marbled through as well as on the outside of roasts and chops melts during cooking, which helps meat to stay moist when cooked by dry heat. Moist heat causes connective tissue to dissolve, and fiber falls apart, making the meat more tender. Acid (lemon juice, vinegar, tomato) added to the liquid hastens the cooking process.

Preparations

Meats to be cooked by dry heat do best if they are brought to room temperature (70°F, 21°C), because they then respond better to heating. Unless a roast is very lean it needs no special preparation. The custom of adding drippings to the pan before putting the roast into it is unnecessary except in the case of lean meat and only means the oven will have to be cleaned more frequently. Basting is also unnecessary, and opening the oven door lowers the temperature drastically, especially in an electric oven. Roasting information for specific cuts of different meats is given in the chart on pages 96 to 98. For broiling and frying, cut excess fat off and score the remaining fat so the edges will not curl. If the tenderness of your meat is in doubt, pound it with a rolling pin, the edge of a heavy plate, or a mallet to crush the fibers and reduce stringiness. It can also be marinated for several hours, then dried well.

Have the broiler or frying pan very hot before introducing the meat. Remember that overcooking toughens meat, especially borderline cuts which are often still tender when they are slightly underdone.

Cuts for braising or pot-roasting do not need any particular preparation, though sometimes they are marinated first, which helps to tenderize them. The vegetables on which the meat will rest in braising should be great enough in number to raise the meat about 1 inch (2½ centimeters); add more if necessary. Fry the vegetables well, but browning or sealing the meat is optional.

Beef

Beef can be more variable in quality than other meats. Obviously, prime tender cuts are always more expensive because they are a smaller portion of the carcass.

When buying beef, look for meat with a fresh red color that has a brownish tinge. Too bright a color means the meat has not sufficiently aged and will be tough and lacking in flavor. The meat should also be marbled evenly throughout with a creamy-colored fat.

The amount of meat you buy depends on your diet and appetite, but an approximate guide is 8 ounces (125-175 grams) of boned meat, or 8-10 ounces (175-225 grams) of meat with bone per person per serving.

The prime cuts of beef include fillet, top rump, sirloin and ribs. These cuts are usually either roasted, broiled or pan fried. Cheaper cuts include round (used mainly for pot roasting or braising), chuck and ground beef.

Lamb

A lamb is a young sheep. In culinary terms the word refers either to an unweaned baby lamb or to an animal less than a year old.

When buying lamb, look for meat with a light color, fine grain and firm texture. It should be creamy-white and soft. Imported lamb has a whiter, firmer fat. Yellowish fat indicates an older animal and brittle white fat one that has been frozen too long.

Serve approximately 6-8 ounces (175-225 grams) of boned meat per person. For meat on the bone, allow 12 ounces (350 grams) of leg, 12 ounces-1 pound (350-450 grams) of shoulder, saddle and loin and 8-12 ounces (225-350 grams) of breast or best end for each serving.

The prime cuts of lamb are the saddle, leg and shoulder. The saddle is the choicest and biggest cut, from which the

76

rib and the loin chops are cut. These are always roasted. The leg, which may be cut into two, the fillet end and the shank or knuckle end, is suitable for roasting, braising and, when boned, for casseroles.

Mutton

Mutton is the flesh of a sheep over one year of age. Good mutton is bright red in color, close grained and firm in texture. The fat is firm and white. In France, where mutton is popular, salt meadow mutton is the most highly praised and is considered a delicacy of Brittany. It comes from sheep reared on the coast where aromatic plants grow.

Mutton, being older than lamb, should be cooked from 5-10 minutes to the pound or half-kilo longer. So if you cannot obtain mutton and have to substitute lamb in any recipe, reduce the cooking time accordingly.

Like most other meat, mutton is cut differently in Britain, the United States and Europe, but as a general guide, the cuts and methods of cooking are as follows: the leg is roasted, boiled or cut into pieces and used in stews, kebabs and curries; the shoulder is roasted and also cut up for curries and stews, the loin is roasted or casseroled, and loin chops are fried or broiled; the neck and breast are stewed.

Pork

Pork is the fresh meat from a pig, as opposed to ham and bacon which are cured before cooking.

When buying pork look for fine-textured, firm, pink-colored, smooth flesh with no gristle. All pork should be thoroughly cooked and never served underdone, because it sometimes harbors a parasite dangerous to man – the trichina worm – which thorough cooking destroys.

Serve approximately 6-8 ounces (175-225 grams) of boned meat or 8-12 ounces (225-350 grams) with bone per person.

The prime cuts of pork are the leg, which is sometimes divided into fillet and knuckle; loin, the best and most expensive joint from which loin chops are cut and which is sometimes divided into hind and fore loin; shoulder or butt, which is a joint cut from the top part of the foreleg. These cuts are usually roasted, broiled or in the case of fillet and chops, baked.

The medium cuts include picnic shoulder, shoulder chops and hind loin chops. Fillet is a fatless cut which is removed from either side of the backbone.

Bacon and Ham

Bacon is the cured meat from a specially bred pig. The meat is immersed in brine, then (in the case of smoked bacon) hung over smoldering oak or hickory sawdust chips; unsmoked bacon, also called green bacon, has a white rind and a milder flavor than smoked bacon.

Ham is the name given to the meat from the thigh of the pig. It is removed from the side of the pig before salting and then cured. There are regional differences in methods of preparation – some hams are smoked before they are cured, others not. A ham should have a thin rind and not be too fatty. When buying cooked ham, look for fresh, pink flesh and white fat.

Veal

Veal is the flesh of calves less than 10 months old. The flesh is pale pink in color and darkens as the animal gets older. It has little fat and because of this, the leanest cuts should be barded, that is, covered with salt pork or bacon, before cooking. Good veal is soft and moist in texture. If the flesh has a blue or brown tinge, it is stale and should not be bought. Veal bones contain a large amount of gelatin, and this makes veal stock ideal for molds and pies.

Two kinds of veal are available: from milk-fed calves and from grass-fed calves. Milk-fed calves are considered to have the more delicate flavor and finer texture, and are more expensive. Serve approximately 4-6 ounces (125-175 grams) of boned meat per person; for meat on the bone, allow 8 ounces (225 grams) of leg; and ¾-1 pound (350-450 grams) of shoulder, shank, hock and knuckle per person.

The prime cuts of veal are the legs, rump, loin, shoulder and saddle. Loin chops, chump chops and cutlets are cut from the loin and should be broiled or shallow-fried. Leg, rump, loin and saddle are usually roasted. The cheaper cuts breast, shank, hock and knuckle, are suitable for roasting when boned, stuffed and rolled, and for braising, boiling and stewing. Shank is suitable for molds and pies.

Beef – a T-bone steak

Veal – an escalope

Pork – two loin chops

Lamb – three loin chops.

Variety meats or offal

Liver

The liver of calves, oxen, pigs, sheep, poultry and game are all used in cooking, but calf's liver is generally considered to be the best and is the most tender. Serve approximately 4-8 ounces (125-250 grams) per person.

Preparation: Add a little butter and oil to the frying pan and preheat. Lightly coat the liver with flour before frying.

Cooking: Frying and broiling are the best ways of cooking tender liver slices. When done, liver should be pale brown on the outside and slightly rare in the center. If it is overcooked it will be tough.

Kidneys

Lamb and veal kidneys are the most delicate in flavor. They are suitable for broiling and frying, and need only a short cooking over medium heat. When cooked centers should remain slightly pink, since overcooking toughens them. Never boil them in a sauce; instead remove them, thicken the sauce and return them for 2-3 minutes to warm through.

Ox, pork and sheep's kidneys are tougher and have a stronger flavor. They benefit from soaking in acidulated water and from slow moist cooking.

Preparation: The white membrane around kidneys should be removed along with the fat, which is highest quality suet and should be rendered down. Allow 2-3 lambs' kidneys per person, $1\frac{1}{2}$-2 mutton, 1 small veal or pork, and $\frac{1}{2}$ or less of ox. Lay the kidneys on a wooden board and, with a pair of scissors or a sharp knife, nick the skin. Peel off the skin with your fingers, taking care not to break the flesh beneath. Remove as much of the fatty core as possible.

If the kidneys are to be broiled, slice them almost but not quite through, so that the two halves of each kidney open out flat. Wash the kidneys in cold, salted water and dry thoroughly with paper towels before using.

Cooking: Brush with melted butter before broiling, or shallow fry in half butter and half oil. Cook for about 6 minutes, turning them once.

Sweetbread

Sweetbread is the culinary name for the neck (thymus) and the stomach (pancreas) glands of lambs, calves and bullocks.

They have a delicate flavor, a close, smooth texture and are rich and filling to eat. Allow between 4-6 ounces (125-150 grams) per person.

Lamb sweetbreads are considered the finest in texture; calf sweetbreads are more economical, and also have a good texture; bull's sweetbreads, although larger and coarser, can be made tender by cooking them for 3-4 hours. They are ideal for dishes with sauces. Neck and stomach sweetbreads are both readily available, but stomach sweetbreads are more sought after because they have a smoother texture and are regular in shape.

Preparation: Place the sweetbreads in a mixing bowl and nearly fill it with cold water. Soak for 3 hours, drain and discard the water. Remove the sweetbreads from the bowl and drain them on paper towels. Remove and discard the skin and any membranes. Place the sweetbreads in a large saucepan and cover with cold water. Place the pan over moderately high heat and bring the water to the boil. Remove the pan from the heat and set aside for 10 minutes. Remove the sweetbreads from the pan and drain them on paper towels.

Cooking: Sweetbreads may be cooked whole, sliced or chopped into pieces. Alternatively, they can be braised in butter and stock, shallow fried in butter or poached in various sauces.

Brains

The brains of calves, sheep and pigs are considered culinary delicacies. Calves' brains are the most popular. They are bland and need a sauce with a definite flavor. Allow 1 pound (450 grams) for four people.

Preparation: Soak the brains in cold water for at least 4 hours, changing the water frequently. Remove and discard any loose skin. Rinse the brains in tepid water to remove any clots of blood.

Cooking: Poach the brains in well-flavored stock. Sheep's brains 15 minutes; calf's and pig's brains, 20-25 minutes. Once poached and drained, brains may be cooked in a variety of ways. One popular way is to dip them in seasoned flour, beaten egg and breadcrumbs and shallow fry until golden.

Heart

Use the hearts of calves, oxen, sheep and pigs for economical, tasty dishes. The meat is firm, lean and close in texture.

Ox hearts weigh between 3-4 pounds ($1\frac{1}{2}$-2 kilograms) and serve four to six people. A calf's heart is usually enough for two and a sheep's heart will serve one. Since hearts are a lean, dry meat they are best cooked by braising, though they can also be baked, stewed and fried. When cooked whole, they are usually stuffed.

Preparation: Cut away the veins, membranes and gristle. Wash thoroughly in cold running water to remove all blood. Soak the heart in cold, salted water, or water and vinegar (1 tablespoon of vinegar to $2\frac{1}{2}$ cups [600 milliliters] of water). Soak a sheep's heart for 2 hours, calf's heart for 4 hours and ox heart for 8 hours or overnight. Cooking time: ox heart, 2 hours; calf's heart, 1-$1\frac{1}{2}$ hours; sheep's heart 45 minutes-1 hour.

Ox tongue

Ox tongue may be bought either fresh or salted from most butchers, and weighs between 4-6 pounds (2-$2\frac{3}{4}$ kilograms).

Preparation: To prepare a fresh tongue for cooking, place the tongue in a large mixing bowl, covered with water and set aside for 3 hours. Drain the tongue. Scrape the skin and remove any surplus gristle. Wash the tongue and drain it.

Cooking: To cook a tongue, place it in a large, deep pan and add enough water just to cover. Place the pan over moderate heat and bring the water to a boil, removing the scum as it rises to the surface. When the water boils, cover the pan and reduce the heat to low. Simmer the tongue for 5-6 hours or until the bones can be pulled away easily, and the tongue is tender when the thickest part is pierced with the point of a sharp knife. Remove from the heat and allow the tongue to cool 30 minutes in the cooking liquid. Drain and discard the cooking liquid. Place the tongue on a board and remove the skin, bones and gristle from the meat. To serve the tongue hot, serve it whole or sliced with mushrooms or Madeira sauce.

Salted tongue: To prepare a salted tongue for cooking, place the tongue in a large mixing bowl, cover with water and soak for 24 hours, changing the water twice. Drain the tongue, scrape the skin and remove any surplus gristle. Wash the tongue with fresh water and drain it again. Cook as for unsalted ox tongue.

Tripe

Tripe comes from the stomach linings of cattle and oxen. This lining is made up of

four different parts, only three of which are sold as tripe. This explains the varied appearance of the meat. The most common varieties are honeycomb, which resembles a honeycomb, and blanket, which is fairly smooth with a slightly velvet surface.

Preparation and cooking: Tripe requires prolonged cooking, but is usually sold partly cooked, so cooking time varies according to the tripe bought. Ask the butcher for advice on its cooking time. Wash under cold running water until the water runs clear. In general, if the tripe is bought completely uncooked, it will require 3-$3\frac{1}{2}$ hours simmering in salted water and or milk, or, if prepared, 1-$1\frac{1}{2}$ hours cooking.

Oxtail

Oxtail has a strong, meaty taste. Allow one ox tail for four people.

Preparation: Oxtail is sold already skinned and chopped into serving pieces.

Cooking: It is best cooked by 'moist' methods of cooking – such as braising and stewing. Prepare the day before eating, so that all excess fat may be removed. It also makes a rich meaty soup.

Feet or trotters

Pig's feet are nutritious and inexpensive. They are generally sold cleaned and prepared for cooking.

They come in two main sizes, medium or large. (The very small pig's feet, called pettitoes, come from suckling pigs.) Pig's feet are usually cooked whole, but they are sometimes split in half if they are very large. Allow two medium sized feet per person.

Calves' feet are also used in cooking and prepared in the same way as pig's feet. They are especially rich in gelatin and are therefore added to any savory you want to gel, especially aspic.

Preparation: If the pig's feet have been split, tie them together.

Cooking: To boil pig's feet, pour 4 quarts ($3\frac{3}{4}$ liters) of water into a large, deep pot and add flavorings such as scraped and sliced carrots, a large chopped onion, a *bouquet garni*, a few black peppercorns and salt to taste. Bring the water to a boil and add the feet. Reduce the heat to low, cover the pan and simmer for 3-4 hours (depending on the size of the feet), or until they are very tender. Drain in a colander and discard the cooking liquid. The pig's feet are now ready to be eaten. They can also be cooked further – fry, broil or cut them into pieces to use in stews.

Head

The heads of animals – ox, calf, sheep and pig – are a source of much well-flavored nutritious meat, such as tongue and brains. Pickled and boiled heads make very good pies and casseroles. Brawn, or head cheese, is jellied head, usually made with calf's or pig's head, and is known as *fromage de tête* in France.

Sausage

There are two major categories of sausage: 'dry' sausages, that is sausages that, generally, may be eaten uncooked, and 'wet' sausages, which need to be cooked in some way before they are eaten.

Most sausages are made from minced pork, fat or lean, and usually seasonings and preservatives as well – the ingredients that make up commercially sold sausages are usually stated on the label in descending order by volume.

'Dry' sausages include salami, mortadella, garlic sausage and liver sausage. 'Wet' include frankfurters, bratwurst, Italian sausages and chorizo. Wet sausages may be boiled, broiled, baked or fried.

Poultry and Game

Poultry is the collective term used to describe domestic birds which are reared for the table. Game, on the other hand, is defined as being wild animals and birds which are hunted for sport and then prepared for eating.

Poultry includes chicken, turkey, duck, goose, guinea fowl and pigeon. Game includes grouse, partridge, pheasant, rabbit, hare and deer (which provides venison).

Poultry must be plucked, hung and drawn before cooking – jobs done these days by the butcher before the poultry is sold. Game is usually hung after it has been shot to allow the flesh to mature – the length of time depends on the game in question and, to some extent, the time of the year. Game is plucked and gutted just before it is sold – a service again performed by the butcher.

When you are buying fresh poultry, look for chickens with tender, firm flesh and plump breasts. Ducks should have rich, fatty flesh, while good-quality turkeys can be recognized by their firm white flesh. When you are buying fresh game, look for hare with dark flesh and plump rabbits with pale meat. Venison should be dark red with creamy white fat.

Frozen poultry and game should be thoroughly thawed before cooking. The best method for poultry is to thaw it in the refrigerator, unwrapped, which takes from 12 hours to 3 days, depending on size. Poultry giblets are usually found in a bag in the neck cavity, and the neck is placed in the body cavity.

Roasting times for individual poultry or game is given in the chart on pages 98 to 100.

Chicken

Chicken is the most frequently served poultry and the most versatile. It goes well with many different sauces and vegetables and can be cooked by all the dry and moist heat methods described earlier.

Two types of chicken are on the market. Battery chickens have been raised indoors on a controlled diet that puts on maximum weight in minimum time, but they do not develop much flavor. However, this does not matter if it is being served with sauce and strongly flavored. They are the least expensive sort to buy. Free-range, or farmyard, chickens mature more slowly, living outdoors, and supplement their diet by whatever they find around to eat. They have a stronger, more interesting flavor which is better for simple unadorned cooking – roasting, broiling, etc. They are, however, more expensive.

Chickens have a number of other names which denote size and age. A **poussin** is a very small chicken, aged between 6-8 weeks, and weighing between $\frac{3}{4}$-$1\frac{1}{2}$ pounds. It can be roasted, fried or broiled and is generally served either whole or split in half. **Broiler** chickens are 3 months old and weigh between 2-2$\frac{1}{2}$ pounds. **Roasting** chickens are up to 9 months old and weigh 3-4 pounds. They are also called **cockerels, pullets** and **fat fowls. Capons** are castrated young cocks which have been specially fattened. Their flesh is white and delicate and they usually weigh from 6-10 pounds and are no more than 10 months of age. **Stewing fowl** are larger, older birds which are tougher and therefore require longer, slower cooking. They are excellent for chicken fricassee.

Even though the poultry you buy is supposedly oven-ready, a number of things need to be done. First, remove from the skin any remaining feathers and feather sacs. Next, cut out the oil sac at the base of the tail (it is the bump on the tail) by making a semi-circular cut above it and scraping out the yellowish oily substance, which can give the flesh an unpleasant flavor. Finally, with your fingers explore the body cavity, removing excess fat, blood vessels and soft, dark red matter from between the ribs. Sometimes the lungs have not been removed. Inspect the neck cavity. If you wash the bird, make sure the skin is thoroughly dry before roasting, or it will not brown well. Never soak it in water.

Remember that stuffing should be put into poultry only at the last minute to remove the possibility of spoiling.

Poultry placed on a high roasting rack need not be turned in order to brown evenly, although sometimes the pan needs to be turned around. To turn unstuffed poultry thrust a large wooden spoon into the cavity, lift, and rotate.

No poultry should be overcooked, because it dries out, loses flavor and becomes stringy. Therefore, knowing how to test for doneness is important. A boiled chicken is done when the meat feels tender when pierced with a skewer. Other chickens are done if their juices run a clear yellow rather than rosy when pierced deeply. With a whole chicken, pierce the thickest part of the thigh, since this is the slowest cooking part. A meat thermometer inserted into the thigh should read 175°–180°F (80°–82°C).

While the poultry is cooking, make stock for the gravy. Use the neck, gizzard, which should have been cut open and contents discarded (if the butcher has not done this, do the cutting well away from other cooking), feet (ask the butcher for them) and wing tips. Cut the wing tips off at the first joint before cooking; they lack meat and are not worth eating, yet they will give flavor to stock. Simmer for an hour or more with the usual ingredients (see stock page 108). Under-season if the stock is for gravy.

Turkey

What has been said about chicken – cleaning, doneness, stock – also applies to turkey. Modern turkeys differ from those of a generation ago in having much smaller body cavities in relation to total weight and in being more tender. The effect of this is that they hold much less stuffing than formerly. For families who like stuffing, the bird never holds enough. Therefore, place extra stuffing in a small casserole, moisten it with a little strong turkey stock, cover tightly with aluminum foil, and put in the oven for the last hour.

The fact that today's turkeys are more tender also means that they cook through more quickly than they did formerly. So you should be prepared to stop the cooking process a little early. Check in the last hour or so to judge how close to doneness the bird is. Should you judge the turkey to be finished and decide to remove it from the oven, keep it loosely covered with tinfoil which will maintain the warmth for at least half an hour.

Duck

Duck is prized for its rich, succulent, fatty flesh. It has far less meat in relation to weight than a chicken, however. A 4 pound (2 kilogram) duck is only enough for two people, and a 6 pound (2½ kilogram) one will do for four or five.

To prepare a duck for roasting, clip the wing ends and neck, and truss it so that the wings and legs are close to the body. Prick the skin around the thighs, back and lower breast so that during roasting excess fat can run out.

Ducks are usually stuffed before roasting. After stuffing, close the cavity with needle and thread or with a skewer.

Goose

Choose a goose which is not more than one year old and which has yellow feet.

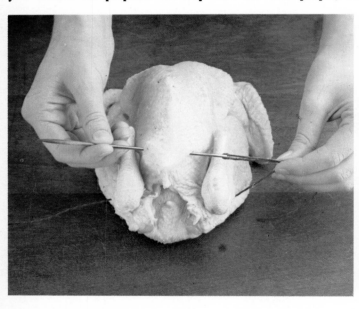

Push the needle through the lower part of the carcass. Pass the string over one drumstick, through the tip of the breastbone and over the other drumstick. Tie firmly.

Then re-thread the needle and thrust it through the top of the carcass, above the wings, where the drumstick and the second joint meet, and then out the other side.

Turn the bird over and carefully push the needle through the wing, the neck flap and, finally, through the outer wing. Then secure the string, tying it firmly.

Tie the string ends together firmly. Rub salt and pepper (and any other herb of your choice) over the skin of the bird. It is now ready to be cooked.

80

Since goose is not meaty allow an 8 pound (3½ kilogram) goose for four people, and a 10 pound (4½ kilogram) goose for six people.

Geese are usually roasted, but most methods of cooking turkey can be applied to goose. The basic method of roasting is to prick the bird all over with a fork and rub it with lemon juice, salt and pepper. The goose is placed on its breast on a rack in a roasting pan. Remove the fat from the roasting pan frequently. When the goose is half cooked, turn it over onto its back.

To test if the goose is cooked, prick the thigh with the point of a sharp knife. The juices that run out should be clear.

Game

The classic way of cooking game birds is to roast them in the oven. Begin the process by covering well with salt pork or bacon and baste them frequently during cooking because they are generally rather lean and can be dry. Often, because of their uncertain age and tenderness it is best to cook them slowly in moist heat. Braising either whole or cut into pieces is often the most satisfactory method.

Trussing Poultry

Poultry is trussed so that it keeps its shape during cooking and is therefore easier to carve.

The simplest way to truss a bird is with a skewer and a piece of string. Push the skewer through the bird just below the thigh bone. Turn the bird onto its breast. Catch the wing pinions with the string, pass the string under the ends of the skewer and cross it over the back. Turn the bird over, pass the string over the drumsticks and tie under the tail.

To truss poultry in the traditional way you need to have a long trussing needle and strong fine string or trussing thread.

Carving meat and poultry

Carving, the cutting or slicing of large cuts of meat or whole game, is a necessary skill. Correctly carved meat prevents waste, improves presentation, saves time (thus avoiding bringing cold meat to the table), and helps make the most of leftovers.

If you have any doubts about your prowess as a carver, or if you are relatively

Pull the leg away from the body and sever it through the joint.

Carve the breast meat in slices, parallel to the breastbone.

Or cut the breast off in one piece with scissors, then halve.

81

Carve the shoulder of lamb from the blade end, cutting the slices as thinly as possible, with the grain.

Turn the shoulder over and carve it into thin slices, across the thicker end of the meat.

Turn the shoulder over once more, fatty side down, and cut the meat, with the grain, into thin slices.

Leg of lamb, on the bone. Begin carving from the shorter, or knuckle end in short, thick slices.

new to the craft, test your expertise (or conduct your experiments, depending on how confident you are of your prowess!) in the safety and privacy of the kitchen. To make a first attempt at the table, with all hungry eyes upon you, takes courage; and in such circumstances even the strongest nerves can fail.

The most important point to remember is that each type of meat has a particular grain which, generally speaking, runs lengthwise along the carcass. The meat is usually carved against the grain, because this shortens the length of the fibers and produces more tender slices. One of the few exceptions to this rule is loin of veal, which is carved with the grain.

Before carving the meat, remove and discard any trussing thread, string or skewers used to close up the cavity.

Avoid cutting the meat in short or deep cuts – aim for large, thin, even slices.

The pictures and directions shown are a guide to carving cuts of meat which have been cooked with the bone. Directions for boned or rolled cuts of meat are not given, because carving is simple – just remember that slices should be fairly thin.

Game

Small game birds such as pheasant, grouse and partridge are served in three different ways, according to the size and toughness of the bird – whole (very small birds only), jointed, before or after cooking, or carved in the same way as poultry, although sometimes only the breast is eaten.

To carve poultry

With the exception of very small birds, the legs are removed first before you carve. To do this, pull the leg away from the body with a two-pronged fork and sever through the thigh joint. Separate the drumstick from the thigh by cutting through the knee joint. To remove the wings, use the fork to hold down the pinion and cut through the shoulder joint. If the fowl is large the breast may be carved in thin slices, parallel to the breastbone. With a smaller bird, the breast is removed in one piece and then cut in half.

If the bird has been stuffed, then this is removed after carving and a small amount is served with the meat. When you're serving poultry, especially chicken and turkey, it is traditional to serve a little

Continue carving the leg from the knuckle, graduating to longer, thinner slices, toward the rump bones.

For loin of veal turn the meat onto its side and steady it with a carving fork. Cut off the shin bone.

Now turn the loin over so that the fatty side is upper most and carve towards the knuckle end.

To carve ham, grasp the knuckle bone and carve thinly toward the knuckle end, down to the leg bone.

white meat (meat from the breast area) plus a little dark (from around the thighs, wings and legs) per serving – always allowing for personal preferences, of course.

Fish and Shellfish

Fish

Fish is a readily available source of protein, vitamins and minerals. It is classified by its source, either fresh or salt water, and by type, white, oily or shellfish.

Since fish is extremely perishable, it must be cooked as quickly as possible after being caught, and in the interim must be kept cold.

Packages of frozen fish are a convenient way of buying. Frozen fish is often fresher than that bought from a fish store, because it was quick-frozen as soon as it was caught. Fresh bought fish can be recognized as fresh if it has a clear, shining eye and fresh-smelling flesh, and is firm when pressed.

Fish can be bought whole, in steaks or in fillets. A fish store owner will clean, dress and cut the fish; in a supermarket it comes prepared. However, if you catch your own fish, preparation at home is not difficult.

Preparing flat fish and round fish

Scaling: To scale a fish, dip it first in cold water and lay it on a board. Grasp the fish by the tail and, with a sharp knife,

scrape from tail to head against the grain of the scales. Wash the fish thoroughly in cold water.

Cleaning or gutting: To clean the fish, cut off the head (if the recipe does not specify leaving it on) and make one long cut down the underside. Using a spoon, scrape out the intestines, which should come out in one piece. Wash the inside of the fish well, holding it under cold water to get rid of any remaining blood.

To clean a fish which is to be kept whole, the easy way is to slit the fish along the belly from under the head to the anus, or you can remove the intestines through the gills. Next, cut away all the fins – the pelvic fins on the underside next to the head, the pectoral fins on either side behind the gills, the dorsal fin on the back and the ventral fin on the underside of the back. The fish is now ready to be cooked.

Filleting: To fillet a fish is to remove the flesh from the backbone in lengthwise pieces. Some fish provide two fillets, some four. First make an incision right down the backbone. Then with short, sharp cuts, separate the flesh from the bone and carefully work the flesh away. Drop the fillets into a bowl of cold water and dry them with a clean cloth or on paper towels.

To skin the fillets, place, skin side down, on a board with the tail towards you. Put some salt on the board. Start at the tail and scrape the flesh loose with a heavy knife. Hold the salted tail with your left hand and, keeping the knife blade perpendicular to the board, push down and towards the head end while moving the knife slowly back and forth in a sawing motion. Always grasp the skin close to where the knife is.

Cut fish is usually improved if the fillets or steaks are sprinkled with a little salt and left for a few minutes before cooking. They should also be rinsed in cold water to reduce cooking odors. If they are to be fried, dry them well with paper towels. As a general rule, you will require between 6-8 ounces (175-225 grams) of fish steaks or fish fillets or 1 pound (450 grams) of whole fish per person.

Cooking fish

Fish can be cooked in numerous ways – frying, broiling and poaching are perhaps best known, but steaming and baking are also suitable. The most popular methods of cooking fish are shallow and deep-frying.

The length of the cooking time varies according to the method used and the type of fish, but generally the fish is cooked if it flakes easily when tested with a fork, and the flesh has turned white and opaque. Try not to overcook fish because it becomes dry and tasteless.

Fish which is to be fried is usually coated in seasoned flour, egg and breadcrumbs, or batter. It is best to deep-fry fish in vegetable oils, since they are lighter and leave the surface of the fish crisp and dry. The thinner the fish, the higher the temperature of the fat should be. Fill a large frying pan one-third full of oil. Heat the oil over moderate heat until

Make an incision down the backbone and carefully ease the flesh away.

Turn around so the head is facing you and remove the other fillet in the same way.

Turn the fish onto its front and remove the remaining fillets, with roe.

Carefully ease the flesh off the skin in one piece.

it reaches 370°F (188°C) on a deep-fat thermometer, or until a cube of stale bread dropped into the oil browns in 45 seconds. Successful deep-frying requires a frying basket which fits easily into the pan. This should be heated before the fish is put in so that the fish does not stick to the basket. Depending on the size, the coated pieces of fish will take about 3-7 minutes to cook through. The breadcrumbs should turn a light golden brown in color. Drain the fried fish on paper towels before serving.

To broil, preheat the broiler to high. Brush the fish with melted butter and place under the broiler. Cook for 10-15 minutes, depending on the thickness of

the fish. Fish steaks and fillets only need to be broiled on one side until cooked through whereas whole fish must be turned to brown evenly on both sides. Whole fish should be scored with three shallow slits on each side to speed up the cooking process and to prevent curling.

Fish is poached in milk, *court bouillon* (see page 111), fish stock, wine or water. It can be done on top of the stove or in the oven. To poach in the oven, preheat it to moderate 350°F (180°C). Lay the fish in a shallow baking dish. Heat up the poaching liquid until it is boiling and pour it over the fish. Cover the dish loosely and place it in the oven. When poaching on top of the stove, place the fish in warm, not boiling, liquid and bring it near to boiling. Reduce the heat to low and poach the fish until it is cooked. Allow 8-10 minutes per pound (10-12 minutes per half-kilo) for large whole fish, 15–20 minutes in all for small whole fish like fluke, flounder or sole, 8–12 minutes for fillets and 10-15 minutes for steaks lying in a single layer in the dish. An onion, lemon slices, chopped carrots and celery may be put in the poaching liquid to add flavor to the fish. For the jug method of poaching smoked fish fillets, see page 74.

Steaming is the best way of retaining flavor in a delicate lean fish. Put the fish on an ovenproof plate or dish and moisten with water, *court bouillon*, etc. Either put into the top part of a double boiler or put into a colander set over a pan half full of simmering water. Cover tightly and cook for the same time as for poaching.

To bake a whole fish, lay the fish on a large piece of aluminum foil. Place a bay leaf, salt, pepper and thin slices of onion and lemon inside the fish. Rub the fish all over with oil, if you are eating it cold, or butter if it is to be served hot. Wrap the fish well, leaving space inside for the air to circulate, and carefully fold the edges to seal. Place the fish in a roasting pan and bake it in the oven preheated to 300°F (150°C). A 2-3 pound (1-1½ kilograms) fish will take about 1 hour. Carefully remove the fish from the foil and, while it is still hot, remove the skin gently with a knife. This is a particularly good way of cooking salmon and salmon trout.

Shellfish

Shellfish is the collective term for all edible crustacea and mollusks. Among these are found clams, crabs, lobsters, mussels, oysters, and shrimp. Overheating and overcooking both ruin the delicate flavor and texture of shellfish. Therefore use low heat and cook the minimum time possible. Serve hot dishes at once.

Bivalves
Bivalves or two-shelled mollusks, include clams, cockles, mussels and oysters. All are prepared in the same way, and all can be eaten raw or cooked.

To prepare bivalves, wash thoroughly in several changes of cold water and scrub with a stiff brush to remove all mud and seaweed from the shells. On mussels, use

---

Types of Fish

White Fish	Oily Fish	Other
Bass (sea wolf, sea perch sea salmon, white salmon)	Carp	**Salted:**
	Conger eel	Bloater (herring or mackerel)
Catfish	Eel	Kipper (herring)
Cod	Herring (sprat, whitebait)	
Coalfish		**Smoked:**
Dab	Mackerel	Cod
Dogfish	Mullet (red, gray)	Haddock
Flounder	Perch	Mackerel
Fluke	Pilchard	Salmon
Haddock	Salmon	Trout
Hake (silver hake, white hake)	Sardine	
Halibut	Smelt	Octopus
Minnow	Trout (brown, salmon or sea, lake)	Squid
Pike	Tuna	
Salmon		
Skate (ray)		
Sole (Lemon or gray)		
Turbot		
Whiting		

---

a sharp knife to scrape off the tufts of hair, or beards, that protrude from between the closed shells. Discard any shells that are not shut tightly or do not close when tapped; also discard those with broken shells. After cleaning place the bivalves in a bowl of lightly salted cold water and let them stand for an hour. If they are to stand longer than this some people add a little cornmeal, oatmeal or flour to the water.

Opening the shells is something of an art, since you must slide a knife between the shells and break the hinge. If you do this often a special oyster knife is a great help. Always open bivalves over a basin in which to catch the juice, which should be kept frozen to add to, or use in place of, fish stock.

To steam, pour barely enough water into a large saucepan to cover the bottom. Add a teaspoon of salt, bouquet garni, and any other flavorings, depending on the ultimate use. Place the bivalves in the pan, cover tightly and place over high heat. Shake the pan frequently so that the shells move around. Cook until the shells open, which is generally 6-10 minutes. If any shells are still closed, discard them. Either serve the cooking liquid with the

bivalves or save it for another use later on.

Shrimp
The shrimp family – shrimp, prawns, butterfly shrimp or Gulf shrimp are free-swimming crustacea with soft, translucent shells. They come in sizes ranging from about 1 inch (2½ centimeters) shelled to more than 4-5 inches (10-12 centimeters), and have flavors that differ somewhat depending on variety and location. Cold-water shrimp are supposed to have more flavor than those from tropical waters.

Shrimp are available throughout the year. They are sold fresh, canned, frozen, dried, potted, and cooked and peeled. Unfortunately uncooked shrimp are hard to find in many areas.

Raw shrimp can be cooked either before or after shelling. If they are to be used cold they are cooked in the shell.

To cook, first rinse the shrimp well under cold water, which not only cleans them but will virtually eliminate cooking odors. Bring water to a boil, add the shrimp and simmer for 3-6 minutes depending on size. Stop the cooking as soon as they have changed color. Do not overcook, for this makes them rubbery.

Lobster

A selection of shrimp

Mussels, scallops and clams

Drain the water, cool and peel the shrimp.

To peel either cooked or raw shrimp pull the head end off gently with the fingers, remove the legs and then the back shell. Depending on the recipe leave the tail on or gently pull it off. Unless the vein running along the top of the back is black, do not remove it. If it must be removed, scrape it out with the sharp point of a knife. Cooked shrimp should be added to sauces at the last minute and cooked only long enough to heat them through.

Scallops

Scallops (*pectens maximus*) are shellfish found around the coasts of France (where they are called *coquilles*) and the United States. They have two shells, one flat and one concave, which contain edible muscle flesh – bright white when fresh. **Sea scallops** are in-season most of the year and are much larger and not nearly so tender as the small **bay scallops,** which have a much shorter season and are considered a delicacy.

Scallops are usually sold clean and out of the shell. If not, however, treat as you would any other bivalve. Remove the flat shells with a knife or place them with the flat shell uppermost in a warm place, where they will open of their own accord. Using a sharp knife, remove the flesh from the shell and cut away the black gristly fiber attached to the flesh. The scallops are now ready for cooking. Do not discard the scallop shells; they may be washed, scrubbed and used as containers for scalloped dishes.

Poach in *court bouillon* or lightly salted water, for 8-10 minutes or until the flesh is firm. To fry scallops, either marinate them in a mixture of olive oil and lemon juice for 30 minutes or poach and drain them. Coat the scallops in either case with beaten egg and breadcrumbs or batter and fry them for 8-10 minutes or until they are lightly browned all over.

Lobsters and crabs

Lobsters and crabs may differ in appearance, but both can be treated in the same manner. Also given similar treatment are crawfish and crayfish. The crawfish, or spiny lobster (*langouste* in France), differs from the lobster in that its front legs do not have enlarged pincers. Crayfish are small fresh-water creatures resembling lobsters.

If you are buying live lobsters or

crabs, see that they are active. A dead or dying one should never be cooked. The most usual way of cooking lobster is to boil it. There are several ways of doing this. The first, and reputedly more humane, method is to place the lobster or crab in a large, deep pot. Cover it with cold salted water and bring it to a boil very slowly over moderately low heat. When the water comes to a boil, increase the heat to moderately high and boil the lobster for 20 minutes, the crab for 10-15 minutes per pound or half kilo.

The second method is to plunge the lobster head-first into boiling water and then cook it for 20 minutes. Cool the lobster in the cooking liquid. This is no suitable for crab.

Alternatively, it may be killed before cooking. Tie the claws together and lay on a chopping board. With a towel wrapped around one hand for protection, first grasp the lobster firmly. With a large, heavy, sharp knife, cut through behind the head to sever the spinal cord. Sever the lobster's spinal column just behind the eyes.

Lobster may also be broiled. First kill it, then slit in two lengthwise. Remove the sac and the intestines. Brush the lobster halves with butter or oil and season with salt and pepper. Preheat the broiler to high. Place the lobster in the broiler pan, shell side down, and broil for 12-15 minutes or until it is cooked through. Serve the lobster halves in their shells, garnished with parsley and lemon wedges.

To prepare a boiled lobster for the table, first twist off the large claws. Crack them with a nutcracker or a light hammer through the center and at the joint. Remove the smaller claws which are used for garnishing. Using a large pointed knife, split the lobster from head to tail down the middle. Remove the sac, intestines and gills. Retain the liver. To serve, arrange it with the head upright and the split tail and claws around it. Garnish with parsley and lemon wedges.

To prepare the crab, follow the step-by-step instructions on the right.

Crabmeat is generally mashed and seasoned with salt, pepper, mustard and vinegar. The meat can then be piled back into the shell and garnished. Most fish sellers will 'dress' a crab in this way if given adequate notice.

Fresh crayfish are green or brown, but turn bright red in cooking. If they are

To extract meat from a crab, remove the legs and pincers, then pull the body away.

Carefully remove the stomach bag and any spongy matter from the shell.

Pull off any gills or "dead man's fingers" and scoop out meat from the claws.

Scoop out the flesh from the shell and add it to the claw meat.

very fresh and have recently been in flowing water they do not need to be gutted before boiling. Otherwise they should be washed under cold running water before cooking, and the bitter-flavored intestinal tube beneath the tail should be removed. Then place them in salted water or *court bouillon*, bring to a boil and simmer for 5-7 minutes.

To gut the crayfish, hold it firmly in the left hand and with the fingers of the right hand pull the middle fin on the tail with a sharp twist, removing the stomach and intestines with it. Wash the crayfish well in running water.

Snails
Both land and sea snails are eaten throughout the world. In size they range from the giant conch of tropical waters to small periwinkles.

Periwinkle, also called **winkle,** is the common name of small edible sea snails. There are 80 species but the Common

Periwinkle is the largest in size and the one found in the greatest numbers around the coasts of Northern Europe and North-eastern North America. Periwinkles are known as *vignots* in France, where they are sold cooked on the streets or made into soup. To cook periwinkles, first wash them in plenty of water. Soak them for 10 minutes and wash them again to remove any sand. Drain the periwinkles and cook them in plenty of boiling, salted water for 20 minutes.

The **whelk** is another small marine mollusk found along the Atlantic coasts of Europe and North America. They are a popular food, especially in parts of northern Europe, and have a hard, chewy texture, even when they are cooked. To prepare whelks, wash them thoroughly several times in clean water to remove all the sand, then simmer them in boiling salted or sea water for 30 minutes. Drain them and remove the flesh from the shell by inserting a pin and pulling.

Vegetables and fruits

Vegetables and fruits require far more careful handling than other foods. Many are delicate, bruise easily, and must be used as soon after purchase or picking as possible. Both contain a high percentage of water, many vitamins and minerals but little fat. Thus they supply essential nutrients and some roughage without many calories, and so make good between meal snacks.

Vegetables

Vegetables are probably the most neglected and badly prepared items in our diet. They often seem less interesting and more fussy to cook than other parts of the meal, because they must be done quickly at the last minute when other things also need attention.

Vegetables are versatile; they can be served alone or in combination, raw or cooked, with sauce or plain. Some, like eggplant, dried beans and onions, are notable for blending well with other ingredients and are used in casseroles, quiches and other cooked dishes; others, like fresh peas and string or snap beans, do best on their own. Most vegetables can be cooked by several methods. Almost all can be either boiled or steamed. Most root and non-green vegetables can also be braised and sometimes fried, baked and roasted. For specific information on cooking methods and times see the chart on pages 100 to 107.

Always check vegetables for doneness before the minimum suggested cooking time is up, and stop the cooking if they seem done. Timing is difficult to judge because so many variables are involved: age, freshness, variety (for instance, main-crop potatoes take longer than new ones of the same diameter), size and thickness. Even weather plays a part. Often, owing to plant breeding, modern vegetables (like modern poultry) take less time to cook than the old varieties.

Ideally, vegetables should be eaten immediately after picking, though some, especially roots, store well. Since most people, most of the time, find self-picking impossible, you should look for a supplier – local grocer, supermarket – with good produce and get to know the days when fresh supplies arrive; for those are the days on which to shop. Vegetables with a lot of natural sugars should be eaten quickly; foremost among these are corn on the cob and peas followed by leafy vegetables like spinach and collards, asparagus, string and other fresh beans, zucchini and eggplant. Green vegetables should be stored unwashed in a plastic bags to retain moisture. Keep them at a temperature of about 45°F (7°C), which generally means the vegetable bin in the refrigerator. Certain thick-skinned vegetables like potatoes, turnips and onions should be stored in a cool dark place between 55°-65°F (12°-18°C). But remember that onions hasten the spoilage of potatoes; likewise apples cause carrots to take on a bitter taste.

Other things to remember are:
1. Never wash vegetables until you are ready to use them, because water dissolves away water-soluble vitamins.
2. Never soak vegetables in water after preparing them for the same reason; instead place in a plastic bag if you have to prepare them in advance. A few exceptions are noted in the table on pages 100-107.
3. Make sure the entire top of root vegetables has been removed before storage, or the root will continue to supply the stem with nutrients. One exception is the red beet whose skin should not be damaged in any way or the beet will 'bleed' and lose its color during cooking.
4. Try to use vegetable cooking water when making sauces or soups; in this way nutrients that are leached out can still be used.

Preparation differs greatly from vegetable to vegetable (see table, pp. 100-107 for details). Most should be carried out as close to cooking time as possible. Invest in a good peeler, and peel vegetables thinly, since flavor and nutrients are just under the skin. Do not bother to peel young carrots, especially for stews; new potatoes can be roasted, cut but unpeeled, and baked. When you trim (take off ends of long vegetables like string beans) or cut off dried up surfaces (eg Brussels sprouts bases), remove as little as possible. Cut vegetables into uniform lengths or chunks, so that all will cook in the same length of time. Do not salt the water until the cooking process is underway.

Boiling is the most common method of cooking vegetables, but you are unlikely to find much agreement about methods. The major controversy is how much water to use. On one side stand those who believe in a minimum: they claim that fewer vitamins are lost in this way and in fact since this method requires that the pan be tightly covered, the vegetables are as much steamed as boiled.

On the other side are the believers in the French method, which uses large pans and lots of boiling water. They claim the vegetables are in the water for less time, since the water returns to a boil more quickly after the vegetables are added. A third school uses just enough water to cover the vegetables. The last method, most agree, is suited for long-cooking, starchy vegetables.

Faced with these choices, you need to take into account your own preferences and equipment. If your saucepans are small, opt for the first method, or for the third if you tend to burn things. You may find that you prefer to cook different vegetables by different methods.

A second area with many opinions is whether to start in cold or boiling water. One general rule followed by some says root vegetables, because they grow underground, should be started in cold water with a lid on the pan, whereas above ground vegetables, which grow in the sun, should be put into boiling water and cooked uncovered or partly covered. When you consult cookbooks, you will find each one has its own unique exceptions to this general rule. So it's probably best to try the various methods and decide which one gives *you* the best results.

Vegetables should be cooked at just above simmer after being brought rapidly to a boil. Many cannot stand fierce or prolonged heat.

Agreement is closer to universal on when vegetables are done: tender but still firm, not soft and mushy. Ideally, at the point of doneness, you should drain the vegetables and serve them at once. Even if they must wait a few minutes, drain them immediately, since as long as they are in hot water they continue to cook. Here the sequence becomes drain, refresh in (that is, place under) cold running water for a brief minute to reduce the temperature to just below the cooking point, and put in a warmed serving dish in a warm place, no more than partly covered to allow steam to escape. Remember the longer your vegetable waits, the more tired and less delectable it becomes.

If your vegetables are going to have a long wait, refresh them until cool while they are still slightly underdone. This will stop the cooking completely. Then just before serving either plunge them into lots of rapidly boiling water for just long enough to heat through, or toss them in melted butter until they are hot and well coated.

Steaming vegetables takes a little longer than boiling them. They are placed in a steaming basket or pan and set over boiling water, tightly covered. This method gives consistently good results and is supposed to retain more nutrients than boiling.

Other cooking methods are braising, baking, roasting and frying. These are not suitable for all vegetables but are useful. Braising requires a frying pan with a tightly fitting lid. You begin by coating uniformly sized and preferably thin vegetables with a minimum of hot fat, then adding a little liquid, covering tightly and bringing to a boil. Reduce heat and steam the vegetables. Shake the pan regularly to prevent sticking. An alternative but slower method is to place the covered vegetables in the oven after they have come to a boil.

Roasting and baking are used mostly for root vegetables such as potato, onion, parsnip, turnip. In roasting, the peeled vegetables are coated with hot drippings and placed either under or alongside the meat or poultry or in a separate pan. They are then cooked in the oven for 45 minutes-1 hour or more depending on oven temperature and vegetable size. Baste several times with drippings and turn over to ensure even browning.

Sometimes to achieve faster cooking and greater heat penetration, the vegetable is first parboiled (partly cooked) for 5-15 minutes. Baking is done with the skin still on (although it is often pricked with a fork) and in dry heat. The vegetables are placed on a rack so air can circulate around them and cooked for about an hour, timing depending on size and temperature. They are done when they feel soft when squeezed (pick them up in a potholder). Sometimes skin is removed before serving (onions); at other times it is left on (potatoes).

Frying of many sorts is popular. Deep-frying is used mainly for potatoes, parsnips and other hard vegetables. The requirements are the same as for meat and fish – fat heated to the correct temperature, vegetables absolutely free of water, and batter coating left to dry for about 10 minutes.

Stir-frying is an Oriental method of quick cooking which has become popular in the West. A little oil is heated, in a shallow pan, until very hot, then thinly sliced vegetables are added. These are stirred and turned constantly using two spoons or spatulas. With mixed vegetables, longer cooking types are added first, shorter cooking ones later. When the vegetables are barely tender, about $\frac{2}{3}$ of a cup (150 milliliters) of stock is added and the pan tightly covered, allowing the vegetables to steam for 2-8 minutes. The pan is uncovered and a teaspoon of cornstarch mixed with water or soy sauce is stirred in to thicken the liquid. The vegetables should be only crisp tender.

Vegetables are also excellent raw. Indeed far more vegetables than most people realize can be enjoyed in this way, and these are listed in the vegetable table (pp. 100-107). Raw vegetables can be used in salads and as garnishes. They can also be served with pre-dinner drinks as a healthy low-calorie substitute for potato chips, and as between meal snacks. As a drink accompaniment, raw vegetables should be chilled and cut into bite-sized pieces. Serve them alone or accompany with a dip – or variety of dips. However, if you base your dips on sour cream or cream cheese both the fat and calorie intake are increased. By substituting yogurt for sour cream and low-calorie for ordinary cream cheese, you can make a more healthful dip.

Dried Legumes

Dozens of varieties of dried beans and peas are available at the supermarket and health food stores. Most packages indicate how long to soak and cook. They are a major source of protein for vegetarians and give every indication of becoming an important part of everyone's diet.

Beans are a good source of vegetable protein, though none contains all the essential amino acids (see p. 140) and therefore they should not be your only protein source. They benefit from good seasoning including tomatoes, onions, garlic and chili.

Cooking times for beans are difficult to determine because they depend on so many variables: where they were grown, weather during the growing season, time elapsed since drying, length of soaking. Most of these are unknown to the cook. Also significant is how you are using them. If they are for a purée or soup you will cook them longer than if they are to

Top left : to prepare asparagus, peel and scrape the stalks thickly at the bottom and very thinly towards the tip.

Bottom left: wash the stalks and tie them into neat bundles with string – not more than 10 stalks to a bundle. Trim to even sizes.

Above : stand in a jar of boiling water and cover with pierced foil. Place in a pan of boiling water for 15–20 minutes or until tender.

be served whole as a vegetable.

Unless the beans are preprocessed (which is commonly the case in North America), they will need to be washed and then soaked in three to four times their volume of water for at least six hours but for less than 12 – a longer soaking period leads to fermentation. Discard any that float. As an alternative to soaking put the washed beans in cold water to cover, bring them to a boil and simmer them for 2 minutes. Cover and remove from the heat; then let stand for 1 hour. The beans are then ready for cooking. Lentils need little or no soaking.

Unless the soaking water has become bitter, use it for the long slow simmering, since it contains nutrients leached from the beans. Remember 1 cup of dried beans expands to 2-2½ cups while cooking. Therefore start with the pan less than half full.

Frozen vegetables

Frozen vegetables with the exception of spinach, should not be thawed before cooking. Drop into a minimum of boiling water and cook, covered, for only a short time – indeed, generally less time than the package suggests. Spinach as it thaws produces a lot of water, so you need add no more. Cook it uncovered to heat it through and allow most of the moisture to evaporate.

Preparing vegetables

Certain techniques are used time and again in cooking, for instance mincing and dicing vegetables and parsley, preparing mushrooms, peeling and seeding tomatoes, and parboiling, blanching and refreshing vegetables.

Mincing or dicing: Mincing or dicing means cutting into small cubes. This technique is used especially for onions, garlic, carrots, celery and sometimes green or red peppers. Mincing parsley means a much finer preparation.

Minced onion is the most frequently called for in recipes. First cut off the brown tip of the onion and peel off the skin; do nothing to the root end where the tear-inducing oils are located. Next cut the onion in half through the root end and tip. Place the onion, cut side down, on a cutting board with root to your left. Make many parallel cuts from root to tip without cutting through the root. Hold the onion together with your fingers while you make several slices

To prepare artichoke hearts, bend back the lower leaves of each artichoke until they snap off.

Remove all the outer leaves until you reach those bending inwards. With a sharp knife slice off the stalk.

Arrange the artichoke on its side and cut off the remaining leaves just above the white heart.

Rotating the base of the artichoke against the knife blade, trim off all the green leaf bases.

parallel to the cutting board. Again, make sure not to cut through the root end. Finally, starting at the tip end and, still holding the onion together with your left hand, cut down towards the board. Discard the root. The fineness of the mincing depends on how close to each other the cuts are. To slice an onion, cut the onion in half and then make cuts at right angles to the board.

Garlic and shallots are minced in the same manner, though fewer cuts can be made. To remove onion and garlic smells from your hands, wash them in cold water, sprinkle with salt and rub into the skin well, rinse again in cold water. Repeat if necessary. Avoid getting salt in open cuts, since it burns them.

Carrots and celery use a modified version of the onion technique. Hold one end in the left hand and make lengthwise cuts through the vegetable. With a carrot or thick celery, slice through parallel to the table once or twice. Lastly, slice down starting at the right end and working to the left. Use the parsley technique below to turn diced celery into a finer mince. Minced or chopped parsley implies flakes so fine you can't see the leaf

structure. It is advisable to wash parsley well ahead so that the leaves will be dry when you begin chopping. Break off the stems (save them in the freezer for *bouquets garnis*) and gather the rest into a small pile. With a very sharp knife make many cuts through the leaves.

The technique is to hold the knife point loosely in the left hand and move the handle up and down with the right hand. Slightly change the location of the handle with each stroke. Frequently gather up the parsley and cut some more.

Preparing mushrooms: Cultivated mushrooms are sorted into three grades: button (small, unopened), cup (slightly opened), and flat (completely opened). The cups and flats can be large or small. Both the caps and the stalks are used in cooking.

Mushrooms that are to be fried or broiled should not be washed under running water. Instead they should be wiped clean with dampened fingers or a cloth. Washing does not affect those which are to be boiled or put in stews as much.

Mushrooms should be peeled only if a very white surface is needed or if the

To peel a mushroom, hold the stem in your hand, gill side down.

Put your thumb under the edge of the cap and pull gently toward the center.

Chinese mushrooms need to be soaked gently before being used.

To peel a tomato, put it into a pan of boiling water and leave for a little.

Drain, then carefully nick the skin at the stem end with a knife.

Pull the skin off gently with your fingers —it should come away easily.

peelings are needed for another purpose (perhaps a stuffing for tomatoes or mushrooms). Under no circumstances should peelings be discarded, because they are full of flavor.

The peeling technique is simple for flats and rather open cups. Hold the mushroom in the left hand with the gill side down. Place the right thumb under the edge of the cap, grasping the black edging found on many mushrooms. Pull up and toward the center, and the skin will peel off in thin strips. To mince the peels and stems as well, use the parsley technique described on the previous page.

Dried mushrooms of both the European and Chinese types require a preliminary soaking in cold water for 30 minutes before they can be used. Often the stem does not soften and must be cut off. Use the soaking water sparingly, since it is strongly flavored.

Peeling and seeding tomatoes: The skin and seeds are removed from tomatoes because they tend to be tough and bitter. Do the seeding over a small strainer and bowl to save the juice for cooking.

Fill a small saucepan with enough water to cover a tomato and bring it to a boil. Drop one tomato at a time into the boiling water and count to eight slowly. Remove it with a slotted spoon and drop it into cold water. This stops the cooking. When all the tomatoes are done it is time to peel them. Nick the skin at the stem end and with the fingers pull off the peel. Cut into quarters and with your thumb, scoop out the seeds. If the tomato is to be used whole, cut off the top (which is at the end opposite to the stem) and use a spoon to scoop out the seeds.

Alternatively, cover the tomatoes with boiling water for 2 to 3 minutes, during which time the skin will loosen. Proceed as above.

Parboiling, blanching and refreshing: Parboiling and blanching both refer to the partial cooking of foods, usually vegetables. Parboiling means the cooking process is begun in boiling water and continues only for a short time, usually no more than 10 minutes. The food is then drained and finished by another method, usually roasting or baking. Vegetables receiving this process are long-cooking ones, such as potatoes.

Blanching means to plunge a vegetable or fruit directly into boiling water to partly cook it. Most vegetables must be blanched before freezing to retard enzyme action and prevent 'off' flavors. Blanching also removes too strong a taste, such as for cabbage, onions and smoked bacon.

Generally, after vegetables have been blanched, they are refreshed. To refresh means to plunge hot foods into cold water, thus stopping the cooking process. In some cases refreshing means to thoroughly cool the food, in others it means only to reduce temperature below the cooking point but to leave it hot. In the latter case putting the vegetable under cold running water is usually enough.

Salad Greens

Salad greens consist mainly of lettuces, which range from crisp in texture to soft, but also include watercress, endive, chicory and spinach. All should be washed in a minimum amount of water and then dried thoroughly before use, so that the dressing will adhere well. Sometimes salads are made from whole leaves, but large leaves can make serving awkward. Always tear salad greens into pieces rather than cut them.

If you are preparing in advance, the washed, torn greens can be stored in the refrigerator for up to four hours in a plastic bag, and for up to two in the salad bowl. Other vegetables, except tomatoes and olives, can be added at preparation time. Incorporate non-vegetables and olives just before dressing, tomatoes after dressing. The salad dressing can be made in advance too, but it should be added only at the last minute. (Dressing added in advance makes the lettuce go limp.)

Tossing the salad means lifting the lettuce up with two forks or a salad serving set, and letting it fall back into the bowl. This should be done until the dressing lightly coats the surface of the

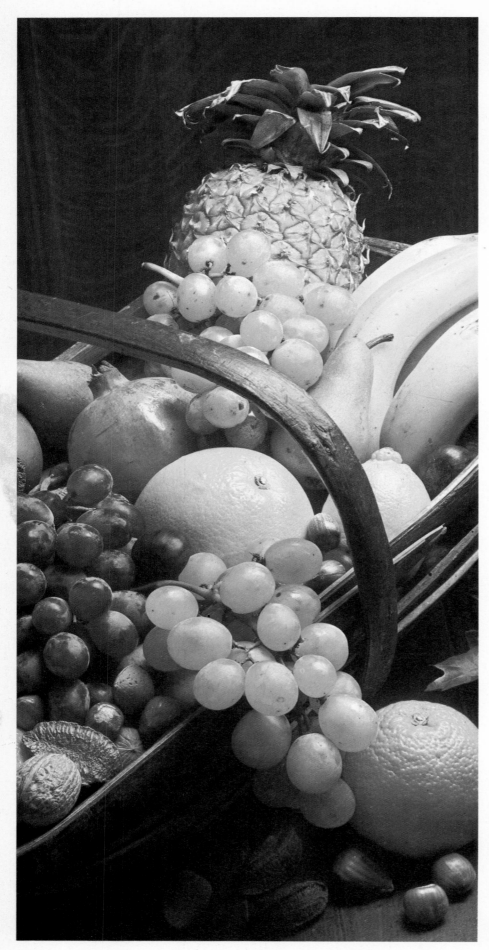

leaves. There should be no excess in the bottom of the bowl. Allow about two tablespoons of dressing for four people. (see also salad dressing, page 120.)

Fruits

Fruits are one of the most versatile and enjoyable elements in our diet. Most contain necessary vitamins and minerals, and with a few exceptions they are low in calories but have enough carbohydrates (sugars) to satisfy hunger and provide pick-up energy. They are welcome at the end of a heavy meal, because they are light and easy to eat. Fruits can be used in appetizers and in refreshing summer salads. Some are also used as accompaniments to meat and fish.

All fruits are at their best when tree- or vine-ripened and freshly picked. Then they are unsurpassed eaten raw and virtually unadorned. But fruit is also good cooked and processed in other ways.

Storage

Fruits differ greatly in how they should be stored and how long they will keep. Most fruits when fully ripe should be refrigerated or placed in a cold place to retard spoilage. Fruits that need to ripen should be kept at about 68 F (20 C) in a dark place. Avocados and bananas both ripen more quickly in a paper bag. The major exception to refrigeration is bananas, which blacken when chilled. Under normal kitchen conditions few fruits will keep more than a week.

The following points are worth remembering:
1. Store under-ripe fruit at a warm room temperature in a dark place. Examine twice a day for ripeness and refrigerate when ripe.
2. To test large fruits for ripeness, gently press the flesh at the stem end; when ripe it will feel soft.
3. Handle all fruits with care because bruised areas spoil. Buy fruit last so it will be at the top of your shopping bag; never drop fruit into a bag, and avoid stores where the help tend to do this.
4. Berries and other small, soft fruits spoil rapidly, so refrigerate and use within 36 hours. Spread highly perishable fruits, like raspberries and blackberries, in a single layer on a tray to retard mold;

A varied selection of succulent fresh fruit in season.

To prepare a fresh pineapple, first cut off a 1 in (2½ cm) slice from both the top and the bottom.

Stand the pineapple upright on a board and, using a sawing motion, cut thick strips downwards.

Turn the pineapple on its side and cut out the prickly pieces in a spiral, following the shape of the fruit.

Using a small pastry cutter or knife, remove the center core as this is hard and unpleasant to eat.

To prepare a fresh pineapple as a container, cut between the flesh and the peel, following the fruit's contours.

Carefully ease the flesh from inside the peel. The flesh can now be chopped with other fruit and returned.

you should always inspect before using.

5. Some fruits, notably melons and pineapple, have a lovely aroma when ripe.

6. Citrus fruit and pineapple do not continue ripening further after picking; green peaches will soften but won't ripen.

Many raw fruits become quickly discolored when peeled and sliced, unless countermeasures are taken, namely placing in acidulated water (which will lead to some loss of nutrients) or sprinkling with lemon or pineapple juice. The quickest to discolor are apples, avocados, bananas and pears. Be sure to use a stainless steel knife which does not discolor fruits.

Frozen fruits tend to become mushy and lose their shape when thawed. They are fine for cooking or sauces, but if you want to use a few for garnishes be sure they are still partly frozen – that is, still contain ice crystals. Chill canned fruits before serving.

Cooking fruit

Cook fruit by poaching (see page 74) rather than boiling or simmering. Drop the fruit into the boiling liquid and reduce the heat to low. Do not allow the fruit to overcook; it should remain firm but tender. Remove from the liquid the

instant it has cooked enough. If the fruit is to be served in the cooking liquid, cool that rapidly by putting the saucepan bottom into cold water. Cooking time will depend on the hardness of the fruit and its size. Not surprisingly, ripe peaches need only a few minutes whereas apples take much longer.

Puréed fruits are cut into small pieces and cooked in only enough water to cover the bottom of the pan to ½-1 inch (1-2½ centimeters), depending on the amount of moisture in the fruit. Again, cooking should be over low heat. The fruit should be stirred several times during cooking since that on the bottom will soften first. The fruit is cooked when it is very tender and mashes easily. Add sugar at this point rather than earlier; less will be needed to achieve the same amount of sweetness.

If you wish to remove the skin from fruit, such as peaches, plunge into boiling water and follow the instructions given for tomatoes (see page 92).

Dried fruits

Many common fruits can be dried at home, while others are bought easily. Most dried fruits can be used either before or after soaking and cooking.

Soaking should not be for longer than necessary for softening, since the water-soluble nutrients are being leached out. With experience you can learn to use just enough water so that all but a little has been absorbed when the soaking period is up. Try to use any remaining water in the recipe. If you are stewing the fruit use the soaking liquid, adding more if needed.

Store dried fruits, tightly covered, in a cool, dark place. Once opened, packages of dried fruits will begin to deteriorate after a few months. Keep them in a tightly closed plastic bag or other airtight container.

If the fruit becomes too dried out, it can be 'revived' by steaming. One method is to put the fruit in the top of a double boiler, sprinkle with a liquid, cover tightly and place over hot, not boiling, water for 10-15 minutes. Alternatively the fruit can be placed in a steamer over a little boiling water, which also tenderizes.

Raisins can be plumped by washing briefly, draining and spreading them in a single layer in a tightly covered pan. Put the pan in a 350°F (180°C) oven for 10 minutes or more until they are fat and unwrinkled. Or soak them for 10-15 minutes in the cooking liquid.

Meat chart

Meat	Suitable for	Cut
Beef	**Roasting**	Ribs (top, fore, back), sirloin, top round, fillet
	Braising or pot roasting	Brisket, rump, bottom round, top round
	Stewing	Chuck (also called shoulder, necks, short ribs), leg, oxtail, shank, skirt, bottom round, salted brisket or rump
	Frying or broiling	Fillet, entrecote, rump, porterhouse and sirloin steaks, minute steak, club steak
Lamb	**Roasting**	All cuts except neck and chops or cutlets
	Braising	Leg, boned and stuffed; shoulder, stuffed breast
	Boiling	Leg (bone-in or boned and stuffed)
	Stewing	Breast, neck and shoulder
	Frying or broiling	Loin, English lamb chop, rib chops and cutlets
Pork	**Roasting**	Leg, loin, shoulder butt, picnic shoulder and pork hock, shoulder and jowl butts, chops, head
	Braising	Shoulder and jowl butts, cutlets
	Stewing	Ham butt (has little fat) or braising cuts (fatty, so cook a day in advance)
	Boiling	All cuts especially salt pork

Preparation	Cooking Time	Internal Temperature
Preheat oven to 425°F (220°C). After cooking for 15 minutes reduce temp to 350°F (180°C).	Rare: 15 minutes to the pound (16 " " " half kilo) Medium: 25 minutes to the pound (27 " " " half kilo) Boned and rolled: 30 minutes to the pound (32 " " " half kilo) plus 30 (32) minutes over.	140°F (60°C) 160°F (72°C) 175°F (80°C)
Preheat oven to 350°F (180°C).	For thinner cuts 40 minutes to the pound (44 minutes to the half kilo). For thicker or stuffed cuts 40 minutes to the pound (48 minutes to the half kilo).	
Preheat oven to 300°F (150°C) or cook on top of stove over low heat.	Most require at least 2½ hours.	
Preheat broiler for 3-5 minutes. Add a little butter and oil to frying pan and heat. Add meat when butter foams.	4-8 minutes on each side depending on thickness and degree of doneness required: rare, 3-4 minutes each side; medium, 5-6 minutes each side; well done, 7-8 minutes each side. Minute steak, 1 minute each side.	
Preheat oven to 400°F (200°C). After cooking for 20 mins reduce temp to 325°F (170°C).	20 minutes to the pound (22 " " " half kilo) plus 20 (22) minutes over.	175°–180°F (80°–82°C)
Preheat oven to 350°F (180°C).	Leg and shoulder: 20 minutes to the pound (22 minutes to the half kilo). Breast: 15 minutes to the pound (16 minutes to the half kilo).	
Bring salted water to boil before adding lamb. Maintain at a slow simmer during cooking.	15 mins to the pound (16 minutes to the half kilo) plus 15 (16) mins.	Well-done: 160°-165°F (74°-75°C) Medium: 145°-150°F (62°-64°C)
Preheat oven to 300°F (150°C) or cook on top of stove over low heat.	At least 2 hours.	
Preheat broiler for 3-5 minutes. Add a little butter and oil to frying pan and heat. Add meat when butter foams.	10-20 minutes for chops; 7-10 mins for cutlets. Reduce heat to medium after cooking each side for 2 minutes.	
Preheat oven to 375°F (190°C).	For bone-in joints: 35 minutes to the pound (38 minutes to the half kilo) plus 30 (32) minutes over. For boned and rolled joints: 40 minutes to the pound (44 mins to the half kilo) plus 40 (44) minutes over.	190°F (88°C)
Preheat oven to 350°F (180°C).	For spare ribs: 25-30 mins to the pound (27-32 minutes to the half kilo). For cutlets and chops; 20-25 mins to the pound (22-27 mins to the half kilo).	
Preheat oven to 300°F (150°C) or cook on top of stove over low heat.	At least 1-1¼ hours.	
	30 mins to the pound (32 minutes to the half kilo) plus 30 (32) mins over.	

Meat	Suitable for	Cut
Pork	**Frying or broiling**	All chops and cutlets, fillet, leg steaks
Bacon and Ham	**Baking and boiling**	All ham cuts
	Frying or broiling	Bacon (all cuts) and ham steaks
Veal	**Roasting**	Leg, fillet, loin, saddle, breast, shoulder and shank
	Braising	Breast, shoulder and shank
	Boiling	Cheaper cuts
	Stewing	Cheaper cuts and more fatty cuts
	Broiling or frying	Loin chops and loin steaks, cutlets and escalopes

Poultry	Suitable for	Cut
Chicken	**Roasting**	Whole: poussin, roasting chicken, capon
	Braising	Roasting chicken, capon
	Stewing (fricassée)	Roasting chicken or young fowl cut into 4 or 8 pieces
	Sautéing (fried or stewed in butter)	Spring or roasting chicken pieces

Preparation	Cooking Time	Internal Temperature
Preheat broiler for 3-5 mins. Add a little butter and oil to frying pan and heat. Add meat when butter foams.	Broil for 15-20 mins on each side depending on thickness. Fry for 5 mins on each side or until well browned. Cover pan and reduce heat to low simmer for 25-35 mins depending on thickness of chops.	
Soak ham for at least 6 hours or overnight to reduce saltiness, or put in saucepan of water and bring slowly to boil. Drain, add fresh water and bring to boil again; simmer required time. Unsmoked ham soak 2 hrs. To bake: simmer for half the cooking time, wrap in foil and bake in oven preheated to 375°F (190°C). A half hour before done, remove foil and peel off skin. Make a diamond pattern in the fat, insert whole cloves and cover with brown sugar to glaze. Bake for last half hour at 425°F (220°C).	Boiling or baking time: 20 minutes to the pound (22 minutes to the half kilo) plus 20 (22) minutes over.	
Heat frying pan without fat for bacon; add a little fat for ham steak. Preheat broiler for 3-5 minutes.	Fry until fat has entirely lost its transparency. Grill steaks for 5 minutes on each side.	
Preheat oven to 400°F (200°C). After cooking for 20 mins reduce to 325°F (170°C). Baste every 20 minutes.	Bone-in: 20 mins to the pound (22 mins to the half kilo) plus 20 (22) mins. Boned and rolled: 30 mins to the pound (32 mins to the half kilo) plus 30 (32) minutes.	185°F (85°C)
Preheat oven to 375°F (190°C).	30 mins to the pound (32 minutes to the half kilo).	
Start in cold water and bring to a boil. Maintain at a slow simmer.	15 mins to the pound (16 minutes to the half kilo) plus 15 minutes.	
Preheat oven to 300°F (150°C) or cook on top of stove over low heat.	At least 1 hour.	
Preheat broiler for more than 5 minutes. Melt butter and oil in frying pan until it foams, then add meat.	Broil for 3-5 mins on each side, reduce heat and cook till done. Fry over moderate heat for 3-5 mins on each side, reduce heat to low and cook till done. Total time: 15-30 mins for chops and cutlets; 6-8 mins for escalopes.	
Preparation	**Cooking Time**	**Internal Temperature**
Preheat oven to 425°F (220°C). After cooking 15 mins reduce temp. to 350°F (180°C).	Unstuffed ready-to-cook weight: 2lb (1kg) – 50-60 mins. 3lb (1½kg) – 1hr + 10-20 mins. 4lb (2kg) – 1hr + 15-30 mins. Stuffed: add 10-30 mins to roasting time.	180°F (82°C)
Preheat oven to 325°F (170°C). Brown chicken in casserole in hot fat.	Same cooking times as for roasting.	180°F (82°C)
Brown pieces in butter and oil, add hot liquid and simmer.	Simmer 1 hour or longer, until tender. Time depends on size of pieces and age. Place leg and thigh meat below breast and wing.	
Heat 2 tbsp butter and 1 tbsp of oil in frying pan or casserole until it foams.	Cook in butter for 8-10 mins, until lightly browned. Cover and simmer 20-25 mins until tender.	

Poultry	Suitable for	Cut
	Boiling	Fowl
	Broiling	Pieces, or halved spring chicken or poussin
	Frying	Spring or roasting chicken cut in 8 pieces off bone
Duck	**Roasting**	Whole
	Braising	Whole, halved or quartered
Goose	**Roasting**	Whole
Turkey	**Roasting**	Whole
	Broiling, sautéing, frying	Pieces

Vegetable chart

Vegetable	Description	Preparation
Artichoke, Globe	Large, thistle-like head of closely packed leaves. Where bud joins stem is fleshy area called the heart.	See page 91. Rub cut edges with lemon juice to maintain color.
Artichoke, Jerusalem	Thin skinned, knobbly either purple or white skin, white flesh. Distinctive, delicate flavor.	Wash well. Peel under running water. Drop into acidulated water (vinegar or lemon juice added) until ready to use.
Asparagus	Either white or green in color. Older stalks will be tougher than young ones.	See page 90.
Beans, Broad	Have either long pods with kidney-shaped beans or shorter pods and round seeds.	Young beans: cook in pods after topping and tailing (removing ends). Older beans remove seeds from pods (and use pods for soup).
Beans, French and Runner	Many shapes and colors. Most common has long thin pod, dark green in color.	Remove stringy edges if necessary. Top and tail. Leave whole if young.

Preparation	Cooking Time	Internal Temperature
Place fowl in cold water and bring to a boil.	Simmer 1½-2 hours until tender.	
Preheat broiler for 3-5 mins. Reduce heat to mod after 2 mins. Butter skin, baste.	Legs: 10-15 mins each side. Breast: 8-10 mins each side.	
Heat 3 oz (75 g) butter and oil in frying pan until it foams. Reduce heat to low.	With bone: cook pieces for 20 mins, turning several times. Off bone: cook 5-10 minutes.	
Preheat oven to 450°F (230°C). After cooking for 15 mins reduce temp to 350°F (180°C).	Unstuffed ready-to-cook weight: 3½lb (1½kg) 1hr + 15-20 mins 4½lb (2kg) 1hr + 25-35 mins 5½lb (2½kg) 1hr + 35-45 mins. Stuffed: add 20-30 mins to time.	180°-185°F (82°-85°C)
Preheat oven to 325°F (170°C). Brown duck in casserole in hot fat.	Same cooking time as for roasting.	As for roasting
Preheat oven to 450°F (230°C). After cooking for 15 mins, reduce temp to 350°F (180°C).	Stuffed: 20-25 mins to the pound (22-27 mins to the half kilo).	185°F (85°C)
Preheat oven to 450°F (230°C) etc as above.	Weight as purchased, then stuffed: 6-8lb (2¾-3½kg)-2½-3 hrs 8-10lb (3½-4½kg)-3-3½ hrs Add an additional ¼ hour for each pound or ½ kilo unstuffed.	180°-185°F (82°-85°C)
Follow directions for chicken.	Increase cooking time, depending on size and thickness.	

Boiling Time	Other Methods	Other Comments
Cook whole in plenty of salted water to cover – 30 min; choke removed – 15 min. Leaf pulls away easily from heart when done. Flesh soft.	Steam – 50 min whole. 25 min choke removed.	Do not use aluminum or iron saucepan, which will discolor flesh. Choke can be removed before cooking: spread top leaves apart and pull out prickly leaves surrounding hairy choke and with teaspoon scrape out choke. Squeeze on lemon juice, press leaves back together again. Rich in Vitamin C.
?0 min in acidulated water.	Steam – 35 min. Deep-fry – parboil 15 min; dry, cut into sticks, dip in batter. Fry for 3 min.	Good for soups. Rich in iron, thiamine, niacin.
Stand upright in pan so stems are in water, tips out – cover loosely with aluminum foil and steam 15-20 min use glass jar method (see page 90).	Sauté, quartered, over moderate heat for 30 min.	Average serving is six stalks per person. Use tough stalks in soup stock. Serve hot with melted butter or hollandaise sauce; cold with vinaigrette. Good alone as a first course or as a vegetable accompaniment to meat, fish and chicken dishes. Rich in Vitamin A, thiamine, riboflavin, Vitamin C.
?-30 min depending on age and size.	Steam – 15 min or more depending on size.	Rich in iron, thiamine, riboflavin, niacin and Vitamin C.
?5 min.	Steam – 10-20 min.	Rich in Vitamins A and C.

Vegetable	Description	Preparation
Beets	Red bulbous root, also a white variety.	Remove leaf stalk 2in (5cm) above root so it won't bleed. Do not trim off root ends. Wash carefully so skin is not damaged.
Broccoli, Calabrese or Italian green sprouting, purple, green, white	Some types mostly stem with a few flowering shoots, other types mostly a head of flowerets. Purple types (almost unknown in U.S.) turn green on cooking.	Cut off lower tough part of stalks; remove wilted leaves. Peel stalks if old from butt upwards. Separate flowerets from old stalks, cut stalks into lengths.
Brussels Sprouts	A variety of miniature cabbage – choose small, solid heads with tightly folded leaves, green and very fresh.	Cut off old-looking base, with sharp knife make deep cross in center of large ones – do not split circumference of base. Remove yellowed leaves.
Cabbage, Savoy and White	Savoy has green wrinkled leaves, is milder in flavor than white which has smooth leaves and a tight head.	Remove coarse outer leaves, cut into quarters and remove hard core. Either cook quarters or finely shred.
Cabbage, Red		Cut into quarters and shred.
Carrot	Orange variety most popular (also white, yellow and purple varieties – mainly European).	Scrape rather than peel since vitamins and flavor are close to skin, or for casseroles just scrub well. Cut large ones into quarters, sticks or rings.
Cauliflower	Hard white head made up of many flowerets. Should be white and firm with fresh green leaves.	Cut off green leaves, trim stalk. Either leave whole or separate into flowerets – cut from base to outside.
Celery	Long white or green stalks rising from a base and ending in curly yellow-green leaves. Best when young.	Remove outer stalks if old and tough. Trim off top and base. Peel off strings with a knife if necessary. Cut into quarters lengthwise or separate stalks.
Corn	Corn should be cooked within a few minutes or hours of picking. Look for ears whose husks are green and fresh.	Just before cooking pull off husk and remove silk.
Cucumber	Most popular type is long and thin with bright, dark green skin and seeded core.	Peeling optional. Sprinkle with salt and let stand 20 min before cooking to remove excess water.
Eggplant	Mainly pear-shaped and purple, but from dark purple to mauve and yellow to white, and from long and thin to quite round. Select firm, smooth, shiny ones of uniform color – no wrinkles.	Slice thinly across, arrange flat on plate and sprinkle with salt. Leave 20 min for excess moisture to come out. Squeeze and pat dry.
Endive	Conical white head of crisp tightly packed leaves. Best heads are tightly closed at top.	Remove damaged or wilted leaves. Leave white, quarter or separate into leaves.
Kale	Member of cabbage family with green curly leaves.	Discard coarse outer leaves. Chop and place in saucepan with just enough water to cover.

Boiling Time	Other Methods	Other Comments
Simmer 1-2 hours, depending on size. Do not pierce with fork. Cooked when skin peels off easily.	Steam – 2 hours.	Often sold ready cooked. Also sold marinated in vinegar.
10-15 min – cook tough stem longer than tender top.	Steam – 20 min.	Flowerets also good eaten raw. Member of cauliflower family. Rich in Vitamin A, riboflavin and Vitamin C.
10 min. Long cooking brings out cabbage smell.	Steam – 15 min.	Member of cabbage family. Also good eaten raw. Good source of Vitamin C if not over-cooked. Rich in iron, Vitamins A and C.
Quarters – 10-15 min. Shredded – 5 min.	Steam – quarters 20 min. Shredded – 10 min. Braise – parboil 10 min, braise 1 hour.	Used raw in salads when shredded. Short cooking and crisp texture enhance vitamin content and improve flavor. Rich in Vitamin C.
	Parboil 10 min. Layer in casserole with apple slices and sliced onion, sprinkle with vinegar and sugar. Add stock and braise 1 hour or more.	Benefits from long slow cooking. Vinegar added to maintain the red color. Rich in Vitamin C.
Simmer 10-20 min. Add sugar if old.	Steam – 15-30 min. Oven braise. Braise on top of stove in butter, stock and sugar for 10-20 min. Liquid should just evaporate.	Excellent raw. Very rich in Vitamin A.
Whole – 15-20 min. Flowerets – 8-12 min. Be careful not to overcook.	Steam – whole 25 min flowerets 15 min.	Excellent raw. Rich in Vitamin C.
Blanch for 10 min before cooking by any other method. Boil 18 min. Fry tightly covered, in butter for min.	Braise in white stock with herbs for about 45 min.	Excellent raw – keep prepared in plastic bag or iced water in refrigerator until ready to use. Use leaves and outer stalks in stocks and sauces; also in soups and stews. Rich in Vitamin C.
For older corn only, add 1 tbsp sugar to the water. 10-20 min depending on age and size. Done when kernels turn bright yellow.	Steam – for young fresh corn – 5-7 min, or until kernels take on bright translucence. Roast – for young, sweet corn, remove silk but leave on husk, wash under running water. Roast over hot coals for 20-25 min, turning occasionally or bake on rack in 400°F (200°C) oven.	Overcooking makes corn tough. Has many uses and combines well with other vegetables. Rich in thiamine and Vitamin C.
Not recommended.	Sauté – 7-10 min over moderate heat. Bake – in butter in 375°F (190°C) oven for 1 hour or until crisp tender.	Used mostly raw in a variety of salads. Rich in Vitamin C; also A, if not peeled.
	Sauté – in butter and oil; turn occasionally; cook 10 min. Deep-fry in batter for 3 min. Broil after dotting with butter and oil.	Skin can be bitter and tough. To remove place eggplant directly on gas or electric burner and char skin, turn often; skin will peel off easily with knife and fingers. Absorbs great quantities of fats. Combines well with meat, cheese and tomato.
min for whole heads.	Braise in butter for 1-1¼ hours.	Frequently used raw in salads. Boiled endive is usually served with béchamel or cheese sauce.
5 min or until tender but still slightly crunchy. Drain and squeeze all water.		Finish off with sauce (velouté, cheese) or serve with pats of butter. Combine with cooked onions and Italian sausages and serve hot. Rich in calcium, iron, Vitamins A and C.

Vegetable	Description	Preparation
Leek	Smaller paler varieties are often more tender.	Cut off roots and remove tops 3in (8cm) above white stem. Remove coarse outer leaves, wash well to remove grit between layers.
Lettuce family (also chicory)	Many varieties from tight crisp heads to soft open leaves. Green (some European varieties are red or copper colored).	Remove coarse or damaged outer leaves. Wash well and drain thoroughly.
Mushroom	Comes in 3 grades: button – small, unopened cup – slightly opened flat – completely opened	Wipe clean rather than washing under water. Trim off dry base of stem. See page 92 for peeling and chopping.
Okra	The long thin green pods can reach 8in (20cm) in length. When overcooked become gummy, therefore, are used to bind stews, sauces and soups.	Leave small pods whole; if large cut into pieces. For braising cut crosswise into thin slices.
Onion	Comes in various sizes from pickling (tiny, used whole) to large Spanish and Bermuda.	Remove outer skin and brown top end; do not cut off root end before all other preparations are done because it contains the eye-irritating oils. See pages 91.
Parsnip	Carrot-shaped root with a pale yellow exterior.	Trim off both ends and peel off coarse outer skin. Cut in half lengthwise and remove hard center core.
Pea	Young small freshly picked peas are sweetest.	Shell peas.
Pepper, sweet or bell	Green (unripe) or red (ripe). Choose those with shiny smooth skins.	Cut off stalk end and remove white pith and all seeds, which are painful to eyes and lips.
Pepper, Chili	Small and elongated, either green (unripe) or red (ripe). Seeds are very hot. Red chillies are hotter than green.	Chillies can burn, so wear rubber gloves or touch only with fork and knife. Cut off stalk end and remove seeds and pith.

Boiling Time	Other Methods	Other Comments
Whole – 12 min. 2in (5cm) lengths – 8 min.	Steam – 20 min whole. Braise – cover with white stock and cook for 30 min in 350°F (180°C) oven.	Allow 2 per person. Rich in iron and Vitamin A.
Not suitable. Blanch old, opened-out endive for 10 min.	Braise – blanch for 5 min, refresh under cold water. Place leaves in baking dish with a little white stock and onions, parsley and cloves. Cook 45 min at 375°F (190°C) oven.	Sometimes cooked with fresh peas. Most frequently used raw in salads. Loose headed varieties rich in iron, Vitamins A and C. Chicory high in Vitamins A and C.
In butter and 1-2 tbsp water, tightly covered, for 5 min.	Broil – brush with melted butter and broil for 5 min. Sauté – for 3 min using 1oz (25g) butter for 4oz (100g) of mushrooms. Steam – 10 min.	Wild mushrooms need to be gathered by experts who can distinguish between both poisonous and non-poisonous. Lemon juice helps to keep white. Cooked mushrooms give off a lot of moisture – do not overcook. Can be used raw in salads, marinated in oil, vinegar and herbs. Rich in iron, thiamine, riboflavin and niacin. Excellent stuffed as hors d'oeuvre.
Whole – 8 min. Cut – 5 min. Cook, covered in a layer no more than 1in (2½cm) thick.	Braise in frying pan with tight fitting lid for 10 min, stirring frequently. Remove cover and cook until tender and golden brown.	Less sap is released by whole okras. Used in Indian and Creole cooking. Rich in Vitamin A, thiamine, riboflavin and Vitamin C.
15–30 min at very low heat.	Steam – 30-35 min. Sauté – sliced or chopped (diced), for 5–7 min or until translucent. Braise – whole small onions are browned in a little butter, a small amount of beef stock is added and onions are cooked 30-40 min. Bake – peeled at 350°F (180°C) oven for 2 hours or until tender. Cut off root and gently squeeze out onion.	See page 63 for description of various members of onion family and other uses. Frequently used as a seasoning to flavor casseroles and other dishes; large ones can be stuffed. *Scallion:* a very young onion with a fresh, tender long green top. Both bulb and stalk are used in salads and as a garnish. They can also be used in cooking. Rich in Vitamin C if green tops are used.
5–30 min.	Steam – 35 min – use only young parsnips. Roast – parboil for 5 min, then roast with joint of meat. Deep-fry.	Root discolors when exposed to air – drop into acidulated (vinegar or lemon juice) water when peeled and cut. Rich in Vitamin C.
0–12 min.	Steam – 20 min. Braise – line casserole with lettuce leaves add peas, chopped onion, and enough white stock just to cover. Bake for 35 min at 350°F (180°C) oven.	The mange-tout or snow pea has an edible pod. Cook whole or quartered like French beans; serve while still crisp. Rich in iron, Vitamin A, thiamine, niacin and Vitamin C.
ot suitable. anch for 5 min before stuffing with t precooked food. uté – in hot oil for 10 min.	Bake – blanched stuffed peppers at 350°F (180°C) oven for 10–15 min. Broil – blanched, stuffed peppers to brown topping.	Used raw in salads. To peel, put under broiler and turn often until skin blisters then pull off. Overcooking causes bitterness. Can be frozen without blanching. Red ones go bad quickly. Green variety rich in Vitamin C; red very rich in Vitamins A and C.
		Seeds are far hotter than pod. Oils cause burning so touch as little as possible with hands, avoid putting hands to face. Wash hands well in hot, soapy water. Green rich in Vitamins A and C, niacin; red seedless variety very rich in Vitamin A and C, niacin; seeds themselves very rich in thiamine, riboflavin and niacin.

Vegetable	Description	Preparation
Potato	Many varieties, some best for boiling, others for baking. New potatoes are small early potatoes often boiled in their skins.	Scrub but do not peel new potatoes; peel all potatoes thinly. Baked – prick each deeply with a fork to allow steam to escape during baking.
Pumpkin	Usually has orange skin.	Cut open and remove seeds and pith. Cut flesh from skin.
Radish	Most common types have red or red and white skins (other varieties may be all white or dark skinned).	Cut off tops just above bulge, remove hairy roots.
Rutabaga	Closely resembles turnip in shape, but is larger, has purplish-brown skin; flesh is yellow in color.	Peel and slice off skin. Wash flesh and slice or chop it.
Spinach	Leaves range in color from pale to dark green; dark type is slightly coarser.	Remove wilted leaves, cut off discolored bases of stem. Cut off stems at base of leaf. Always wash thoroughly before cooking.
Squash	Color of skin ranges from off-white and yellow to dark green, many shapes. Smaller sizes are better than large.	Peel, halve lengthwise and scoop out the seeds. Slice or dice, sprinkle with salt and let stand 10 min if braising or sautéing to remove some water, dry.
Sweet Potato and Yam	Both are tubers with reddish skin and either white or yellow flesh. They are both tropical plants, but are not related.	Before boiling, peel and halve or quarter or remove skin afterwards for other methods, blanch for 10 min, cool and slip off skin with knife and fingers.
Tomato	Red or golden in color when fully ripe. Salad variety is round; cooking variety (plum tomato) is oval.	For peeling, seeding, juicing, see page 92.
Turnip	Bulbous white root with a smooth leafy green top. Both root and top are edible.	Prepare and cook roots like rutabaga. Prepare and cook tops like cabbage or kale.
Zucchini	Best young, no more than 1in (2½cm) in diameter and 6in (15cm) long. Has edible light green skin.	Trim ends and wipe clean. Leave small ones whole – slice larger ones into rounds or cut lengthwise into sticks. Sprinkle with salt and let stand for 20 min remove excess water.

Boiling Time	Other Methods	Other Comments
15–20 min. Mashed – cook and drain potatoes – mash with a fork, masher or electric mixer. Just before serving add 1¼ cups (300ml) hot milk to 2lb (1kg) potatoes. Beat until light and fluffy. Alternatively, add ½ stick (4oz) butter or margarine and cold milk. Beat thoroughly. Keep warm on stove over low flame (for a short time).	Steam – 15-20 min. Bake – arrange in hot oven so they do not touch. Bake 45 min-1½ hours, depending on size and oven temperature; 375°F (190°C) is best. Roast – under or alongside meat for 1 hour turning and basting twice or in separate pan (preheat pan with ¼in [½cm] of oil or drippings until very hot) rolling potatoes in oil – turn and baste several times. French-fried – cut into long, thin strips and fry to golden in hot oil; Idaho potatoes best. Sauté – add single layer of potatoes, sliced or diced, to hot butter and oil. Fry, turning frequently, for 10-15 min.	Potato skin is good to eat and unpeeled potatoes are more nutritious since most vitamins and minerals lie just under the skin. Baked potatoes cook faster when a metal skewer is thrust through the center before cooking. To have tender boiled potatoes return drained potatoes to saucepan and shake over heat until a film begins to form on pan and potato surface is no longer moist. For baked in skin: rich in thiamine, niacin and Vitamin C, boiled peeled reduces vitamin content though it still remains high.
20 min or until tender.	Bake – place halves face down on baking sheet, add ½in (1cm) water and bake 30 min in 375°F (190°C) oven.	Serve seeds, wash and dry thoroughly, fry and salt; use as a snack. Pumpkin is seldom served alone as a vegetable but is used in casseroles or other prepared dishes and as pie filling.
6-8 min depending on size.		Mainly eaten raw alone or in salads. Rich in Vitamin C. Serve cooked with béchamel or parsley sauce.
20-30 min.	Roast – parboil thick slices for 12 min, drain. Arrange around meat for last hour of roasting.	Boiled rutabaga is usually mashed with butter, salt and pepper. Rich in Vitamins A and C.
Use no water at all or only enough to cover bottom of pan. Boil 10 min. Drain, press down hard with wooden spoon to get all liquid out.		Allow 8oz (225gr) of fresh spinach per person since it cooks down greatly. After draining, chop, purée in electric blender or force through a coarse strainer. Spinach can be mixed with a béchamel or cheese sauce; blends well with many things, especially eggs. Good raw in salads. Rich in iron, Vitamins A and C.
0 min.	Steam – 20 min. Braise – half cover with white stock and cook for 40 min. Sauté – over moderate heat for 15 min.	Combines well with other ingredients, especially onions and tomatoes. Rich in Vitamin C, though amount differs with variety.
0-40 min if peeled use a minimum of water.	Baked – see potatoes Sauté – see potatoes Roast – see potatoes	Sweet potatoes have a sweet flavor and are rich in Vitamins A and C. They spoil rapidly. Yams keep well but are low in nutrients and relatively high in carbohydrates.
ot suitable.	Bake – whole, placed stalk end down on baking sheet, brush with oil, bake 15 min in 375°F (190°C) oven. Broil – halve, place cut side up on broiler pan and place under moderate heat for 5-10 min.	Baked and broiled tomatoes should not be overcooked or they will collapse. Goes well with many herbs and other vegetables, cheese. Excellent raw, seeds if in a green 'jelly' can be bitter, discard. Oval (or plum) tomatoes make stronger, more flavorful sauces.
		Roots rich in Vitamin C. Turnip greens: rich in Vitamin A, thiamine, riboflavin and Vitamin C.
-15 min if whole.	Steam – whole for 20 min. sliced 10 min. Sauté – 7-10 min over moderate heat.	Excellent combined with onions, tomatoes, eggplant and cheese; makes good soup.

ote: "Rich in Vitamins" means that at least 10 per cent of the recommended daily intake is supplied by 100 grams ounces) of the cooked vegetable. In many cases the amount supplied is far higher.

Chapter Six

Stocks

Your own stock makes a world of difference in the flavour and texture of many basic dishes. Soups, gravies, gelatines and aspics all take on memorable new dimensions.

Stock is worth making on a large scale because of its many uses and any surplus can be frozen in suitably sized containers. When estimating final results, remember that stock is always reduced by at least half and sometimes more to concentrate the flavour. Although stock may take up to five hours to cook, cooking can be stopped at any time and continued again when it suits you.

Stocks are made from a variety of ingredients, depending on how they are to be used. The four major categories are meat, chicken, fish and vegetable. It is important to keep in mind how you are going to use a particular stock and to select your stock ingredients to complement those dishes.

Choosing ingredients

The best are made from fresh bones (or fish trimmings), fresh meat (or fish) and vegetables bought specifically for the purpose. A more economical stock can be made from leftover or surplus ingredients which might otherwise be wasted. For instance, chicken carcasses and meat bones can be wrapped and stored in the refrigerator until you have enough to make stock, and certain vegetable peelings and some vegetable cooking liquids are also worth saving. But be selective: the stockpot is not a dustbin; throwing all your scraps into it indiscriminately will only produce poor results.

Meat and bones

When the butcher bones and trims meat for you, be sure to take everything home.

After all, you have paid for the bones and trimmings and most of them are ideal for the stockpot. Have the butcher cut large bones into short convenient pieces. Wash all bones well before use.

Beef and veal bones make the best all-purpose stock. Ham, gammon, pork and lamb bones all have distinctive flavours. They are excellent for specific purposes, but don't use many in a general-purpose stock. If you have a freezer, make pork or lamb stock with bones left when the joint is eaten, freeze and use for gravy stock next time you have the same type of meat. Veal bones, pigs' trotters and calves' heads produce gelatinous stocks, so include one if you want to make aspics and jellied soups.

The addition of raw meat gives stocks a stronger flavour and makes them nourishing. The cheapest cuts such as shin and neck are suitable, especially for long cooking. Sometimes better cuts are simmered in the stock and then used to provide a family meal.

The vegetables most commonly used in meat and fish stocks are onions, leeks, carrots and celery. Always use fresh vegetables and especially avoid old celery stalks which have an unpleasant flavour. Mushroom peelings add colour as well as flavour as do tomatoes, though the latter can sour stock that is kept for more than a day. Parsnips should be used sparingly. Turnips, cauliflowers and members of the cabbage family can be used for vegetable stock, but their flavour is too strong for meat or fish stock. Cooked vegetables make stock cloudy, as do potatoes and other starchy vegetables such as peas and beans.

Parsley, marjoram, thyme and bay leaf (either fresh or dried) are used to flavour most stocks. Salt and peppercorns are also used, and occasionally mace. Never season stock heavily, however. Wait until the liquid has been reduced or add when you are making the final dish.

Basic methods

Meat stock, white or brown

Simple meat stock is made from a collection of meat and bones consisting mainly of beef, veal and chicken, though a small amount of pork could be added. For white stock, the meat and bones are placed in water and brought to the boil. When the liquid comes to the boil, skim away fat and scum with a slotted spoon (you may need to skim again during cooking). Reduce heat, add herbs, salt and peppercorns. Add vegetables and half-cover the pan with a lid. For brown stock an additional step is needed. The meat, bones and vegetables are placed in a roasting pan and browned in a hot oven for about 40 minutes. They are then transferred to the stockpot. Pour off the accumulated fat, add some water to the roasting pan and scrape up the brown juices. Add these to the stockpot. Fill the pot with cold water and bring to the boil.

Simmering: Never let the stock boil; if it does, fat and scum amalgamate with the stock and make it cloudy. Simmer gently until the liquid has reduced by one-third and you feel maximum flavour has been extracted from the ingredients. This may take up to five hours, but cooking can be stopped at any time and continued later. Never cover airtight unless the contents have cooled completely, or the stock will sour. Skim as necessary during cooking and top up with boiling water if the liquid has evaporated below the level of the ingredients.

Degreasing: When the stock has cooked enough, strain through a fine sieve into a bowl. Discard bones, vegetables and herbs. Keep the meat to use for potting, making into a cottage pie or Bolognese sauce if it has any flavour left.

If the stock is not for immediate use, refrigerate it as soon as it has cooled. Leave the bowl uncovered until the fat has hardened and formed a seal which

To make basic white stock, first chop the vegetables. Put them into a heavy saucepan with meat or fish bones.

Add water and bring to a boil very slowly. When the foam forms a definite scum, remove it with a slotted spoon or skimmer.

When the scum has stopped rising in large quantities, add herbs (bouquet garni, for instance, as here) and seasonings.

Half-cover the saucepan, then simmer the stock for the amount of time specified in the recipe being used.

Skim and fill up with boiling water if the liquid falls below the ingredients. Then pour through a colander into a clean bowl.

If the stock is to be used immediately, mop up the fat with kitchen paper towels, or a slice of bread.

Or cool it a little, then take off fat with a skimmer. Or leave it until completely cold (as above) and scrape off solid fat.

Strain the de-greased stock through a strainer, lined with a layer of cheesecloth, back into a clean saucepan.

Reheat the stock. If the flavoring seems weak, boil rapidly to reduce and concentrate the flavor. Season to taste.

the stock to stay fresh longer. Scrape the fat off only when the stock is needed. Then cover the bowl with foil to prevent the stock absorbing or passing on smells and flavors to other foods. Stock kept in the refrigerator must be brought to a boil every three or four days.

Straining and final flavoring: Pour degreased stock through a strainer lined with fine cheesecloth. Reheat and, if the flavor is too weak, boil down to concentrate its strength. Correct seasoning if necessary by adding salt or pepper.

Meat glaze: At this point a meat glaze can be made by reducing 3 quarts (3 liters) of stock to about $1\frac{1}{2}$ cups (400 milliliters) of glaze. Boil slowly until most of the liquid is gone and the stock becomes a syrup which coats a spoon nicely – watch closely at the ends so it doesn't burn.

Meat glaze will keep for weeks in the refrigerator. If a mold should develop, wash it off with warm water, then simmer the glaze with a spoonful of water until a syrup forms. It can also be frozen. A spoonful of glaze dissolved in hot water will take the place of a stock cube. A half teaspoon stirred into soups and sauces boosts flavor marvellously.

Clarifying: Stock for aspic or clear soup should be sparkling and clear. Clarifying is quite simple when both stock and whisk are absolutely grease free. Turn the cold stock into a pan set over low heat. When the stock is liquid but still cool, whisk in one large egg white for every quart (liter) of stock. Continue whisking until frothy white globules form on the surface. Boil for 2-3 minutes, then turn off the heat and leave for about 10 minutes. The egg whites, acting as a magnet for all the minute cloudy particles, turn a dirty brownish-gray and leave a clear stock below.

Line a strainer with a double layer of damp cheesecloth and place over a large bowl. Slowly pour the stock through the strainer to get rid of the scum. If necessary, repeat the process until the stock is completely clear.

Other stocks
Chicken stocks can also be either white or brown. However, never brown chicken parts in the oven, where they tend to burn. Instead, brown the chicken and vegetables, cut into small pieces, in hot oil or drippings.

Fish stock is a white stock made with

fresh fish, fish heads, bones and trimmings. It needs only a short simmering.

Storage
Most meat and chicken stocks can be kept in the refrigerator for up to 10 days, but must be degreased and brought to a boil after four days and boiled up again every three or four days thereafter. Meat or vegetable stocks that include cabbage, lots of onion or other strongly flavored vegetables will not keep as long as meat stock without such ingredients. Fish stock should always be used within a few days. Otherwise they can be frozen.

White Beef Stock
There is really no substitute for a well-flavored, homemade beef stock. It is an essential ingredient in many dishes, sauces and soups, and it is simple to make.
Makes $7\frac{1}{2}$ cups ($3\frac{3}{4}$ liters)

2 lb (1 kg) beef shin bones, cut into pieces
1 marrow bone
4 quarts ($3\frac{1}{2}$ liters) water
1 large onion, cut in half
2 carrots, scraped and cut in big pieces
1 large leek, washed thoroughly and cut in half
1 celery stalk, trimmed
8 peppercorns
4 cloves
1 bouquet garni
1 tablespoon salt

In a large saucepan, cover the bones with the water and bring slowly to a boil. Skim the surface with a slotted spoon to remove the scum. Continue to remove the scum as it rises.

When the scum stops rising, add the remaining ingredients, partly cover and simmer gently for 4 hours, or until the liquid is reduced by half.

Pour the stock through a strainer lined with two layers of cheesecloth into a large bowl. Set the stock aside to cool, then store it in the refrigerator or use as required.

Brown Stock
Brown stock is the base for sauces and gravies.
Makes 10 cups ($2\frac{1}{2}$ liters)

6 lb ($2\frac{3}{4}$ kg) veal and beef shin and marrow bones, broken or sawn into short pieces

5 quarts ($4\frac{3}{4}$ liters) cold water
6 peppercorns
6 cloves
1 bouquet garni
1 carrot, scraped and diced
1 turnip, peeled and diced

Preheat the oven to moderate 350°F (180°C).

Place the bones on a baking sheet and put them in the oven to brown for about 40 minutes.

Remove the baking sheet from the oven and transfer the bones to a large stockpot or saucepan. Add all the remaining ingredients. Place the pot over high heat and bring the liquid to a boil. Skim the surface with a slotted spoon to remove the scum.

After the stock has reached boiling point reduce the heat and simmer, partly covered with the lid at an angle, for $2\frac{1}{2}$-3 hours, or until the stock has reduced to half the original quantity.

Strain the stock into a large bowl. Set the stock aside to cool, then store it in the refrigerator or use as required.

Veal Stock
Veal stock is an essential part of many classic recipes. Make the stock the day before it is needed, so that it may be chilled, the fat removed and the stock reheated as required.
Makes $7\frac{1}{2}$ cups ($1\frac{3}{4}$ liters)

2 lb (100 kg) veal bones, cut into 2 in (5 cm) pieces
1 lb ($\frac{1}{2}$ kg) knuckle of veal, cut into 1 in ($2\frac{1}{2}$ cm) pieces
2 onions, sliced
1 small turnip, peeled and chopped
4 carrots, scraped and chopped
1 cup (125 g) button mushrooms, sliced or 1 cup (125 g) mushroom stalks, chopped
1 bouquet garni
2 fresh marjoram sprays
8 peppercorns, crushed
1 strip lemon rind
3 quarts (3 liters) water

In a large saucepan, blanch the veal for 5 minutes, drain and rinse. Wash out the saucepan. Return the veal to the pan along with the rest of the ingredients. Bring to a boil. Partly cover the pan, reduce the heat and simmer the stock for 3 hours.

Remove the lid, increase the heat and boil the stock for 15-20 minutes or until it has reduced by one-third of its original quantity. Remove the pan from the heat. Pour the stock through a strainer into a large mixing bowl. Discard the contents of the strainer.

Set the bowl aside to cool. Chill the stock in the refrigerator for at least 3 hours or until the fat has risen to the surface and set.

Remove the bowl from the refrigerator. Remove and discard the fat and reheat the stock as required.

Chicken Stock

A well-flavored homemade chicken stock is invaluable. It forms the basis for many sauces and soups and is used in a wide variety of other dishes.
Makes 1¾ quarts (1½ liters)

Carcass, bones and giblets (excluding the liver) of a cooked or raw chicken
1 carrot, scraped and sliced
4 celery stalks, trimmed and sliced
1 onion, stuck with 2 cloves
1 bouquet garni
Grated rind of ½ lemon
1 teaspoon salt
10 peppercorns
2 quarts (1¾ liters) water

In a large saucepan, bring all the ingredients to a boil. Remove any scum that rises to the surface with a slotted spoon.

Half-cover the pan with the lid, reduce the heat and simmer the stock gently for about 2 hours.

Strain the liquid into a bowl. Set the stock aside to cool. Store it in the refrigerator or use as required.

Fish Stock

To make a good fish stock, it is preferable to use the bones and trimmings from a firm-fleshed fish, such as sole or flounder. Shells of shrimp, crabs and lobster may also be added.
Makes 5½ cups 1¼ liters)

3 lb (1¼ kg) fish bones and trimmings, washed thoroughly
1 bouquet garni
1 celery stalk, trimmed and chopped
1 large onion, sliced
2 carrots, scraped and sliced
Salt
6 peppercorns
Juice of ½ lemon
2½ quarts (2½ liters) water
1 cup (225 milliliters) white wine

In a large saucepan, bring all the ingredients to a boil. The liquid should

cover the bones and vegetables, so add more if necessary. Remove any scum that rises to the surface with a slotted spoon. Simmer the stock for 30-40 minutes.

Remove the pan from the heat and strain the stock into a large mixing bowl. Use it immediately or allow it to cool and store in the refrigerator for a day only.

Vegetable Stock

For this recipe, whole vegetables have been used. For a more economical stock replace some of them with celery leaves and trimmings, and peelings from root vegetables. Vegetable stock makes a nourishing thin soup when served with grated cheese, or use it in sauces and vegetarian dishes.
Makes 7 cups (1¾ liters)

4 tablespoons (50 g) vegetable fat
1 large onion, finely chopped
3 large carrots, scraped and chopped
3 celery stalks with leaves, trimmed and chopped
1 large turnip or parsnip, peeled and chopped
1 teaspoon brown sugar
2½ quarts (2½ liters) hot water
1 bouquet garni
6 white peppercorns
1½ teaspoons salt
2 whole cloves

In a large saucepan, melt the vegetable fat. Add the onion, carrots, celery, turnip or parsnip and sugar and cook, stirring frequently, for 8-10 minutes or until the onion is golden brown. Pour in the hot water and add the *bouquet garni*, stirring frequently. Reduce the heat to moderately low and simmer, stirring occasionally, for 45 minutes.

Remove the pan from the heat and pour the stock through a fine wire strainer into a large mixing bowl. Press down on the vegetables to extract all the juices.

Set the stock aside to cool. Store it in the refrigerator or use as required.

Court Buillon

Court bouillon is an acidulated stock, which is used for poaching fish. It can be reused, providing it is strained after use and stored in the refrigerator.
Makes about 2½ quarts (2½ liters)

2½ quarts (2½ liters) water, or water and wine mixed
1 lb (½ kg) carrots, scraped and sliced
2 medium-sized onions, sliced

4 celery stalks, chopped
1 bouquet garni
2 teaspoons salt
⅔ cup (150 ml) cider or wine vinegar

Pour the water or water and wine mixture into a saucepan and add the vegetables, *bouquet garni*, salt and vinegar. Bring the liquid to a boil. Reduce the heat to low and simmer the mixture for 1 hour.

Remove the pan from the heat and strain the mixture through cheesecloth or a fine strainer set over a large bowl or pan. Use immediately, or allow it to cool and store in the refrigerator until required.

Types of stock and their uses

Brown stock: So called because ingredients are colored by browning before water is added. It is usually made exclusively with beef bones and meat (but sometimes includes veal and/or chicken) plus celery, root vegetables and herbs. It is ideal for brown sauces as well as kidney, tomato and other vegetable soups requiring good color and strong flavor; for adding to red meat casseroles and pies. A very strong meaty stock (aspic) is used for clear hot and cold jellied soups.

Game stock: This is made from game carcasses and meat scraps plus beef bones (fresh or saved from making brown stock) plus a few vegetables, notably celery and herbs. Most distinctive flavor, medium color. Use for game soups, sauces to serve with game, to moisten game pâtés, pies and casseroles.

White stock: This is usually made from the bones and meat scraps of one or several of the following: veal, chicken, rabbit, pork, mutton, lamb and ham (occasionally beef is used), plus celery, root vegetables and herbs. Omit mutton, lamb and ham from a general purpose stock and only use pork sparingly. Delicate meaty flavor and pale color if based on veal and/or chicken. Use for cream soups, fine white sauces and aspics. The predominance of lamb or mutton makes stock ideal for Scotch and barley broths. Use ham stock for purées and soups made with lentils or dried beans.

Chicken stock*: This is made with stewing fowl and knuckle of veal for maximum flavor; chicken carcass, skin and giblets plus poultry scraps; or giblets only. Always includes celery, a few root vegetables and herbs. Poultry flavor, pale color. Excellent general-purpose stock for

111

all types of soups, sauces for vegetables and white meat dishes, moistening white meat casseroles and pies.

Fish stock*: Use fish heads, bones and trimmings, lemon, celery, a few root vegetables and herbs. Turbot and flounder or halibut heads, and sole bones are best. Add fresh, cheap white fish to bolster flavor if bones are few. Almost colorless. Quickly made. Delicately flavored. Wine can replace some of the water. Use for fish soups, poaching fish, fish aspics and sauces or rice to accompany fish dishes.

Vegetable stock: A good way to use up scraps. Can be made from one or several of the following: celery stalks and leaves, trimmings from leeks and carrots, outer leaves, watercress stalks, mushroom peelings, outer lettuce leaves, young pea or broad bean pods and some vegetable cooking liquids. Mostly used in vegetarian cookery. Color and flavor can be strengthened by lightly browning vegetables in butter before water is added. Blend all ingredients in a blender to make an instant soup. Or strain off vegetables and use liquid for soups, braising vegetables, cooking lentils, dried beans and rice.
*NB Strictly speaking, chicken and fish stocks are types of white stock.

Soups

Soup is normally served as the first course, in which case it should stimulate the appetite rather than satisfy it. The richer and heavier the main course, the lighter the soup should be. Conversely, creamy soups with a lot of body to them are most suitable when a simple, light main course is planned.

Very substantial soups, such as *bouillabaisse* or minestrone, are really more like stews than soups and can be a meal in themselves. Use them for informal occasions to replace the first and main course and follow with something light. On average allow $\frac{2}{3}$ of a cup (150 milliliters) of soup per person when served as a first course or a generous 10 fluid ounces (300 milliliters) when the soup is the main part of your meal.

Soups are either thick or thin.

Enriching soup

This is an optional extra, done just before serving to add creamy flavor and improve

texture. Simply stir in small pats of butter or a little cream or soured cream. Cook over gentle heat until warmed through but on no account allow to boil.

An egg yolk beaten into cream will thicken as well as enrich the soup. Allow 1 egg yolk and $4\frac{1}{2}$ tablespoons cream per $2\frac{1}{2}$ cups (600 milliliters) of soup. Blend the yolk and cream in a small bowl. Stir in a spoonful of hot soup. When blended, add another spoonful. Continue adding and blending in the hot soup until the bowl is full. Remove from the heat and gradually stir the contents of the bowl into the soup. Pour into warmed soup plates or a tureen and serve immediately.

Making thick soups

Thick soups can be divided into three categories: purées, creams and veloutés. The basic difference among them is the thickening agent used.

Purées are made with fruit or vegetables and are usually substantial enough to need no additional thickening. Ingredients are simply reduced to a purée in a blender or rubbed through a strainer with the cooking liquid.

Cream soups can be made from fish, shellfish, poultry or vegetables. The flavored cooking liquid is strained off after the basic ingredients have been cooked. The liquid is then thickened with a mixture of butter and a cereal product (usually flour). Often some of the original ingredients are stirred into the soup just before serving for added flavor.

Veloutés are velvety smooth and thick luxurious soups usually made with a vegetable, though sometimes white fish or poultry are used. They are made by a combination of puréeing and thickening.

Basic method for purée soups

This is the simplest method of making a soup and is used exclusively for vegetables and fruit. Potatoes, Jerusalem artichokes, carrots, parsnips and peas, beans and lentils will all purée to a thick soup after cooking.

Vegetables such as mushrooms, lettuce and watercress do not have much substance in themselves. If used alone, large quantities would be needed to create the right consistency for a purée soup. Therefore, a vegetable, such as potato is usually added to give the starchy ingredient necessary for thickening.

Fruit soups usually produce a slightly

thinner purée, which can be thickened with a little arrowroot or cornstarch if wished or simply enriched with a little cream or sour cream just before serving.

It is difficult to approximate the proportions of vegetable or fruit, butter and liquid needed to make a purée soup because they vary so much depending on chosen ingredients and consistency required. As a rough guide, allow 2 tablespoons (25 grams) butter and $2\frac{1}{2}$ cups (600 milliliters) liquid to each 1 pound (450 grams) of vegetables or fruit.

Sweating the vegetables: Clean and dice or slice the vegetables. Put them in a saucepan with a little melted butter over very low heat. Shake the pan or stir to coat the vegetables all over with the butter. Cover and cook very gently for 5-10 minutes to soften the vegetables and let them absorb the butter without browning. This process is called sweating and must be done very slowly over gentle heat. Fast cooking will fry the vegetables, giving them a hard outer skin so the butter cannot be absorbed. Frying will also spoil the color of the soup.

Adding the liquid: After 5-10 minutes, add the liquid. For vegetable soups, chicken or other white stock is generally used. Vegetable stock and vegetable cooking water are other possibilities or for a creamy vegetable soup, milk diluted with a little stock. Season lightly with salt, pepper and complementary herbs and spices.

For fruit soups, use fruit juice or water with sugar, lemon zest and spices such as cinnamon or cloves for added flavor.

Bring to a boil and simmer, covered, until the ingredients are quite tender, about 15-25 minutes depending on varieties used. Do not overcook, especially when green vegetables are used, or flavor and color will be lost. In plain and chilled soups, fat tends to coagulate when cold, spoiling texture and appearance, so sweating is usually omitted when the soup is to be served chilled. It may also be omitted when a plain, easily digested soup is being prepared. In this case, the vegetables or fruit are cooked directly with the liquid.

Making the purée: Purée vegetables or fruit with their cooking liquid, using a strainer or a blender.

Place a large strainer over a bowl or clean saucepan. Pour in the contents of the soup pan, pressing the vegetables through with a wooden spoon. Discard any fibrous pieces remaining in the strainer. Scrape the purée from the underside into the soup bowl. In some cases, a nylon strainer is necessary to avoid discoloration of ingredients.

Using a blender is the quickest and easiest way to reduce fruit or vegetables to a purée with their cooking liquid (although it may be necessary to strain the soup after blending to remove fibers). A blender produces consistently smooth results which are ideal for a velouté or cream soup but, from a purist's point of view, are rather too textureless for a purée soup.

Potage Parmentier, a delicious soup served either hot or cold.

Serving: If the soup is to be served hot, reheat gently after puréeing and adjust seasoning to taste. Add more liquid if the consistency is too thick. If too thin, the soup can be simmered to reduce the quantity of liquid by evaporation – but this process is not effective when a lot of thickening is needed. Enrich, as already described, if wished.

If the soup is to be served cold, the consistency can be slightly thinner, and the seasoning should be a little stronger since flavors appear to diminish when ingredients are chilled. Cool the soup, cover and chill thoroughly before serving.

Potage Parmentier

This traditional purée soup proves you don't need exotic or expensive ingredients to make a really delicious and nourishing soup. It tastes just as good served cold as hot – when cold it is called Vichysoisse.
Yields 6 servings

$\frac{1}{2}$ **cup (125 g) butter**
2 lb (1kg) leeks, washed, trimmed and chopped
1 lb ($\frac{1}{2}$ kg) potatoes, peeled and chopped
2 celery stalks, trimmed and chopped
2$\frac{1}{2}$ cups (600 ml) chicken stock
2$\frac{1}{2}$ cups (600 ml) milk
Salt and pepper
$\frac{1}{2}$ **teaspoon sugar**
$\frac{1}{4}$ **teaspoon grated nutmeg**
1$\frac{1}{4}$ cups (300 ml) heavy cream

In a large saucepan, melt the butter, add the leeks, potatoes and celery and sweat for 8 minutes, stirring occasionally.

Pour on the stock and milk and bring to the boil. Season with salt, pepper, sugar and nutmeg. Cover the pan and simmer for 30 to 40 minutes, or until the vegetables are soft. Reduce to a purée in a blender or rub through a strainer.

If serving hot, return the purée to the pan. Reheat and enrich with the cream. If serving cold, put the purée into a bowl and stir in half the cream. Chill in the refrigerator for 4 hours and stir in the remaining cream before serving.

Basic methods for cream soups

Cream soups are finer in texture and richer than purée soups. They can be made from fish, shellfish, poultry or vegetables. A higher percentage of the basic ingredient is needed since only the cooking liquid is used for the final soup, although reserved pieces are sometimes used to garnish it.

Any vegetables used are sweated in butter as described for purée soups (page 112), then simmered in liquid (usually a suitable stock or milk diluted with stock). Fish or poultry, if used, are added to the simmering liquid; they are never sweated. Cooking is longer than for a purée soup, to extract maximum flavor from the ingredients. The flavored liquid is then strained off and thickened.

Thickening cream soups: A cereal product (usually flour) and butter are used to thicken cream soups, using the roux method, beurre manié blended flour.

The roux method of thickening is also widely used in sauce-making. (See page 117 for a detailed description.)

Beurre manié is flour and butter mixed together before cooking. Use a fork or palette knife to blend butter and flour to a paste, using the same amounts as for a roux. Form the mixture into small pellets and stir into the soup, a few at a time, until the desired consistency is achieved. The flour thickens the soup as it disperses. Bring the soup to simmering point.

Blended flour is the easiest method and particularly suitable when a plain soup is wanted or if the soup is to be enriched before serving. Mix flour allowing $\frac{1}{4}$ cup (25 grams) flour to $2\frac{1}{2}$ cups (600 milliliters) soup to a smooth paste with 1-2 tablespoons of cold liquid in a small bowl. Gradually blend in a ladle of hot soup,

114

then slowly stir the contents of the bowl into the soup pan. Bring to a boil, stirring until thickened.

Cornstarch or arrowroot can be used in place of flour; they are useful when a very smooth result is required. Arrowroot, in particular, is ideal for fish soups and fruit soups since it remains clear and uncloudy on thickening.

Serving: Check seasoning and consistency as for purée soups and enrich just before serving if wished.

Cream of Chicken Soup

This is a good way to produce a cheap meaty soup.
Yields 4 servings

5 tablespoons (60 g) butter
$\frac{1}{2}$ onion, diced
$\frac{1}{2}$ carrot, scraped and diced
1 chicken part, weighing about 8-10 oz (225-275 g)
1 bay leaf
2 whole cloves
2 peppercorns
1 quart (900 ml) chicken stock
$\frac{1}{3}$ cup flour
$2\frac{1}{2}$ cups (300 ml) milk, warmed
Salt and pepper

Sweat the onion and carrot in 1 tablespoon (15 grams) butter for 5 minutes. Add the chicken, bay leaf, cloves, peppercorns and stock. Bring to a boil, cover and simmer for 30 minutes. Strain off the stock and reserve. Discard the seasonings. Skin and bone the chicken. Cut the flesh into bite-sized pieces and reserve.

Melt the remaining butter in a clean saucepan. Stir in the flour and cook without browning. Blend in the milk, stirring, and bring to a boil. Add the strained stock, stirring well. Adjust seasoning to taste.

Stir in the chicken just before serving.

Basic method for velouté soups

Veloutés are made by combining the methods used for purée soups and cream soups. In addition they can be enriched and thickened with egg yolks and cream.

Poultry or white fish can be used but vegetables are the usual main ingredient. Those with a distinctive flavor (such as asparagus, Jerusalem artichokes, celeriac, leeks and Florence fennel) are particularly suitable.

Sweat the vegetables (see page 112), add the liquid (and poultry or fish if used) and simmer as for a purée soup. Because

several thickening agents will be used, a smaller than usual quantity of the basic ingredient will be needed but those choosen need to be well flavored. Reduce to a purée (in a blender for really smooth results), strain if fibrous and then thicken with a roux or, for the finest results, with blended cornstarch as described for cream soups. Check seasoning and enrich with cream and egg yolks just before serving.

Fennel Velouté

The smoky aromatic flavor of Florence fennel makes it an ideal vegetable for a luxurious velouté soup.
4-5 servings

$\frac{3}{4}$ lb (350 g) Florence fennel, thinly sliced, green fronds reserved for garnish
1 small onion, chopped
3 tablespoons (40 g) butter
$3\frac{3}{4}$ cups (900 ml) chicken or white stock
Salt and pepper
$2\frac{1}{2}$ tablespoons cornstarch
2 egg yolks
5 tablespoons heavy cream

Melt the butter and sweat the vegetables for 5 minutes. Stir in the stock. Season, cover and simmer for 15-20 minutes.

Pour off about half the cooking liquid into a clean saucepan. Reduce the vegetables with the remaining cooking liquid to a purée in a blender. Pour through a strainer, to remove fibers, into the saucepan.

Blend the cornstarch with 3 tablespoons of cold water in a small bowl. Gradually stir in a ladle of hot soup, then stir the contents of the bowl into the saucepan. Bring to a boil and cook for 1 minute. Adjust seasoning to taste.

Blend the egg yolks with the cream, stir in a ladle of hot soup and then stir back into the pan. Heat through gently but do not boil. Serve at once, garnished with green fennel fronds.

Making thin soups

Thin soups, like thick soups, can be divided into three categories – broths, thin soups and clear soups.

Basic methods for broths

Broths are made with water and meaty bones, and given a long slow cooking to extract maximum flavor from the ingredients. The liquid is not thickened in any way, but meat is picked off the bones, which are then discarded, and the meat (and often vegetables) is stirred into the broth before serving. A classic broth is cock-a-leekie which is made with chicken, veal knuckle and leek.

Broths can also be made using fish as the main ingredient (*bouillabaisse* and *moules à la marinière* are two examples). If a lot of fish is included, supplementary vegetables, pulses and cereals are quite unnecessary. Fish broths are more quickly cooked than meat broths because fish bones give off a bitter flavor if cooking is prolonged.

Cooking: Dice or slice a few firm vegetables, such as carrots, turnips, a potato and onion or leek for flavoring. You can sweat them in butter, although this is not essential. If a richly colored soup is required, let them fry to a golden brown.

Add a meaty bone, raw, to the pan. Cover the ingredients with water, add barley and any pre-soaked dried vegetables (about 2 tablespoons [25 grams] to 2½ cups [600 milliliters]), such as lentils, haricot beans and split peas. Season lightly with salt, pepper and suitable herbs, such as thyme, basil, oregano or mixed herbs.

Bring slowly to a boil, skim the surface if any scum rises, then cover the saucepan and simmer for 2-3 hours. Lift out the bone, take off any meat and cut it into bite-sized pieces. Discard the bone. Skim off any fat from the soup and return the meat to the pan. Add any fresh green vegetables such as peas or cabbage which need only a short cooking time (they would lose color, texture and freshness if added earlier); complete cooking.

Scotch Broth

A filling, meaty soup, Scotch Broth is thickened with pearl barley and dried peas. If you wish to remove all the fat from the broth, allow the broth to cool for at least 8 hours or overnight. Remove and discard the fat that rises to the surface. Reheat the broth before serving.

4-6 servings

3 lb (1¼ kg) neck of mutton or lamb, chined and trimmed of excess fat
7½ cups (1¾ liters) water
Salt and black pepper
¼ cup (50 g) pearl barley, blanched
¼ cup (50 g) green split peas, soaked overnight in cold water and drained

1 large carrot, scraped and chopped
1 large onion, chopped
2 leeks, washed thoroughly and diced
2 celery stalks, trimmed and diced
1 large turnip, peeled and diced
2 tablespoons chopped fresh parsley

Cut the meat into 4-5 inch (10-13 centimeter) pieces. Place the meat in a large saucepan and pour over the water. Set the pan over moderately high heat and bring the liquid to a boil. Skim off and discard any scum which rises to the surface. Add the salt, pepper, barley and peas. Reduce the heat to low, cover and simmer 1½ hours. Add the carrot, onion, leeks, celery and turnip. Re-cover the pan and continue cooking for a further 1 hour or until the vegetables are very tender. Remove the pan from the heat. Using tongs, transfer the meat to a chopping board and slice the meat from the bones. Discard the bones and return the meat to the pan.

Return the pan to moderate heat and cook for a further 5 minutes. Taste and add more salt and pepper if necessary. Sprinkle with parsley and serve.

Basic method for thin soups

Thin soups are made by cooking ingredients in stock, but there is no need to clarify the stock. The liquid is not thickened, except when added ingredients do this naturally (as when a potato disintegrates). Chicken, meat, game, fish or shellfish stock can be used.

Thin soups give plenty of scope for your own recipe ideas. The soup can have a variety of ingredients added to give bulk and substance: for example rice or pasta, grated or diced cheese, slivers of ham or bacon, eggs, bread and vegetables.

Both broths and thin soups tend to be substantial. Although it sounds contradictory to describe, say, minestrone as a thin soup, this is technically correct. While a bowl of minestrone is full of vegetables and pasta, the liquid element is thin. The consistency of the liquid and not the other ingredients differentiates a thin soup from a thick one.

Thin soups containing fish or shellfish are often called chowders. Pork or bacon is sometimes added too.

Cooking: The success of a thin soup lies in the quality of the stock from which it is made. It is essential to have a well flavored stock, since cooking time is considerably shorter than for a broth.

This means that ingredients added either during the cooking or at the end do not impart as much flavor to the liquid as they would with longer, slower cooking.

The basic method is much the same as for broth, and a wide range of vegetables can be used. Quickly cooked vegetables such as peas and beans should be added towards the end of the cooking time, so that they remain whole.

Minestrone
6-8 servings

¼ cup (50 g) dried beans, soaked in cold water overnight
5 cups (1¼ liters) beef stock
1 large carrot, scraped and diced
1 onion, sliced
3 slices bacon
1 garlic clove, finely crushed
Salt and pepper
1 celery stalk, trimmed and sliced
1 leek, washed thoroughly and sliced
3 tomatoes, blanched, skinned and quartered
⅓ cup (25 g) spaghetti, broken into short lengths
Freshly grated Parmesan cheese

Drain and cook the beans in fresh water until tender (do not add salt). Drain and turn the beans into a large clean saucepan. Add stock, carrot, onion, bacon, garlic and seasoning. Cover and simmer over low heat for 20 minutes. Add the celery, leek and tomatoes and continue cooking for 10 minutes. Taste and adjust seasoning.

Bring the soup to a boil and add the spaghetti. Lower the heat and simmer for 10-12 minutes.

Stir in 3 tablespoons of grated Parmesan cheese and serve with additional Parmesan in a separate serving bowl.

Basic method for clear soups

Clear soups, or consommés, make excellent appetizers. They are not too filling, but because the flavor is savory and strong, you only need a little for each person – about ⅔ of a cup (150 milliliters). They can be served hot or cold.

When cold, consommé is a soft jelly which is usually chopped before serving. It should not be ice-cold, and can be garnished with lemon quarters or chopped anchovy fillets and sour cream. When hot, consommés are often garnished with croûtons or strips of meat, or blanched julienne strips of vegetables. To blanch the julienne strips, put the prepared vegetables into a strainer or frying basket. Plunge into boiling water for 30 seconds, then refresh in cold water. Drain and dry immediately.

Since clear soups are essentially twice refined stocks, they are, in fact, very simple. But like all simple things they must be perfect to be really good. Flavor, color, clarity and texture (if the soup is to be served cold) are all important. Clear soup is simply not worth making if you are going to rely on a commercial stock cube. Homemade stock is the essential ingredient of a consommé. Use a really good beef or chicken stock. Be sure to include chicken or veal bones, a pig's foot or half a calf's foot when making the stock, since these ingredients provide a gelatinous texture. Browning the bones is also important, for it gives the rich color so characteristic of a good consommé.

In addition, after the initial browning, you can add a little sugar and cook, stirring, for a few minutes before pouring on the liquid. The sugar will caramelize giving the stock an extra-rich golden color. Finally, remember to strain, degrease and clarify the stock thoroughly (see page 110).

Cooking: Your stock should be further enriched by cooking fresh meat and vege-

To make minestrone (a thin soup), first cook the dried, soaked beans in fresh water until tender.

Drain, then add the beans to a saucepan with the other long-cooking vegetables (carrot, onion), bacon, stock and seasoning.

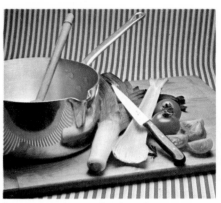

Cover and simmer for 20 minutes. Add the short-cooking vegetables (celery, leek, tomatoes) and cook for 10 minutes.

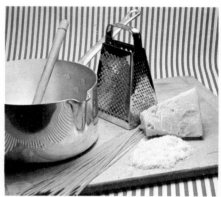

Finally, bring to a boil, add the spaghetti and simmer for 12 minutes. Stir in 2 tablespoons of grated cheese before serving.

tables in it, clarifying it again and, finally, flavoring it with sherry or Madeira. Port may be used with game stock.

For beef consommé, use lean meat to impart a strong flavor and grind or dice it so that all the nourishment is drawn out during the cooking. Economical cuts, such as shin or stewing beef are just as suitable as a more expensive roast. The higher the proportion of meat to liquid the better the flavor of the consommé. (The meat itself can be used afterwards, but since little flavor is left in it choose a recipe such as shepherd's pie or spaghetti sauce and add plenty of extra spices and flavorings.) For chicken consommé, use fresh uncooked chicken legs or thigh joints to give maximum flavor.

Beef Consommé

This is just a basic guide – add more or less vegetables if you like. Chicken consommé is made in the same way.

6-8 servings

$\frac{3}{4}$ **lb (350 g) lean beef, ground**
7½ cups (1¾ liters) bouillon (clarified beef stock)
1 small carrot, scraped and diced
1 small onion, diced
1 celery stalk, trimmed and diced
1 bay leaf
1 whole clove
6 peppercorns
Salt
2 egg whites and shells
3 tablespoons sherry or Madeira

Place the meat in a large saucepan with the stock and set over low heat. Add the vegetables together with the bay leaf, clove, peppercorns and a little salt.

Lightly beat the egg whites to a soft foam, slide into the soup and add the shells crushed. Whisk with a balloon whisk until the soup comes to a boil. Set the whisk aside and allow soup to rise slowly to the top of the saucepan. Carefully remove the pan from the heat and let the soup subside – but do not break up the foam covering the surface. Return the pan to very low heat, and leave to simmer gently, uncovered, for 1 hour.

Strain the soup through a fine cloth or jelly bag into a clean bowl, sliding foam, egg shells and other ingredients out of the saucepan. Let the liquid drip through by itself. Do not press the bag at all or the consommé may become cloudy.

If time permits, allow the clear soup to become quite cold then lift off hardened

fat from the surface. Alternatively, skim as much fat as possible off the hot soup with a spoon, and draw paper towels across the surface: they will act like blotting paper, absorbing any remaining small globules of grease.

Reheat but do not boil. Taste and adjust seasoning. Stir in sherry or Madeira and garnish if desired immediately before serving.

Sauces

A sauce is a liquid, seasoning or relish, served with food in order to complement, coat, contrast with or garnish it. A sauce can be made separately from the food it is seasoning or used in the actual preparation to bind the various ingredients together. This section comprises only savory sauces; sweet ones are discussed on pages 138-139.

Types of sauces

Sauces may be roughly divided into five categories: white, brown, egg-based, tomato and other (which includes mint, apple and bread). Additionally, there are pan gravy and *vinaigrette* or French dressing. Each of these groups has dozens of variations, so learn to recognize the basic type when you see such names as sauce Mornay and béarnaise.

Both white and brown sauces have a roux base. A white roux is cooked only long enough to eliminate the raw taste of the flour and only 'white' liquids such as milk, chicken and fish stocks, and wine are added. In brown sauces, the roux is cooked until it browns slightly and 'brown' liquids such as brown stock and red wine are added.

Egg-based sauces combine egg yolks and a high proportion of butter or oil, whisked together to become thick and glossy. The two most famous are hollandaise and mayonnaise, which both have numerous variations.

Several general points about sauces are worth emphasizing. Never economize on time or ingredients. For example, use homemade stock instead of a stock cube. Use a heavy-based saucepan, which will distribute the heat more evenly, thus preventing burning. Avoid aluminum pans which tend to discolor white sauces.

Many sauces can be prepared in advance and stored in the refrigerator,

covered closely with a disc of dampened waxed paper. Always reheat a sauce which has been kept in the refrigerator in a bain-marie or double-boiler, because this helps to prevent the sauce going lumpy or burning.

Making a roux: The term *roux* comes from the French and means specifically equal weights of butter and flour cooked slowly together before a liquid is added. This cooking eliminates the raw taste of flour, which can spoil a sauce. Roux are either white or brown.

A white roux is cooked over low heat. First the butter is put in a medium-sized saucepan. When it has melted, slowly blend in the flour. Stir the roux with the back of a metal spoon as it bubbles gently without coloring for 2 minutes. Remove from the heat and cool to well below boiling point before adding liquid. A cool roux reduces the likelihood of a lumpy sauce. Add the liquid and blend well, making sure that all the roux is off the bottom of the pan. Return the pan to the heat, bring the sauce to a boil, stirring constantly, and simmer for about 5 minutes. Season to taste.

The quantities given below are for three consistencies of white sauce. Be a little more generous with butter than flour, and you will find the liquid blends in more easily.

Consistency	Butter and flour to 1¼ cups (300 ml) liquid
Thin, pouring	1 tablespoon (15 g)
Medium, coating	2 tablespoons (25 g)
Thick, panade	4 tablespoons (50 g)

A brown roux is made with cooking oil, vegetable fat or drippings instead of butter, unless it is for a delicate dish. Heat the fat over low heat and blend in the flour. Cook, stirring, for 8-10 minutes or until the flour has turned a pale golden nut brown. It will keep cooking for a few minutes after it is removed from the heat. Cool and add liquid as for white sauce. A brown sauce should simmer for 1 hour or more to bring out its full flavor.

Blending method: Blended sauces tend to contain little or no fat, so the thickening agent, which may be flour, cornstarch or arrowroot is first blended with a little of the cold liquid to make a smooth paste.

For 1¼ cups (300 milliliters) of sauce in a small bowl blend together 4 tablespoons (25 grams) plain flour or 2 tablespoons (15 grams) cornstarch with

4-5 tablespoons of the cold liquid. Bring the rest of the liquid to a boil and pour this into the bowl containing the paste mixture. Return the mixture to the saucepan, bring the sauce to a boil, stirring constantly, and simmer for about 3 minutes, until thick. Season to taste.

Brown sauces

Brown sauces take more time to make than white sauces because they require long, slow cooking. Therefore it pays to make large quantities of basic brown sauce and to freeze most in 1- or 2-cup (300 or 600 milliliter) containers.

Sauce Espagnole (Basic Brown Sauce)

Strong and rich flavored, Sauce Espagnole can be used as an accompaniment to steak, vegetables, game or eggs, and as a base for other brown sauce variations.
Makes about $1\frac{1}{4}$ cups (300 milliliters)

2 tablespoons (25 g) butter
1 carrot, scraped and diced
1 onion, chopped
2 oz (50 g) unsmoked bacon, rinds removed and chopped
$\frac{1}{4}$ cup (25 g) flour
$2\frac{1}{4}$ cups (450 ml) brown stock
1 bouquet garni
2 tablespoons tomato purée
Salt and black pepper

In a small heavy-based saucepan, melt the butter and cook the vegetables and bacon over a low heat for 10 minutes or until lightly browned. Add the flour, and cook for 2-3 minutes, stirring constantly, until the roux is brown.

Remove the pan from the heat and gradually add $1\frac{1}{4}$ cups (300 milliliters) of stock. When the sauce is smooth, return the pan to the heat and bring to a boil slowly, stirring constantly. Add the *bouquet garni* and simmer, covered, for about 30 minutes. Add the rest of the stock and the tomato purée, and simmer, covered, for another 30 minutes, stirring frequently.

Strain the sauce, skim off any fat, adjust the seasoning and serve.

Other sauces on Sauce Espagnole: *Sauce diable*, with wine, vinegar, shallots and cayenne pepper; *Sauce Robert*, with onions, wine and Dijon mustard; and *mushroom*.

Brown deglazing sauce

Brown deglazing sauce is much simpler than brown sauce. Most of the fat is

removed from the roasting pan, and $1\frac{1}{4}$ cups (300 milliliters) of brown stock is added. The coagulated pan juices are scraped up with a wooden spoon, and the sauce is boiled down over high heat until reduced by about half. A lump of butter is stirred in, off the heat, before serving.

Egg-based sauces

Egg-based sauces are made by gradually incorporating butter or oil into well-beaten egg yolks. An egg and oil combination is called mayonnaise, an egg and

Rich, creamy, homemade mayonnaise. For a lighter taste, you can use a combination of half olive oil and half good quality vegetable oil.

butter mixture hollandaise. When finished, both sauces have thickened into smooth creams that hold their shape. Despite their reputation for difficulty, neither sauce is especially hard to make when you understand how egg yolks work. First, in order to absorb a fat the yolks have to be beaten until thick and light in color. Second, the fat must be added slowly and in tiny quantities at first. If either sauce should curdle, there are tried and true methods of rescuing it.

Mayonnaise

For mayonnaise, the oil is added to the well-beaten egg yolks by droplets until the sauce has the thickness of double cream. About half the oil will have been added. Do not stop beating until this point is reached. The rest of the oil can be added by the tablespoonful, making sure that all of it is incorporated before the next spoonful is added. When the sauce is finished beat in 2 tablespoons of boiling water as a further insurance against curdling.

A large egg will absorb no more than $\frac{2}{3}$ of a cup (150 milliliters) of oil, and a novice should use slightly less than this maximum. Trying to add more oil than a yolk can absorb causes the mayonnaise to curdle.

Mayonnaise

Makes 1½ cups (300 milliliters)

2 egg yolks, at room temperature
Salt and white pepper
1 teaspoon dry mustard
1¼ cups (300 ml) olive oil, at room temperature
1 tablespoon white wine vinegar or lemon juice

In a medium mixing bowl, whisk together the egg yolks, salt, pepper and mustard until they are thoroughly blended and have thickened. Add the oil, a few drops at a time, beating constantly with a wire whisk. After the mayonnaise has thickened, the oil may be added a little more rapidly.

Beat in a few drops of vinegar or lemon juice from time to time to prevent the mayonnaise from becoming too thick. When all the oil has been added, stir in the remaining vinegar or lemon juice.

If the mayonnaise does curdle, or if after standing for several days in the refrigerator the sauce has thinned and released oil, take the following steps.

First, warm a small bowl in hot water and dry it thoroughly. Next, place in it a tablespoon of mayonnaise and a teaspoon of dry mustard. Beat these with a wire whisk until they become thick and creamy. Continue beating in the rest of the sauce by the teaspoonful, allowing each addition to thicken before more is

added. Especially at first, add only small quantities. Alternatively, add ice-cold water a teaspoon at a time, whisking constantly, until mixture is smooth.

Other sauces based on mayonnaise are *Tartar sauce* flavored with heavy cream, finely minced capers, gherkins, fresh chives and chervil. Mayonnaise with herbs (chopped fresh parsley, basil, chives, marjoram, tarragon) makes another variation. To keep for more than a few days, however, the herbs must be blanched for 1 minute before being stirred into the mayonnaise.

Hollandaise

Hollandaise sauce is made over hot water so that the eggs are warmed slightly while the butter is added. The eggs must be thick, smooth and light in color before the butter is added to them. At first, add the softened butter by the half teaspoonful, making sure that it has been incorporated fully before the next spoonful is added. When the sauce begins to thicken, you can add slightly larger amounts of butter. Never try to hurry the sauce. A large egg can absorb up to 5 tablespoons (65 grams) of butter, but a novice should use no more than 4 tablespoons (50 grams).

If the sauce must be kept warm for any length of time over hot water, stir in 1½ tablespoons of velouté or béchamel (white) sauce.

Hollandaise Sauce

Traditionally served with asparagus and salmon, Hollandaise Sauce can also accompany other vegetables and fish dishes. It is always served warm.
Makes 1 cup (225 milliliters)

7 tablespoons white wine vinegar
6 peppercorns
1 bay leaf
¾ cup (175 g) butter
3 egg yolks
Salt

In a small saucepan, bring the vinegar, peppercorns and bay leaf to a boil over moderate heat. Reduce the heat and simmer the mixture for 10 minutes, or until it is reduced to 2 tablespoons (25 milliliters). Pour the vinegar mixture through a strainer into a cup. Set aside. Discard the peppercorns and bay leaf.

In a small mixing bowl, cream the butter with a wood spoon until it is soft. In another small, heatproof mixing bowl

To make béarnaise sauce, first strain the vinegar mixture, then cream the butter and beat the egg yolks.

Over warm water, stir the mixture carefully until it thickens. Then stir in the butter, a small piece at a time.

When the mixture is smooth, remove the bowl from the heat and beat in seasonings such as cayenne, tarragon and chervil.

beat the egg yolks to blend them together. Beat in the salt and a heaped teaspoon of the softened butter. Stir in the vinegar.

Put the bowl with the egg yolk mixture over a medium-sized saucepan one-third full with warm water. Place the pan over the lowest heat. The water should heat gradually but never come to boiling point. Whisk the egg yolk mixture until it begins to thicken.

Add the remaining butter, a teaspoon at a time, stirring constantly. When all the butter has been added, taste the sauce. Add more salt if necessary. If the sauce is too sharp, add a little more butter. Pour into a warm sauce boat and serve.

To make French dressing, measure the vinegar into a bowl or pitcher.

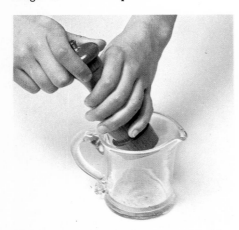

Then add seasoning and beat gently with a fork to dissolve the salt.

Pour over the oil and beat vigorously to mix and thicken the dressing.

If by some chance the sauce will not thicken, the butter has probably been beaten in too quickly. To remedy, warm a bowl in hot water and dry it. Add a teaspoon of wine vinegar or lemon juice and a tablespoon of the hollandaise and whisk until it thickens. Beat in the rest, a tablespoon at a time, making sure each addition has thickened before the next is added.

If a finished sauce begins to separate, you can save it by using the above technique. Also, see cold-water method under mayonnaise.

Béarnaise is probably the most widely used variant of hollandaise. The technique for making it is the same, but the flavorings are sharper: wine vinegar, shallot, bay leaf, tarragon, chervil and peppercorns. Sometimes meat glaze melted in white wine (*Sauce Colbert*) or tomato paste (*Sauce Choron*) is stirred into the *béarnaise*. *Mousseline sauce* is hollandaise with a small amount of whipped cream stirred in just before serving.

If hollandaise is to be used with fish, the vinegar and peppercorn flavoring is replaced by a white-wine fish stock cooked down to concentrate it.

Salad dressings

Although there seem to be many types of salad dressing, most are variations on two basic themes: French dressing and mayonnaise (see egg-based sauces).

The classic French dressing consists of olive oil, vinegar, salt and pepper. Crushed garlic, mustard and/or chopped herbs may also be added, in which case the dressing becomes *Sauce Vinaigrette*.

Basic French Dressing
Makes about ⅔ cup (125 milliliters)

3 tablespoons wine vinegar
1 teaspoon salt
1 teaspoon black pepper
7 tablespoons olive oil

In a small mixing bowl, beat the vinegar, salt and pepper together with a fork. Pour on the oil until well mixed. Use as required.

Other sauces

The category 'other sauces' brings together a necessarily incomplete collection of popular sauces. Given here are tomato sauce and traditional accompaniments for beef, lamb, pork and poultry.

Tomato sauces

Tomato sauces are simple to make and keep well in a screw-top jar in the refrigerator for up to 5 days; they can also be frozen. Sugar is added in the following basic tomato sauce recipes to counteract the bitterness often found in cooked

tomatoes. Dried herbs other than basil can be used, especially marjoram and oregano.

Tomato Sauce I
Makes about 3¾ cups (750 milliliters)

3 lb (1¼ kg) fresh tomatoes, halved
2 teaspoons salt
1 teaspoon sugar
1 teaspoon dried basil
½ teaspoon grated lemon rind

Preheat the oven to warm 325°F (170 C).

Place the tomatoes in a large ovenproof casserole. Cover the casserole with a well-fitting lid or aluminum foil and place in the oven. Bake for 45 minutes or until the tomatoes are very soft. Remove the casserole from the oven.

Place the tomatoes in a large strainer set over a large saucepan. Rub the tomatoes through the strainer until only a dry pulp is left. Discard the pulp. Add the salt, sugar, basil and lemon rind to the pan. Place the pan over moderate heat and cook, stirring frequently with a wooden spoon, for 10 minutes or until the mixture is fairly thick.

Tomato Sauce II
Makes about 3¾ cups (750 milliliters)

1 tablespoon vegetable oil
1 medium-sized onion, chopped
1 large carrot, scraped and finely chopped
1 celery stalk, trimmed and finely chopped
1 garlic clove, crushed
28 oz (600 g) can Italian plum tomatoes
3 parsley stalks
1½ tablespoons sugar
2 teaspoons salt
1 teaspoon pepper
1 teaspoon dried basil, marjoram or oregano

Heat the oil in a large saucepan and add the onion, carrot and celery. Stir to coat the vegetables in the oil, cover and cook slowly until soft, about 10 minutes. Add the garlic and cook for 2 minutes.

Add the tomatoes and can juice, parsley, sugar, salt and pepper. Bring to a boil and simmer, uncovered, for 30 minutes or more. Stir several times. Add basil or other herbs for the last 15 minutes of cooking.

If the sauce is not thick enough, raise the heat and slowly boil off any excess

Stir frequently. Correct the seasoning before serving.

Horseradish Sauce

Horseradish sauce is a classic accompaniment to hot or cold roast beef. It is also excellent with smoked trout.

6 servings

1 teaspoon lemon juice
2 teaspoons vinegar
1 teaspoon prepared mustard
Salt and black pepper (to taste)
1 teaspoon sugar
4½ tablespoons grated fresh horseradish
⅔ cup (150 ml) heavy cream, stiffly whipped

In a medium-sized mixing bowl, combine the lemon juice, vinegar, mustard, salt, pepper, sugar and horseradish. Fold in the cream and spoon the sauce into a sauce boat. Serve cold.

Mint Sauce

The traditional sauce served with roast lamb, this should be made with young, fresh mint.

6 servings

15 tablespoons finely chopped fresh mint
2½ tablespoons sugar
6 tablespoons (75 ml) malt or distilled white vinegar
1½ tablespoons hot water

Pound the mint and sugar together in a mortar with a pestle, or combine them together in a small bowl. Add the vinegar and hot water and stir until the sugar has dissolved. Set the bowl aside and leave it for 1-2 hours before serving.

Applesauce

Serve this tart applesauce as a refreshing accompaniment to pork, goose or duck.

4 servings

1½ lb (700 g) cooking apples
Finely grated rind of 1 lemon
1½ tablespoons water
Salt
Sugar to taste
3 tablespoons (40 g) butter

Peel, core and slice the apples. Place them in a bowl of water with a little salt as they are being prepared to prevent them from becoming brown. Drain and place them in a large saucepan. Bring the apples, lemon rind, water and salt to a boil.

Cover and simmer until the apples are soft. Add sugar to taste, a little at a time, stirring constantly. Allow the apples to cool. Purée the apples in a blender or rub through a strainer. Beat in the butter. If the sauce is to be served hot, return it to a clean saucepan and simmer for 2-3 minutes.

Bread Sauce

Serve with roast turkey, chicken or pheasant.

4 servings

1 medium-sized onion, studded with 2 cloves
1 bay leaf
1¼ cups (300 ml) milk
1 cup (50 g) fresh white breadcrumbs
Salt and pepper (to taste)
1 tablespoon butter
1 tablespoon light cream

Place the onion, bay leaf and milk in a saucepan. Cover the pan and place over very low heat for 10-15 minutes, to infuse the milk with the flavoring. Remove and discard the onion and bay leaf. Bring the milk to a boil, add the breadcrumbs and simmer for 3-4 minutes, or until the sauce is thick and creamy.

Remove the pan from the heat. Stir in the salt, pepper, butter and cream with a wooden spoon. Gently reheat the sauce, but do not allow it to boil. Serve at once.

Marinades

Marinades are used to give foods more flavor, to change flavor, and to tenderize. Meat and vegetables are most commonly marinated; the soaking periods can be from as little as 15 minutes to add flavor, to a week for a large leg of pork or venison to tenderize and improve flavor, to even longer for salting and brining a piece of beef.

Fruit is also marinated, in which case the term used is **macerate**. Macerated fruit is soaked in a liqueur or liqueur and juice combined.

Most but not all marinades are liquid based. (One exception is a herb and salt combination rubbed on meat.) Marinades are generally composed of an acid liquid such as wine, beer, wine vinegar, lemon juice and yogurt. To this base are added salt, a variety of herbs and spices (garlic, pepper, thyme, bay leaf, sage, juniper berries, cloves, allspice, mace, etc.) and

sometimes aromatic vegetables (onion, carrot, celery). Oil is often included to help the mixture adhere to the meat or vegetable.

Short-term marinades (those left for less than 36 hours) are frequently uncooked. Marinades to be used for more than 36 hours are usually cooked; this keeps the vegetables in the marinade from souring. Cooking also makes flavor more available to the food placed in it, and therefore is sometimes also used for short marinades, especially for vegetables. Cooked marinades should be chilled before meat is placed in them unless the recipe specifies otherwise. Sometimes raw vegetables are put into a hot marinade which cooks them slightly before it cools, adding to the penetration of flavor.

The length of marination depends on the result you wish to achieve. A short marinade imparts a mild flavor but will not tenderize much, while a longer one adds a stronger flavor and has greater tenderizing powers. Length of marinade also depends on the size of the food being marinated. Thus cubes of stewing beef would soak for 2-3 hours, whereas a whole pot roast of about 4 pounds (2 kilograms) would require 12 hours or more. Meat can be braised in its marinade, or if the meat is broiled or grilled as in the case of kebabs, the marinade may be used in making a sauce, or for basting. So never throw a marinade away until you decide whether it will be needed at a later stage in cooking.

Since marinades are acid based, the most suitable containers are earthenware, china, glass and enamel. Avoid aluminum and cast iron, which the acid affects.

Stuffing or Forcemeat

Stuffing, or forcemeat, is any sweet or savory mixture which is put inside another food such as poultry, rolled roasts, fish and vegetables both to add flavor and maintain shape. Frequently stuffings are a preparation of ground meat, fish, shellfish, vegetables or fruit, mixed with spices and herbs, which are bound with egg, milk, cream or stock. A breadcrumb or flour mixture, called a *panade*, is sometimes added to give more body.

Stuffing is usually flavored according to its use or accompaniment – for example, chestnuts for turkey, sage and onion for loin of pork, orange or apple for duck, truffle and *fois gras* for game and fish, rice or mushrooms for large fish.

A stuffing should not be soggy; do not, therefore, add all the liquid called for at once. Handle the mixture gently, so it does not become compacted, then pack into the bird or roast lightly, leaving room for expansion during cooking. This ensures a light, moist stuffing.

Although stuffings can be made in advance, they should never be put in the bird or roast until just before cooking because of bacterial contamination.

Thyme Stuffing

Thyme Stuffing is simple to make and reasonably economical, too. It tastes particularly good with fish, veal or poultry. The amount given below is sufficient to stuff a 4 lb (2 kg) fish or chicken.

Makes about 1 cup (225 grams)

2 cups (125 g) fresh white breadcrumbs
2 dessert apples, peeled, cored and finely chopped
1 medium-sized onion, finely chopped
½ cup (75 g) seedless raisins
2 teaspoons finely chopped fresh thyme
2 teaspoons finely chopped fresh lemon thyme
Salt and black pepper (to taste)
1 egg, lightly beaten

Place all the stuffing ingredients in a medium-sized bowl and stir until they are thoroughly combined. If the mixture is still slightly crumbly, add a little water or lemon juice.

The stuffing is now ready to use.

Chestnut and Sausage Stuffing

This is the traditional stuffing for turkey. It is simple to make and adds a delicious flavor to the bird. The amount given below is sufficient for one 10-12 lb (4-5 kg) turkey

1¼ lb (550 g) chestnuts, peeled
2½ cups (600 ml) beef stock
2 tablespoons butter
1 celery stalk, trimmed and chopped
Salt and black pepper
2 tablespoons butter
1 large onion, finely chopped
½ pound (225 g) pork sausage meat
1½ cups (75 g) fresh white breadcrumbs
2 eggs, lightly beaten

Put the chestnuts, stock, celery, salt and pepper in a saucepan. Simmer for 1 hour, or until chestnuts are tender and have absorbed all the stock. Transfer the chestnuts and celery to a mixing bowl and allow to cool. Crumble the chestnuts into small pieces, or mash through a coarse strainer.

In a small saucepan, melt the butter. Add the onion and sausage meat and cook for 8 minutes. Allow the sausage mixture to cool, then add the breadcrumbs and eggs to the chestnuts along with the onion and sausage meat and mix well with a spoon.

The stuffing is now ready to be used.

Bread

Bread is one of our cheapest sources of food energy since it contains proteins, iron, calcium and B vitamins. It is easy to buy a commercially made loaf of bread or even freshly baked bread from a bakery, but neither of these give the satisfaction of bread you have made yourself.

Making bread is an art, but contrary to opinion, it can be easily mastered. Bread recipes vary considerably and the guidelines set out here will not fit all of them exactly, but if you understand what each ingredient is meant to do and what the techniques are, you will be well on your way to successful bread-making.

The techniques discussed below are for yeast-based bread only. Soda and other breads based upon baking soda, or other raising agents, are much simpler to make, require no raising and only one kneading before baking.

Ingredients

Flour: The best flours for both bread and yeast doughs are milled from hard wheat. These flours have a high gluten content which produces an elastic, springy dough; whereas soft-wheat flours make a rather sticky dough. Try to use all-purpose or white bread flour which contains more hard wheat and is particularly good for bread-making. When making bread, it is best if the flour and liquid are at room temperature. Warm flour that is too cold in the oven.

Yeast: The most important thing to remember about yeast is that it is a living cell which must be provided with a 'friendly' environment if it is to do its job

properly. Yeast is destroyed by extreme heat – over 110°F (45°C). If you add hot water to it, or try to speed up the rising process by leaving the dough in a very hot place, it will be killed. You can use cold water to dissolve the yeast and leave the dough to rise in the refrigerator overnight (this prolongs the rising process), but the yeast will develop most satisfactorily if the room temperature and the temperature of the ingredients are between 75°F (24°C) and 85°F (30°C).

Sugar: Sugar provides food for the yeast and also adds flavor to the bread. Sugar also plays a part in browning the crust. If there is not very much sugar in the dough, the yeast will use it all in making carbon dioxide and alcohol, and the baked bread will not be golden brown. Too much sugar, however, retards the yeast's activity and the dough will take longer to rise.

Liquid: The moisture in the dough is supplied by water or milk, or a mixture of the two. It may be added cold; the ideal temperature, however, is a lukewarm 80°F (27°C) to 85°F (30°C). Test the milk on the inside of your wrist. Milk should be scalded (brought to just under the boiling point) and then cooled to lukewarm before being combined with flour. Scalding destroys certain bacteria which can sour the dough and also makes the dough easier to handle.

Salt: Salt should never be mixed directly with yeast because it slows down the fermentation process. But a sufficient amount of salt must be added to the dough or the bread will have an uninteresting flavor.

Eggs and butter or oil are variables. When eggs are added to dough, as in sweet breads or French *brioches*, the finished bread is richer and more yellow. Butter or oil increase the volume of the baked bread because the gluten network of the dough is lubricated so that it expands more smoothly and easily. Butter or oil also improves the flavor and keeping qualities of the bread.

Dissolving the yeast: Crumble fresh yeast into a small bowl. Using a fork cream a small amount of sugar with the yeast and then add a little lukewarm water 85°F (30°C). Mix to a paste and set aside in a warm, draft-free place to ferment. At the end of 15-20 minutes the yeast will be puffed up and frothy.

If you are using dried yeast, dissolve small quantity of sugar in lukewarm

To make bread, put the flour and salt into a warmed bowl. Make a well in the center and pour in the liquid ingredients.

Using your hands or a spatula, mix all the ingredients together until all of the flour is incorporated.

Turn the dough onto a floured board and knead it for about 10 minutes, or until it feels smooth and elastic.

Return the dough to the bowl, cover and leave it in a warm place for about 1 hour, or until it has doubled in bulk.

Turn onto the floured board again and punch down the dough to break up the air pockets. Knead for a further 5 minutes.

Form the dough into the shape required and arrange either in a loaf pan or on a greased baking sheet. Leave to rise again.

water 100°-110°F (38°-42°C) in a small mixing or cereal bowl and sprinkle on the yeast. Leave it for 10 minutes to allow the yeast cells to separate, swell and become active. It should double in volume. The yeast is now ready to begin its work as soon as it is added to the dough.

Mixing the dough: Put the dry ingredients – flour, salt and sugar – in a large, warmed bowl. Make a well in the center and pour in the liquid ingredients – dissolved yeast, milk and/or water, butter melted in the milk, or oil. Then, using your fingers or a spatula, gradually draw the dry ingredients into the liquids and continue mixing until all the flour is incorporated and the dough comes away from the side of the bowl. If the dough is too soft and wet, add more flour.

Kneading: Turn the dough out of the bowl onto a floured board or marble slab to knead. This will thoroughly mix the flour with the liquid. The kneaded dough will hold in the gas bubbles manufactured by the yeast. Fold the dough over onto itself towards you and then press it down away from yourself with the heels of your hands. Turn the dough slightly and fold and press it again. Continue kneading for about 5-10 minutes until the dough feels smooth and elastic. Dough made with hard-wheat flours requires a little more kneading than dough made with soft flour. If the dough feels sticky while you are kneading, you can work in a little more flour, but be careful not to add too much or the dough will become stiff.

Rising: Shape the kneaded dough into a ball and place it in a lightly greased bowl. Sprinkle the surface of the dough with a little flour and cover the bowl with a damp cloth. The flour prevents the dough from sticking to the cloth as it rises and the cloth is dampened to increase the humidity. Do not cover the bowl tightly because to grow the yeast needs air as well as moisture, warmth and food.

Place the bowl in a warm, draft-free place until the dough has almost doubled in bulk. Rising times vary greatly depending on room temperature, the amount of yeast in the dough and the kind of flour used; generally speaking 1-1½ hours is adequate. The longer the fermentation, the better-flavored and better-textured the bread will be. However, the dough should not be left to rise in a warm place for too long or it will become tough. You can tell if this is happening because a crust will form on the top of the dough. If you want to speed up the rising process, place the covered bowl on an oven rack over a pan of boiling water. But be sure that the bottom of the bowl is not too close to the water or the heat will kill the yeast.

To test if the dough has risen sufficiently, press two fingers deep into the dough and withdraw them quickly. If the indentations remain the dough has risen enough.

If you are preparing the dough the day before the bread is to be baked, you can prolong the rising process by putting the covered bowl in a cool place or in the refrigerator for 8-10 hours or overnight. When the dough is fully risen it will be lighter and more spongy than dough which has risen in a warm place. It will require more kneading the second time as well as a longer proving. This slow rising method will, however, produce an excellent bread which will keep well.

. **Second kneading:** Push your fist into the center of the dough and fold the edges to the center. This punching down breaks up the large gas pockets and makes available a new supply of oxygen for the yeast plants. Turn the dough out of the bowl onto the floured work surface. Knead it thoroughly and vigorously for 2-3 minutes (a larger batch of dough requires a longer kneading). This second kneading is more important than the first because it temporarily checks the action of the yeast. Use a sharp knife to cut the dough into the number of loaves you are baking. With your hands, shape these pieces into balls.

Proving: What you are proving is that the yeast is still active. To do this the balls of dough are put into greased pans and pulled out slightly so that they are roughly the shape of the pans. The pans should be only about half full. Sprinkle the surfaces of the loaves with a little flour. Cover the pans with a damp cloth and return them to a warm place for 45-60 minutes. During this time the dough will rise to the tops of the pans.

The proving may be done on an oven rack over a pan of boiling water, but be careful not to place the bottoms of the pans too close to the hot water. If you want your bread to have a shiny crust, instead of sprinkling the dough with flour, just before baking brush the tops of the loaves with a mixture of beaten eggs and milk. A country-style finish can be produced by making a crisscross gash in the top of the dough with a heated, sharp knife or kitchen scissors.

Baking: The bread must always be started in a hot oven. Therefore, preheat the oven to the correct temperature before the dough is put in to bake. Baking stops the fermentation of the yeast and evaporates the alcohol.

Place the pans in the center of the oven and bake for 15 minutes. In this initial stage the loaf rises dramatically, because the leavening gas is expanding rapidly and the gluten cells are stretching to accommodate it. Transfer the pans to a lower

To make the golden crust on this white household bread, brush with egg yolk and milk.

shelf and reduce the oven heat. The gluten cells will gradually be set by the heat, and after 25-30 minutes the bread should be done, having shrunk slightly in the pans.

To increase the crustiness of the loaves, brush the tops with lightly beaten egg white or cold water 10 minutes before the end of the baking time. For a soft crust, brush the tops with melted butter 10 minutes before the baking time is completed.

Remove the pans from the oven and turn the bread out, upside-down, onto a wire rack. Rap the bottoms of the loaves with your knuckles. If they sound hollow, like a drum, the bread is cooked. If they feel soft, return them, upside-down, to the oven with the heat reduced and bake for a further 10-15 minutes.

A shiny, glazed crust, characteristic of French and Vienna bread or rolls, can be obtained by placing a flat pan of boiling water in the bottom of the oven just before the bread is put in, and leaving it in the oven throughout the baking. The steam from the water forms a coating of moisture on the surface of the dough, which gives it time to expand and develop a crust.

Cooling: Bread should be cooled on a wire rack so that the air can circulate around it and prevent moisture from spoiling the crispness of the crust.

Household Bread

This is the white bread most often seen in European shops. But like anything homemade, it certainly looks and tastes better. Bake the bread in different containers, or shape the dough into individual braids, rolls, long French-style loaves or round Italian-style loaves.

Makes four 1 *pound* (450 *gram*) *loaves*

2 teaspoons butter
1 oz (25 g) fresh yeast or $\frac{1}{2}$ oz (15 g) dry yeast
1$\frac{1}{2}$ tablespoons plus 1 teaspoon sugar
3 cups (625 ml) plus 4 teaspoons lukewarm water
12 cups (1$\frac{1}{4}$ kg) flour
1 tablespoon salt

Grease the loaf pans with the butter. Crumble the fresh yeast into a small bowl and mash in 1 teaspoon of sugar. Add teaspoons of water and cream the water and yeast together to form a smooth paste. Set the bowl aside in a warm, draft-free place for 15-20 minutes, or until the yeast has risen and is puffed up and frothy.

1½ teaspoons butter
1 oz (25 g) fresh yeast or ½ oz (15 g)
dry yeast
1 teaspoon brown sugar
3 cups (625 ml) plus 4 teaspoons
lukewarm water
12 cups (1¼ kg) stone-ground
wholewheat flour
1¼ tablespoons rock salt or 1
tablespoon table salt
3 tablespoons clear honey
1 tablespoon vegetable oil

To bake the bread, follow the directions
given under Household Bread.

Standard White Bread

This is a smooth-textured, pleasant-
tasting milk bread. It has a shiny, golden-
brown crust and is excellent for sand-
wiches. This dough recipe can also be
used successfully as a base for fruit or nut
loaves. For a fruit loaf, during the second
kneading add either 1 cup (150 grams)
of raisins or dates; for a nut loaf, 1 cup
(150 grams) of chopped walnuts, hazelnuts, filberts or almonds. For a fruit and
nut loaf, add 1 cup (150 grams) of dried
fruit and ½ cup (75 grams) of chopped
walnuts, hazelnuts, filberts or almonds.
Makes one 1 pound (450 gram) loaf

4 tablespoons (50 g) plus ½ teaspoon
butter
½ oz (15 g) fresh yeast or 1 package
dry yeast
1½ tablespoons plus 1 teaspoon sugar
3 teaspoons lukewarm water
1¼ cups (300 ml) milk
4 cups (450 g) flour
1 teaspoon salt
Glaze:
1 egg lightly beaten with 1
tablespoons milk

To bake the bread, follow the directions
for making Household Bread. In addition,
scald the milk, add the butter to it and,
when it has melted, cool to lukewarm.
The second kneading should last only
4 minutes.

Pastry

Pastry is an unleavened dough, generally
made from shortening, flour and liquid,
which is rolled out and used to line pie
plates and tart pans and envelop or cover
sweet and savory fillings. The eight basic
pastries are: shortcrust, rich shortcrust,

Put the flour, the remaining sugar and
the salt into a warmed, large mixing bowl.
Make a well in the center of the flour
mixture and pour in the yeast and the
remaining lukewarm water. Gradually
draw the flour into the liquid. Continue
mixing until all the flour is incorporated
and the dough comes away from the side
of the bowl.

Turn the dough out onto a floured
board or marble slab and knead for about
10 minutes, reflouring the surface if the
dough becomes sticky. The dough should
then be elastic and smooth. Rinse,
thoroughly dry and lightly grease the
large mixing bowl. Shape the dough into
a ball and return it to the bowl. Dust the
top of dough with a little flour and cover
the bowl with a clean, damp cloth. Set the
bowl in a warm, draft-free place and leave
it for 1-1½ hours, or until the dough has
risen and has almost doubled in bulk.

Turn the risen dough out of the bowl
onto a floured surface and knead for about
8-10 minutes. Using a sharp knife, cut the
dough into four pieces and roll and shape
each piece into a loaf. Place the loaves in
the pans, cover with a damp cloth and
return to a warm place for about 30-45
minutes, or until the dough has risen to
the top of the pans.

*You can make wholewheat bread this shape
by baking it in a clay flowerpot.*

Preheat the oven to 475°F (240°C).
Place the pans in the center of the oven and
bake for 15 minutes. Then lower the
temperature to 425°F (220°C), put the
bread on a lower shelf in the oven and
bake for another 25-30 minutes.

After removing the bread from the
oven, tip the loaves out of the pans and
rap the undersides with your knuckles. If
they do not sound hollow, lower the oven
temperature to 375°F (190°C), return the
loaves, upside-down, to the oven and
bake for a further 5-10 minutes.

Cool the loaves on a wire rack.

Wholewheat Bread

Although it is most delicious when freshly
baked and spread with butter, honey or
cheese, stored correctly this bread keeps
extremely well for up to a week after
baking. For variation, the loaves may be
baked in well-greased clay flowerpots, or
shaped into cottage loaves on a baking
sheet. To make cheese bread, add 3 cups
(350 grams) of finely grated Cheddar
or any similar cheese to the flour with the
yeast mixture.
Makes four 1 pound (450 gram) loaves

puff, rough puff, flaky, suetcrust, hot water crust and choux.

The basic ingredients used to make pastry are:

Flour: In almost every kind of dough, all-purpose white wheat flour is used. Self-raising flour is used only when a heavier ingredient such as suet is incorporated.

Salt: In most doughs, salt is added in amounts varying from $\frac{1}{8}$ teaspoon to 1 teaspoon.

Sugar: Sugar is added to sweet pastry doughs.

Shortening: All dough includes shortening (a general term that comprises all fats) in proportions which vary according to the richness of the pastry – the more shortening, the richer the dough. Generally, butter is used, but margarine, suet, lard, vegetable fat or oil, or a combination of shortenings can also be used.

Liquid: A small amount of liquid is added to the flour and shortening mixture to bind it and make it more pliable. Water is most commonly used, but other liquids such as eggs, milk, cream, sour cream and buttermilk may be used.

Flavorings: Cheese, herbs, spices and essences may be added to the basic pastry dough.

Yeast: In some doughs, such as that used for making Danish pastries, yeast is used.

Techniques

The method by which shortening is incorporated into flour determines the texture of finished pastry. In puff, rough puff and flaky pastry, the shortening, generally butter, is added either in one large or several smaller pieces, and rolled and folded into the flour and liquid mixture. The resulting texture is, as the names of the pastries imply, light and flaky. For closer-textured pastries, such as shortcrust, the shortening is cut into small pieces and rubbed into the flour with the fingertips until the mixture resembles fine or coarse breadcrumbs. For even closer-textured pastry doughs, such as choux or hot water crust, the shortening is melted with the liquid and then stirred or beaten into the flour. The eggs in choux pastry open out the texture.

The basic points to remember when making pastry dough are:

1. Unless the dough is made with yeast

126

or cooked, the ingredients and implements should be kept cool.

2. For some pastry doughs, such as puff, the ingredients should also be chilled.

3. Again with the exception of yeast and cooked doughs, a minimum of handling is desirable. When possible, use a table knife or pastry blender to incorporate the shortening into the flour. When rubbing the shortening into the flour, use your fingertips and work quickly and lightly. The more you handle the dough, the stickier and less manageable it becomes.

4. When rolling out dough place it on a lightly floured working surface and use a floured rolling pin. Make sure that the dough does not stick to the surface as it is rolled out. Roll the dough lightly and evenly away from you. Do not turn the dough over or it will absorb too much flour from the working surface. If the dough is sticky or contains a high proportion of shortening, chill it in the refrigerator before rolling it out to make the handling easier.

5. Generally speaking, pastry should be baked, or at least start its baking time, in a hot oven. Long, slow baking produces hard, flat-tasting pastry.

6. Closer-textured pastry dough, such as shortcrust and rich shortcrust, are more suitable for lining quiches and pie plates and for baking blind (see p. 128). All types of pastry doughs are suitable for covering pies and enveloping sweet or savory fillings.

If you have a freezer, it is well worth your while to make extra dough and freeze it. Wrap it in suitable quantities, for example 1-cup (for single-crust pies) and 2-cup (double-crust) blocks. Remember to remove the dough from the freezer at least 30 minutes before using so that it can thaw out thoroughly. Tarts and pie shells can also be frozen. It is best to freeze the pastry dough uncooked. If the pie has a cooked filling, such as steak and kidney, this should be cooked and cooled before covering with the pastry dough.

When a recipe calls for 1 cup (225 grams) of pastry, it means that that much flour should be used.

Preparing a double-crust pie
Divide the pastry dough into two portions, one slightly larger than the other. Roll out the larger portion to a little less than $\frac{1}{4}$ inch ($\frac{1}{2}$ centimeter) and about

1 inch ($2\frac{1}{2}$ centimeters) wider than the inverted pie plate.

Lift the dough on the rolling pin and place over the pie plate. Lift up the outside of the dough with one hand and press it gently to the sides of the pie plate with the other, taking care not to stretch the dough. Put the prepared filling into the plate, making a slight mound in the center.

Roll out the smaller portion of the pastry to about $\frac{1}{2}$ inch (1 centimeter) larger than the dish. Brush the rim of the dough lining with water, lift the dough lid on the rolling pin and place over the filling. Trim the edges and crimp (see below). Make a small slit in the center of the dough to allow steam to escape during cooking.

Preparing a single-crust pie
Roll out the dough $\frac{1}{4}$ inch ($\frac{1}{2}$ centimeter) thick and 4 inches wider than the pie plate. Lift the dough onto the rolling pin and cover the base and sides of the plate. Trim to $\frac{1}{2}$ inch from the plate edge and fold the dough under to give the edge a double thickness.

For a straight-sided flan ring, which either has a loose bottom or is placed on a baking sheet, do lining in the same manner as for a pie plate. The easiest way to remove excess dough at the edges is to roll the rolling pin across the flan ring, first away from you and then back toward you. Gradually manipulate the dough to smooth out any air bubbles. Repair any holes or cracks, using pieces of leftover dough as patching material. Because of the straight sides take extra care that the dough is not pulled up, for stretching causes the dough to contract and slide downward during baking.

To line a fluted quiche pan, press the dough into the shape of the pan, then take off any surplus by running a rolling pin over the top.

Just before baking run your thumb nail between the edge of the pan and the dough. This will ensure that the quiche slips out easily after baking.

Covering a pie plate
Roll out the dough evenly to about $\frac{1}{4}$ inch ($\frac{1}{2}$ centimeter) thick, and 4 inches (1 centimeters) wider than the pie plate. Place the pie plate upside-down on the dough to check for width. Cut a 1-inch ($2\frac{1}{2}$ centimeter) wide strip from the outer edge of the dough, place it on the moist

To make pastry roses, make slits, about 1 in (2½ cm) apart, along a strip of dough.

Starting at one end, roll the dough strip up, holding the base firmly.

Using your fingers, pull out the cut dough edges to form petals.

To make leaves, roll out dough trimmings and cut strips about 1 in (2½ cm) wide.

Cut diagonally across the dough strips making diamond patterns.

Now, using a pointed knife, mark veins on the dough leaf.

To decorate the edges, make slits around the rim, then fold back to make a triangle.

Hold the rim and, with the back of a knife, make indentations along the edge.

Press your thumb on the rim and mark crimps around the edge with two fingers.

ened rim of the plate, and seal the ends together with a little water. Brush the entire strip with water.

Fill the pie plate to just below the rim of the dish and smooth over the surface. Lift the dough circle onto the rolling pin and place it over the pie plate, taking care not to stretch it. Then press the lid to the rim. Cut off any excess dough.

Lining tart molds

Place the molds closely together on a baking sheet. Roll out the dough until it is thin and large enough to cover the whole area of the tart molds. Lift the dough on the rolling pin and cover the molds. Press the dough into the molds, then take off the surplus with a rolling pin. The molds should now be baked.

Finishing the crust

Crust edges can be finished by fluting or by crimping with a knife. To flute place middle finger of left hand on rim and

Jam tarts – a beautiful, yet simple, dessert, is usually made by filling pre-baked tart shells or molds with delicious fruit jams, which can be either commercially bought or homemade.

press out, while first two fingers of right hand push in on either side. Repeat this around the rim. Two-crust pies can also be sealed by using the back of a knife to make a series of shallow horizontal dents around the crust rim. This causes the crust to expand when baked. Sometimes the knife is held vertically and pressed into the dough at one inch intervals to give a scalloped appearance.

Pastry glazes

Dough is usually glazed with beaten egg yolk, lightly beaten egg white, egg white and sugar or whole beaten egg. Of these, egg yolk usually produces the glossiest finish. Brush the glaze on before baking. Sweet dough can be brushed lightly with water and then sprinkled with sugar for a

pretty sparkling effect. Milk or a mixture of milk and sugar is also a successful glaze, although the result is not as shiny as egg yolk.

Baking a pie shell

Pastry crust is sometimes baked before being filled, in Europe this is called "baking blind". Pie shells and individual tarts are frequently baked in this way.

Preheat the oven to 400°F (200°C). Prick the base of the pie shell all over with a fork. Line the pie crust with aluminum foil or waxed paper and half fill it with dried beans or rice to keep sides in place. Put the pie plate in the oven and bake for 5 minutes. Remove the beans or rice and foil or paper, and bake for 5–10 minutes more, or until the crust is crisp and golden brown. Remove the pie crust from the oven and allow it to cool. The crust is now ready to be filled.

(The beans or rice can be stored in a jar and used again. They will keep for several months.)

Shortcrust Pastry

This is the basic shortcrust pastry used for making sweet or savory pies and tarts.
For one 2-crust 8-9 inch pie

2 cups (225 g) flour
Pinch salt
4 tablespoons (50 g) butter
4 tablespoons (50 g) vegetable fat
5-6 tablespoons iced water

Sift the flour and salt into a medium-sized mixing bowl. Add the butter and vegetable fat and cut them into the flour with a table knife until they form pea-sized globules. Then with your fingertips, rub the fat into the flour until the mixture resembles coarse breadcrumbs.

Sprinkle on 4½ tablespoons of the iced water and, using the knife, mix it lightly into the flour mixture. Mix and knead the dough two or three times or until it is smooth. Sprinkle on more water if the dough is too dry. Form the dough into a ball, wrap it in waxed paper and place in the refrigerator for 30 minutes to chill.

Rich Shortcrust Pastry

Use this pastry as a crust for rich or sweet fillings.
For one 2-crust 8-inch pie

1½ cups (175 g) flour
Pinch salt
6 tablespoons (75 g) butter, chilled
1½ tablespoons sugar
1 egg, lightly beaten
1½-3 tablespoons iced water

Sift the flour and salt into a medium-sized mixing bowl. Add the butter and cut into small pieces. Rub the butter into the flour until the mixture resembles fine breadcrumbs. Mix in the sugar.

Add the beaten egg with a spoonful of iced water and mix it into the flour mixture with a spatula. Add more water if the dough is too dry.

Knead the dough gently and form it into a ball. Wrap it in waxed paper and place it in the refrigerator for 30 minutes to chill.

Puff Pastry

This pastry is generally considered to be the best of all the basic pastries in flavor and texture, and the most difficult to make. It should be made with only the finest ingredients: the flour should be of good quality and the butter unsalted. The amount of water given in the recipe ingredients is only approximate, since different brands of flour may absorb more or less water. The object in making puff pastry is to produce thin layers of dough

To make puff pastry, lightly knead the dough with your hands to make it smooth and pliable.

Beat the remaining butter into an oblong. Roll the dough out and place the butter in the center of the dough.

Fold the four sides of the dough over the butter to enclose it completely, making a neat package.

Place the package, with the folds facing downwards, on the working surface and roll it out away from you.

Now carefully fold the rolled dough into three and then turn it so that the open end is facing you.

Now roll the dough out again into an oblong, fold it as before and chill it in the refrigerator.

interspersed with thin layers of butter. When the dough is cooked, the butter is absorbed by the starch particles when they burst, and the result is a pastry of light horizontal flakes which melt in the mouth.

Puff pastry is used for making patty shells, Napoleons, vols-au-vents and small sweet or savory pastries.

When making puff pastry, it is important that the consistency of the dough and the slab of butter should be the same, that is, pliable but not sticky.

When rolling out the dough use an even pressure, avoid stretching the dough and keep the thicknesses of the dough the same all over. Do not use too much flour to prevent the dough from sticking to the working surface or rolling pin, otherwise the proportions of flour to butter will be altered and produce a less satisfactory pastry.

Once the rolling and folding processes have been completed, the puff pastry dough can be covered and chilled in the frigerator before it is needed so that it can Remember to remove it from the refrigerator before it is needed so that it can become pliable and easy to roll into the required shape. Puff pastry may also be frozen for up to 3 months. If you are freezing puff pastry, pack it in 2-cup (225 gram) or 4-cup (450 gram) portions.

If large quantities of pastry are required it is best to make two batches of 4 cups (450 grams) each.

Makes ten 3½-inch patty shells

4 cups (450 g) flour
½ teaspoon salt
2 cups (450 g) butter
1 cup (225 ml) iced water

Sift the flour and salt into a large mixing bowl. With a table knife, cut ½ cup (125 grams) of the butter into the flour. Rub the butter and flour together and mix to a firm dough with the water. Knead the dough to make it pliable and form it into a ball. Cover with waxed paper and place the dough in the refrigerator to chill for 15 minutes.

Put the remaining butter between two pieces of waxed paper and beat it with the back of a wooden spoon or a wooden mallet into a flat oblong slab about ¾ inch (2 centimeters) thick.

On a floured board, roll out the dough into a rectangular shape ¼ inch (½ centimeter) thick. Place the slab of butter in the center of the dough and fold the

130

dough over it to make a package. Place the dough in the refrigerator to chill for a further 10 minutes.

Place the dough, with the folds downwards, on the board and roll out away from you into a rectangle. Fold the rectangle in three. Turn so that the open end is facing you and roll out again. Chill the dough in the refrigerator for 15 minutes. Then repeat this process twice more.

The dough is now ready for use.

Rough Puff Pastry

A rich pastry which is easy and quick to make, Rough Puff Pastry does not rise as well as puff pastry. It is used, therefore, mainly for pie crusts and turnovers.
Makes one 2-crust 8-10 inch pie

2 cups (225 g) flour
½ teaspoon salt
¾ cup (175 g) butter
6-8 tablespoons iced water

Sift the flour and salt into a medium-sized mixing bowl. Add the butter and work into the other ingredients with a table knife. Pour in 6 tablespoons of the iced water and mix quickly with a knife to form a dough, which should be lumpy. Add a little more of the water if the dough looks too dry.

Shape the dough into a ball and place it on a lightly floured working surface. Using a floured rolling pin, roll out the dough into an oblong.

Fold the dough in three, turning it so that the open end faces you. Roll out the dough again into an oblong shape and fold it in three.

Repeat the rolling and folding process.

Wrap the dough in sheets of waxed paper and chill it in the refrigerator for 30 minutes. Remove the dough from the refrigerator. If it looks streaky, roll it out and fold it once more. The dough is now ready to use.

Flaky Pastry

A light, buttery pastry, Flaky Pastry is most often used for mince-meat or fruit pies.
Makes one 2-crust 8-inch pie

1½ cups (175 g) flour
Pinch salt
4 tablespoons (50 g) butter
4 tablespoons (50 g) vegetable fat or lard
4½-5 tablespoons cold water

Sift the flour into a mixing bowl and add the salt. Divide the butter into two equal pieces and add one piece to the flour. Rub the fat into the flour until it resembles fine breadcrumbs. With a spatula mix in the water to form a firm dough.

Put the dough on a floured board and shape it into a square. Roll out the dough into an oblong and dot two-thirds of it with small pieces of half the fat. Fold over one-third of the dough and then the other third to make a neat, square. Press the edges with the rolling-pin to seal.

Turn the dough around so that the sealed ends are facing you and roll out again into an oblong. Dot with pieces of the remaining fat, fold in three, seal the edges, turn the dough and roll out again.

Repeat this process with the remaining butter. Wrap the dough in waxed paper and place it in the refrigerator for 10 minutes to chill.

Suetcrust Pastry

A simple-to-make pastry (much more common in European cooking), Suetcrust Pastry may be used in sweet or savory steamed layer dishes or as a pastry container for steamed meat puddings. The dough may also be shaped into small balls and cooked in stock to make dumplings.
For one 7-inch steamed pudding

2 cups (225 g) self-rising flour
Pinch salt
½ cup (125 g) shredded suet
¾ cup (150 ml) cold water

Sift the flour and salt into a medium-sized mixing bowl. Stir the suet and water into the flour mixture to form a firm dough. Form the dough into a ball and wrap it in a sheet of waxed paper. Place the dough in the refrigerator to chill for 10 minutes.

Hot Water Crust Pastry

This is the traditional pastry for Old World raised pies made with meats such as pork, veal, ham and game pies.

It is important to note that this pastry be made as quickly as possible, otherwise the fat may solidify.
For one deep 6-7 inch pie

3 cups (350 g) flour
1 teaspoon salt
¾ cup (150 ml) water
½ cup (125 g) vegetable fat or lard
1 egg yolk, lightly beaten

To make a pie case for a raised pie, mold the warm dough around the outside of a lightly greased glass storage jar.

Tie a band of waxed paper around the dough to support it. Place on a baking sheet and spoon in the desired filling.

Dampen the edges of the dough case, fit a dough lid on top to cover completely and, finally, crimp to seal the edges.

Sift the flour and salt into a large mixing bowl.

In a small saucepan, bring the water and vegetable fat or lard to a boil over high heat, stirring frequently until the fat or lard has melted. Remove the pan from the heat.

Make a well in the center of the bowl. Pour in the fat and water mixture and the beaten egg. With a wooden spoon stir the mixture around gently. Let flour wash slowly in from the sides. The mixture will not get lumpy if you keep it thick, and the dough will be smooth.

Turn the dough out onto a floured board and knead it well with your hands until it is shiny.

Roll out the dough into the required shape and use at once.

Choux Pastry

This special light pastry, commonly called 'puff pastry' in the U.S., is used almost exclusively for éclairs and cream puffs, but it is also used in classic French desserts such as Gâteau St. Honoré. French in origin, it is named *choux* because it puffs up during the baking process and sets in the shape of a cabbage. *Makes 10 ounces (275 grams)*

1¼ cups (300 ml) water
6 tablespoons (75 g) butter, cut into small pieces
1 teaspoon salt
2½ cups (275 g) flour
5 extra-large eggs

In a heavy saucepan, bring the water to a boil. Add the butter, and salt. When the butter has melted, remove the pan from the heat and beat in the flour. Continue beating until the mixture pulls away from the sides of the pan.

One by one, beat each egg into the dough until it is well blended, then the

To make pastry for choux puffs, beat the flour into the warm water, melted butter, salt and flavoring.

One by one, beat the eggs into the dough, beating well until the mixture is thick, smooth and glossy.

Fill a piping bag with the mixture and pipe the dough onto greased baking sheets, well apart, in circular mounds.

next. When the eggs have all been completely absorbed, the mixture should be thick and somewhat glossy.

The dough is now ready for use.

Cakes

Cakes seem to come in an infinite number of varieties, but they fall into definite groups or categories. If you look closely at the recipes you will discover not only the

two most common kinds: creamed butter and sugar and beaten eggs (whole or separated), but also rubbed-in fat, melted fat and yeast. The last three are more common in European baking.

Cake making

For the best results when making cakes have all the ingredients at room temperature (about 70°F [21°C]). Preheat the oven to the specified temperature. If the oven is too cool when you put the cake in, the finished cake will have a heavy texture.

Use the correct size tin or pan as specified in the recipe. If the pan is too large, the cake will be thin and heavy. If it is too small, the mixture may overflow as it rises and the cake's texture will be coarse.

Grease and flour the pan before you begin to mix the cake batter.

To prepare the pan, spread only a thin film of lard, oil or butter over the sides and bottom. Sprinkle in a little flour and tip and rotate the pan to distribute the flour evenly. Shake out any excess by turning the pan upside-down and gently knocking on the bottom. Sometimes sugar is added with the flour. This gives a crisper, crunchier crust, which is especially good on plain cakes.

If the cake requires a long baking, the pan should be greased and then lined with buttered greaseproof or waxed paper. For a rich fruit cake, tie a band of brown paper around the outside of the pan as well.

If the recipe specifies cake flour, do not substitute self-rising, because the texture will be too open and the cake will rise too much. If self-rising flour is called for but not available use plain flour with baking powder in the proportion of 1 level teaspoon baking powder to 1 cup (450 grams) cake flour. Flour should always be sifted before use to remove lumps and aerate the flour.

Measure the ingredients carefully and blend them together thoroughly. Do not beat the batter after the flour has been added or the cake will be heavy.

Folding

Many recipes indicate that the flour, eggs or another ingredient should be folded in. This gentle method keeps a maximum amount of air in the cake batter, which leads to better rising.

Every cook should master the folding technique, which consists of two basic steps. First, cut across the center of the mixture with a large metal spoon. Second, run the spoon around the perimeter of the bowl, ending with a folding motion towards the center. Give the bowl a quarter-turn. Repeat these two steps until almost all the substance is incorporated (break up and incorporate the last bits as you pour the batter into the cake pan).

Be sure to get your spoon right down to the bottom of the bowl so that no large pockets of batter or flour remain unincorporated. Be gentle, delicate and even slow in all your motions. For a tender, light cake try to keep the number of folds to eight or ten.

Fill the cake pan only one-half to two-thirds full of batter.

Place the pan in the center of the oven so the heat can circulate around it. In general, small cakes should be baked near the top of the oven, and large cakes in the middle of the oven.

Bake the cake for the length of time specified in the recipe. Before removing it from the oven, test it to be sure that it is done. If not, continue baking for 5 minutes and test again.

To test if the cake is completely baked, insert a metal skewer or thin knife into the center of the cake. If it comes out clean, the cake is done. Alternatively, lightly press the top of the cake with a fingertip. The cake will spring back if it is cooked. The cake should also have pulled away slightly from the edges of the pan.

As soon as the baking is completed, remove the cake from the oven and let it stand for a few minutes. Then loosen the sides by running a knife between the cake and sides of the pan (unless the pan has a non-stick finish). Place a clean cloth over the top and turn the cake out on to the cloth. Then transfer it to a wire cake rack (place the rack, inverted, on the bottom of the cake and turn it over). The cloth will prevent the top of the cake from being marked by the rack.

If the cake is to be iced or frosted, wait until it has cooled to room temperature.

Methods of cake-making

Creaming butter and sugar

This method is used for richer cake when the margarine or butter is creamed together with sugar, using a wooden spoon or an electric mixer. The mixtur should be beaten until it is light and fluffy, because this incorporates air and dissolves the sugar crystals.

The eggs are then beaten in, one at a time, and the flour is folded into the mixture. If the mixture starts to curdle when the eggs are added, beat in a spoonful of the measured flour as given in the recipe.

The creaming method is widely used and is the basis for many popular cakes. Surprisingly, it is also the basis for most fruit cakes. But perhaps the most popular form of creamed cake in America is Devil's Food Cake. Topped and filled with Chocolate Fudge Frosting this cake becomes an irresistible dessert and a splendid finale to any meal.

Devil's Food Cake

4 oz (125 g) semisweet cooking chocolate
1 cup (225 ml) mild chocolate
1 cup (225 g) light brown sugar
3 egg yolks
2½ cups (275 g) cake flour, sifted
1 teaspoon baking soda
⅛ teaspoon salt
½ cup (125 g), plus 2 tablespoons butter
¾ cup (175 g) sugar
¼ cup (50 ml) water
1 teaspoon vanilla extract
2 egg whites
CHOCOLATE FUDGE FROSTING
1 cup (225 ml) light cream
2 cups (450 g) sugar
⅛ teaspoon salt
2 oz (50 g) semisweet cooking chocolate, grated
3 tablespoons butter
¼ teaspoon vanilla extract
⅔ cup (50 g) walnuts, chopped

Preheat the oven to moderate 350°F (180°C). Put the chocolate, milk, brown sugar and one egg yolk in the top part of a double boiler or a bowl placed over a saucepan of hot water. Place the pan over low heat and cook the mixture, stirring constantly with a wooden spoon, until the chocolate melts and the mixture thickens slightly. Remove the pan from the heat and set aside.

Resift the flour with the soda and salt into a medium-sized bowl. Set aside.

Put the ½ cup of butter into a second bowl and cream it with a wooden spoon. Gradually add the sugar, beating constantly. Beat until the butter is light and fluffy. Add the remaining egg yolks one at a time, beating well after each addition.

Lightly mix in one-third of the flour mixture and water and beat well until the batter is smooth. Stir in the vanilla essence. Stirring the batter constantly, add the chocolate mixture.

In a medium-sized mixing bowl, beat the egg whites with a wire whisk or rotary beater until they form stiff peaks.

With a metal spoon, lightly fold the beaten egg whites into the batter.

With half the remaining butter, grease three shallow 8-inch (20 cm) cake pans. Cut three waxed paper circles the same size as the pans and grease them with the remaining butter. Pour the batter into the pans, dividing it equally between them.

Place the pans in the oven and bake for 25 minutes, or until a knife plunged into the center of one cake comes out clean.

Remove the pans from the oven. Loosen the cakes with a knife and turn them out onto a wire rack to cool.

To make the frosting, in a medium-sized, heavy saucepan, bring the cream to a boil over moderate heat. Remove the pan from the heat and stir in the sugar, salt and grated chocolate. Return the pan to the heat and stir to melt the chocolate. Cover the pan and cook the mixture for 3 minutes. Do not stir. Uncover the pan, reduce the heat to low and cook until the mixture reaches 238°F (115°C) on a sugar thermometer or until a teaspoon of the mixture dropped into iced water forms a soft ball.

Remove the pan from the heat and plunge it into a larger pan filled with cold water.

When the mixture has cooled to 110°F (52°C) or the bottom of the pan is cold enough to touch, beat in the butter and vanilla. Continue beating until the frosting thickens and reaches spreading consistency. Stir in the walnuts.

Sandwich the three cake layers together with three-quarters of the frosting and spread the remaining frosting over the top and sides. Using a spatula, or blunt knife, make swirling patterns on the surface of the cake. Leave the frosting to cool and then serve.

Beaten eggs

Cakes made by this method need not contain fat. The basic ingredients are eggs, sugar and flour. The beating of the eggs and sugar should be done with a wire whisk or electric mixer so that as much air is incorporated into the mixture as possible to produce a light, fluffy cake, such as angel cake. In these cakes air is the only leavening agent.

In some recipes the eggs are separated, and only the yolks are beaten with the sugar. The whites are beaten separately until stiff and folded into the sugar mixture along with the flour.

Beaten cakes should be eaten as soon as possible because the omission of fat in the recipe gives them a drier texture. If a sponge cake is to be kept for later use, the same method is used with the addition of melted butter or oil. The best known cake made with this method is called a Genoise Sponge.

Angel Cake

1 cup (225 g) flour
1½ cups (175 g) fine sugar
12 egg whites
1¼ teaspoons cream of tartar
¼ teaspoon salt
1 teaspoon vanilla extract

Preheat the oven to warm 325°F (170°C).

Sift the flour with one-third of the sugar 3 times.

Place the egg whites in a large mixing bowl and, using a wire whisk or electric beater, beat them until they are frothy.

Add the cream of tartar and salt and continue beating until the mixture forms soft peaks. Slowly beat in the remaining sugar. Then stir in the vanilla extract.

Using a metal spoon gradually fold the flour and sugar mixture into the egg whites. With a cutting movement fold the flour and sugar together until they are well blended.

Spoon the mixture into an ungreased 10-inch (25 cm) angel cake pan or ring mold. Bake for about 45 minutes or until firm. Place the pan, cake side down, onto a wire rack. Leave until cool.

Sponge Cake

This is a basic mixture with a high proportion of eggs and no fat, and the result is a very light cake. Serve, sandwiched with whipped cream and strawberry jam.

2 teaspoons butter
¾ cup (75 g) plus 2 teaspoons flour
3 eggs
⅜ cup (75 g) superfine sugar
½ teaspoon baking powder

Preheat oven to a moderate 350°F (180° C). With 1 teaspoon of the butter, grease two 7-inch (18-centimeter) shallow cake pans. Line the bottom of the pans with a circle of waxed paper and grease with the remaining butter. Sprinkle the 2 teaspoons of flour into the pans and tilt and rotate them until they are well-coated, discarding the excess. Set aside.

Place a large, heatproof mixing bowl over a large saucepan half-filled with boiling water. Place the eggs and sugar into the bowl and set the pan over low heat. Using a wire whisk or electric beater, beat the eggs and sugar together for about ten minutes or until the mixture is pale in color and thick, and will leave a ribbon trail on itself when the beater is lifted. Remove the pan from the heat and then remove the bowl from the pan. Continue to beat the mixture until it becomes cool.

Sift the remaining flour and baking powder onto the egg mixture and, using a large metal spoon, fold it in very carefully until the flour is thoroughly combined. Pour the batter into the prepared cake pans and place them in the center of the oven. Bake the cakes for 25-30 minutes or until the surface springs back when gently pressed with a fingertip.

Remove from the oven and turn the cakes onto a wire rack. Remove the waxed paper. Cool completely before serving.

Genoise Sponge
This is a classic French sponge which can be served plain, or filled and iced. The mixture is also used to make small shell-shaped **Madeleines** or cut up into small squares or oblongs and made into petit fours.

1 cup (225 g) plus 2 teaspoons unsalted butter, melted
2 cups (225 g) plus 3 tablespoons cake flour
1¼ cups (275 g) sugar
8 eggs, at room temperature
½ teaspoon vanilla extract
BUTTERCREAM
2 oz (50 g) semisweet chocolate, broken into pieces
¾ cup (175 g) unsalted butter
3 cups (350 g) confectioners' sugar
2 tablespoons heavy cream
½ teaspoon vanilla extract

Preheat the oven to fairly hot 375°F (190°C). Using the 2 teaspoons of butter, grease two 9-inch (23 centimeters) shallow cake pans. Dust them with 2 tablespoons of flour, tipping and rotating the pans so that they are evenly coated. Shake out any excess flour. Set aside.

Place a medium-sized heatproof mixing bowl over a large saucepan half-filled with hot water. Put the sugar, eggs and vanilla essence into the bowl and set the pan over low heat. With a wire whisk or electric beater, beat the mixture for 20-25 minutes, or until it is thick and pale and will make a ribbon trail on itself when the beater or whisk is lifted.

Remove the pan from the heat and the bowl from the pan. Sift in the remaining flour and, with a metal spoon, lightly fold it into the egg and sugar mixture. Gradually pour in the melted butter, stirring constantly. Pour equal amounts of the batter into each of the prepared cake pans. Place the pans in the center of the oven and bake for 20-30 minutes, or until the centers of the cakes spring back when lightly pressed with a fingertip.

Remove the pans from the oven and leave for 5 minutes. Then turn the cakes out onto a wire rack to cool completely.

Meanwhile, make the buttercream. Place the chocolate pieces in a small heatproof bowl set over a pan of simmering water. Place the pan over low heat and melt the chocolate, stirring occasionally. As soon as the chocolate has melted, remove the pan from the heat and set aside.

In a medium-sized mixing bowl, cream the butter with a wooden spoon until it is soft. Sift in half of the confectioners' sugar and beat until the mixture is light and fluffy. Add the cream, vanilla extract and the melted chocolate. Sift in the remaining sugar and blend the mixture thoroughly.

Cut the domed top off one of the cakes

and discard it. Spread the cake with one-quarter of the buttercream, and place the second cake on top, dome side up. Spread the remaining buttercream over the top and sides of the cake, bringing it up into decorative peaks.

Rubbing in

Plainer cakes, scones and biscuits are made by this method. Usually the proportion of fat is one-quarter to one-half of the flour or dry ingredients. The fat is rubbed into the flour until the mixture resembles fine breadcrumbs. Fruit and flavoring are added and then the liquid, generally egg and milk.

Shortbread

Shortbread is often formed into shapes in special shortbread molds. However, it may be shaped on a baking sheet.

1 cup (225 g) plus 1 teaspoon butter
2 cups (225 g) flour
1 cup (125 g) rice flour
½ cup (125 g) plus 1 tablespoon sugar

Using the teaspoon of butter, grease a large baking sheet and set aside.

Sift the flour and rice flour into a mixing bowl and stir in the ½ cup (125 grams) of sugar. Add the remaining butter and cut into small pieces with a knife. With your fingertips, rub the butter into the flour mixture until it resembles coarse breadcrumbs.

Knead the mixture gently until it forms a smooth dough. Turn the dough out onto a floured board and divide the dough in half. Form each piece into a circle about ¼ inch (1 centimeter) thick and 6 inches (15 centimeters) in diameter. Transfer the dough circles to the baking sheet, crimping the edges with your fingertips. Prick the top of the dough with a fork. Place the baking sheet in the refrigerator and chill the dough for 20 minutes.

Preheat the oven to moderate 350°F (180°C).

Place the baking sheet in the center of the oven and bake the shortbread for 10 minutes. Reduce the oven temperature to cool 300°F (150°C) and continue to bake the shortbread for a further 30-40 minutes or until it is crisp and lightly browned.

Remove the sheet from the oven and, with a knife, cut the circles into triangles. Allow to cool slightly on the baking sheet. Sprinkle the remaining tablespoon of sugar over the triangles. Transfer the

shortbread to a wire rack so that it can cool completely.

Store in an airtight tin if you do not intend to serve immediately.

Melting

This method makes moist cakes that keep well. The fat is melted with the sugar, syrup or molasses and then mixed into the dry ingredients. Most recipes use cake flour with the addition of bicarbonate of soda or baking powder as a raising agent. A better result is obtained if moist brown sugar is used, because this gives the cake a rich dark color and increases its keeping qualities.

Parkin

Parkin is a moist cake which should be kept for at least a week in an airtight tin before serving.

1 cup (225 g) plus 2 teaspoons butter
4 cups (450 g) flour
1 teaspoon baking soda
1 teaspoon salt
2 teaspoons ground ginger
6 cups (450 g) rolled oats
1 cup (250 ml) dark molasses
1 cup (250 ml) light corn syrup
¼ cup (50 ml) clear honey
3 tablespoons soft brown sugar
1½ cups (350 ml) milk

Preheat oven to warm 325°F (170°C).

Using the 2 teaspoons of butter, grease two 10-inch (25-centimeter) square cake pans. Line with non-stick silicone paper and set aside.

Sift the flour, soda, salt and ginger into a large mixing bowl. Add the rolled oats and stir well. Set aside.

In a medium-sized saucepan, melt the remaining butter with the molasses, syrup, honey and sugar over low heat. Cook the mixture, stirring constantly for 1 minute, or until all the ingredients are thoroughly combined. Remove the pan from the heat.

Make a well in the center of the flour mixture and pour in the butter and molasses mixture and the milk. Using a wooden spoon or spatula, gradually draw the flour mixture into the liquid.

Continue mixing until all the flour mixture is incorporated. Spoon the batter into the prepared baking pans and place them in the oven. Bake the parkins for 45–50 minutes, or until the cakes are firm when pressed with your fingertips.

Remove the pans from the oven and

baking sheet, well spaced to leave room for them to rise. Cover them with the cloth or plastic bag and place in a warm place to rise for another 30 minutes.

Brush the top with the sweetened egg and milk mixture and sprinkle with the sugar. Place the buns in the oven and bake for 25–30 minutes.

Serve when warm.

Finishing Touches

This section presents some methods to decorate both pastry and cakes. The simplest decorations are a dusting of confectioners' sugar, a little jam and whipped cream. But these are not suitable for all occasions, and numerous others have therefore evolved.

Icings, frostings and fillings

Icing or frostings are the thin coverings that go over the sides and tops of a cake. They can be either firm or soft. Frosting can also be used as a filling. Fillings go between the layers of a cake or into a pie shell. In general, they are soft. Toppings are usually passed separately and are added by the individual. Most, but not all, are thin enough to pour. Meringue is also a topping, though it fits none of these categories.

Glazes

The term 'glaze' is given both to a thin hot mixture of equal parts of water and sugar which is brushed over yeast cakes and buns to give them a shiny surface, and to a modified jam.

A jam glaze is used in various ways. It can be spread over a baked pie shell to prevent any sogginess. Painted over a fruit flan, it gives a shiny finish. Glaze is also used on the top and sides of cakes before icing to hold crumbs in place so they won't spoil the icing. Sometimes it forms a thin filling between layers.

Glazes are spread most easily with a brush – an ordinary 1 inch ($2\frac{1}{2}$ centimeter) brush works quite well.

Apricot jam and redcurrant jelly make the best glazes because they contain sufficient pectin to stiffen the glaze and prevent it from being sticky to the touch. The glaze should be applied while still hot; in the case of a fruit flan while the fruit is still warm. Apricot should be used for yellow and other light-colored fruits,

set the parkins aside to cool in the pan for 15 minutes before turning them out onto a wire rack to cool completely.

Yeast

Yeast cakes and buns are made in the same manner as yeast breads, though the dough is often sweetened more. They usually have a sweet filling, such as raisins and peel or a spice-flavored sugar and butter mixture, which is added before baking.

Bath buns

Makes 12 buns

$\frac{1}{3}$ cup (75 g) plus 1 teaspoon sugar
$\frac{3}{4}$ cup (150 ml) lukewarm milk
$\frac{1}{2}$ oz (15 g) fresh yeast or pkg dried
4 cups (450 g) flour
$\frac{1}{2}$ teaspoon salt
$\frac{1}{2}$ cup (125 g) butter
2 eggs, lightly beaten
$\frac{2}{3}$ cup (125 g) currants
$\frac{1}{4}$ cup (50 g) candied peel
$\frac{1}{2}$ egg, lightly beaten with 1 tablespoon milk and sweetened with 1 tablespoon sugar
$\frac{1}{4}$ cup (50 g) sugar

136

Bath buns – spicy buns made from yeast dough. Candied orange peel and currants are added for flavor.

In a small mixing bowl, dissolve 1 teaspoon of sugar in the warm milk. Crumble the yeast on top and mix well. Leave the milk-and-yeast mixture in a warm place for 15–20 minutes or until it becomes frothy.

Sift the flour and salt into a warm mixing bowl and mix in the remaining sugar. With your fingertips, rub the butter into the flour mixture. Make a well in the center of the flour mixture and pour in the frothy yeast and the beaten eggs. Mix in with a fork and then, using well-floured hands, knead lightly to make a soft dough.

Put the dough in a greased bowl, cover with a cloth or a plastic bag and place in a warm place for 1 hour, or until the dough has doubled in bulk. Turn the dough onto a floured board and knead in the currants and candied peel.

Preheat the oven to a hot 375°F (190°C). Lightly grease a baking sheet.

Divide the dough into 12 pieces and shape into buns. Place the buns on the redcurrant is the most suitable for red and other dark-colored fruits.

Jam Glaze

⅜ cup (125 g) apricot jam or redcurrant jelly
1½ tablespoons water
1 teaspoon lemon juice

With a wooden spoon, press the apricot jam or redcurrant jelly through a strainer into a saucepan.

Add the water and lemon juice. Cook, stirring constantly, for 2-3 minutes, or until the glaze is thick and sticky. Remove the pan from the heat and use the glaze while it is still hot.

Icings

Firm icings are still warm when they are put on cakes; they harden as they cool. An uncooked glacé icing calls for 1½-2 cups (175-225 grams) confectioners' sugar mixed with 3 tablespoons of very hot water, plus flavorings and coloring (if used). Cooked glacé icing is more interesting.

Glacé Icing

Glacé icing is the simplest, quickest type of cooked icing to make and is ideal for topping a plain sponge cake. If you like, add ¼ teaspoon of vanilla or coffee extract at the same time as the syrup. Orange or lemon icing can be made by adding the grated rinds of 2 oranges or 2 lemons to the sugar syrup before it boils.
Makes about 2½ cups (600 milliliters)

2 cups (450 g) sugar
1¼ cups (300 ml) water
2 cups (225 g) confectioners' sugar

In a medium-sized saucepan, dissolve the sugar in the water over low heat, stirring constantly. Increase the heat to moderate, cover the pan and bring the syrup to the boil. Continue boiling until the syrup registers 215°F (105°C) to 220°F (120°C) on a sugar or candy thermometer (about 1 minute), or until a small amount removed from the pan and cooled will form a short thread between your thumb and index finger. Remove the pan from the heat and allow the syrup to cool slightly.

Place the confectioners' sugar in a medium-sized bowl. With a wooden spoon, gradually beat in the syrup. Continue beating until the icing is thick and smooth. Place the bowl over a pan of

simmering water and stir until the icing is warm and of a spreading consistency.

Pour the icing onto the center of the cake and spread it out quickly with a knife dipped in hot water.

Chocolate glacé icing can be made by replacing ¼ cup (25 grams) of the confectioners' sugar with cocoa.

Chocolate Icing

Makes enough for a 9-inch (23-centimeter) cake, top and sides

8 oz (225 g) semisweet chocolate broken into pieces
½ cup (125 g) heavy cream
3 cups (350 g) confectioners' sugar

In a heatproof bowl set over a pan of simmering water, melt the chocolate over low heat. Remove the pan from the heat and remove the bowl from the pan. Set aside to cool for 10 minutes. Beat in the cream and confectioners' sugar, beating until the mixture is smooth. Spread the

To make glacé icing, sift the confectioners' sugar through a fine strainer into a bowl.

Beat the mixture vigorously for 3 minutes until it is shiny and smooth.

icing over the top and sides of the cake using a wide, blunt knife. Be sure that the icing stays smooth as it is spread.

Set the cake aside in a cool place for 2 hours, or until the icing has set.

Buttercream Icing

Buttercream frosting is probably the most versatile of the soft toppings, since numerous flavors can be added.
Makes enough to fill and ice one 9-inch (23 centimeter) cake

6 tablespoons (75 g) unsalted butter, at room temperature
3 cups (350 g) confectioners' sugar, sifted
½ teaspoon salt
1½ teaspoons vanilla extract
2 tablespoons heavy cream or milk

Place the butter in a large mixing bowl and, with the back of a wooden spoon or an electric mixer, cream it. When it is smooth, gradually add half of the sugar

Gradually beat in warm water or any flavoring or color to be added.

Now pour the icing on top of the cake and spread evenly with a spatula.

To make powdered sugar decoration on a cake, place a doily on top and sift on the sugar.

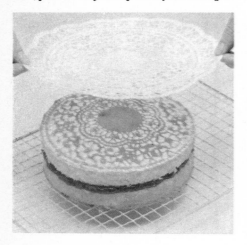

Gently lift the doily off the cake with the tips of your fingers.

and the salt. Cream the butter and sugar together until the mixture is pale and fluffy. Mix in the vanilla extract and cream or milk and beat in the remaining sugar.

Variations: **Chocolate Buttercream Frosting:** Add 2 ounces (50 grams) of melted semisweet chocolate with the cream and vanilla extract to the basic Buttercream Frosting. Alternatively, replace $\frac{1}{4}$ cup (25 grams) of the confectioners' sugar with cocoa.

Orange or Lemon Buttercream Frosting: Substitute the grated rind of $\frac{1}{2}$ orange or lemon and $4\frac{1}{2}$ tablespoons of orange or lemon juice for the cream in the basic Buttercream Frosting.

Fillings

In addition to jam and flavored whipped cream which need no further description, pastry cream (a type of custard) and lemon curd can also be used as cake fillings.

138

Pastry Cream
Makes $1\frac{1}{2}$ cups (12 oz)

2 egg yolks
4 tablespoons sugar
1 tablespoon cornstarch
1 tablespoon plus 1 teaspoon flour
$1\frac{1}{4}$ cups (300 ml) milk
$\frac{1}{2}$ teaspoon vanilla extract
1 egg white

In a medium-sized bowl, lightly beat the egg yolks with a fork. Add the sugar and beat the mixture until it is creamy. Sift in the cornstarch and flour a little at a time, beating constantly, then gradually mix in about one-quarter of the milk and the vanilla extract.

In a medium-sized saucepan, scald the remaining milk over high heat. Pour the hot milk into the egg-and-sugar mixture, beating well with a wire whisk. Return the mixture to the pan and, stirring constantly, bring it back to the boil. Remove the pan from the heat and beat the mixture until it is smooth. Set aside and allow it to cool.

In a small bowl, whisk the egg white with a wire whisk until it forms stiff peaks. Transfer about one-quarter of the warm cream mixture to a medium-sized bowl. Carefully fold the egg white into the mixture. Fold the egg-white mixture into the remaining cream in the saucepan. Return the saucepan to the stove and cook the mixture over low heat for 2 minutes, stirring occasionally.

Pour the cream into a bowl to cool

Lemon Curd
Makes 4 1-lb (2 kg) jars or 6 cups

$1\frac{1}{2}$ cups (350 g) butter, cut into small pieces
4 cups (900 g) sugar
thinly pared rind and juice of 6 large lemons
8 eggs, well beaten

Place a large heatproof mixing bowl over a pan half-filled with hot water. Put the butter, sugar, lemon rind and juice in the bowl. Set the pan over moderately low heat. Cook the mixture, stirring constantly with a wooden spoon, until the sugar has dissolved.

Using a wire whisk or rotary beater, beat in the eggs. Continue cooking, stirring constantly, for 35-40 minutes or until the lemon curd thickens.

Remove the pan from the heat. Lift the bowl out of the pan. With a slotted spoon,

remove and discard the lemon rind.

Ladle the lemon curd into clean, dry jam jars. Lightly press a circle of waxed paper onto the surface of the curd in each jar.

Cover the jars with plastic wrap and secure them with rubber bands. Label and store in a cool, dark, dry place.

Sauces

Sauces are the most frequent type of topping. They can be served hot or cold to enhance ice cream, crêpes, bread and rice puddings among many other desserts. Thin custard tastes best when made fresh.

Vanilla Custard
Makes about $2\frac{1}{2}$ cups (600 milliliters)

2 cups (450 ml) milk
1 vanilla bean
4 egg yolks
$\frac{1}{4}$ cup (50 g) sugar

Place the milk and vanilla bean in the top of a double boiler or in a heatproof bowl placed over a saucepan of water and heat to just below boiling point over moderate heat. When bubbles form at the edge of the pan, remove the milk from the heat. Cover the pan or bowl and set it aside for 10 minutes. Remove the vanilla bean with a slotted spoon, wash and set it aside for future use.

In a large bowl, beat the egg yolks and sugar together with a wire whisk until they are smooth and creamy. Gradually strain in the milk, stirring constantly. Pour the custard back into the top of the double boiler or bowl and cook over hot (not boiling) water for 3-5 minutes, or until the custard begins to thicken, stirring constantly with a wooden spoon. Care should be taken not to overcook the custard or it will curdle. The custard should be thick enough to coat the back of the spoon. Remove the pan or bowl from the heat and pour the custard into a bowl or pitcher. Serve warm or chilled.

Fresh fruit sauce

Fruit sauces can be made with fresh fruit, canned fruit or jam. Fresh fruit sauces can be frozen. Soft fruits such as raspberries, strawberries, plums, peaches and apricots are best for sweet fruit sauces.

To make a fresh fruit sauce, the fruit must be ripe and firm. Place the chosen fruit in a saucepan with just enough water to cover the bottom of the pan. Cook the fruit over moderate heat for 10-15 minutes, or until it is tender. Transfer it to a strainer placed over a bowl. With a wooden spoon, press the fruit through the strainer into the bowl. Add at least 1½ tablespoons or more of sugar or to taste. The juice of half a lemon will sharpen the flavor if it is weak.

Pour the sauce back into the saucepan if it is to be served hot and cook over moderate heat, stirring frequently, for 2 minutes, or until it is heated through. Place the strained sauce in the refrigerator to chill for 30 minutes if it is to be served cold.

Canned fruit sauce

This can be made with any sort of small canned fruit – berries, cherries, black currants. Serve as an accompaniment to ice cream, filled choux puffs or meringue chantilly.

28-ounce (1 kg) can of fruit
Peel and juice of 1 lemon
2 teaspoons arrowroot
2 tablespoons water

Drain the fruit and put it aside. Put the grated lemon peel and juice into a saucepan and bring slowly to a boil. Mix the arrowroot with the water until it has dissolved and add it to the boiling syrup. Stir vigorously until the mixture thickens slightly. Remove from the heat and extract the lemon peel. Add the reserved fruit. Serve hot or cold, but not chilled.

Jam sauce
Makes about 1½ cups (350 milliliters)

6 tablespoons jam
Grated rind and juice of 1 lemon
6 tablespoons sugar
1½ cups (800 ml) water
2 teaspoons cornstarch dissolved in 1½ tablespoons water

In a small saucepan, melt the jam with the lemon rind and juice, sugar and water over moderate heat, stirring with a wooden spoon until the sugar has completely dissolved. Remove the saucepan from the heat and set it aside for 10 minutes.

Add the cornstarch mixture to the jam mixture and stir well. Return the saucepan to the heat. Bring the sauce to the boil, stirring constantly. Remove from the heat and pour into a warmed sauce boat. It is excellent, when hot, served over ice cream or rice pudding.

Chocolate sauce

This is a semisweet sauce, suitable for using on ice creams, puddings, meringues and cakes.
Makes 2½ cups (600 milliliters)

6 oz (175 g) semisweet or cooking chocolate, broken into pieces
14-oz (425 ml) can evaporated milk
1 teaspoon vanilla extract
¼ teaspoon almond extract

In a double-boiler or in a heatproof bowl

Finished, luscious choux puffs, filled with a rich pastry cream mixture and topped with chocolate sauce.

placed over a pan of hot water, melt the chocolate with the milk, stirring occasionally. As soon as the chocolate has melted, remove the bowl or pan from the heat. Beat the vanilla and almond extracts into the chocolate mixture. Continue heating until the sauce is smooth. Serve warm.

Meringue topping
Meringue topping can be either the soft, melt-in-the-mouth type or crunchy depending on how long it is cooked and at what temperature. For either type of meringue use from 2-4 tablespoons (25-50 grams) of sugar for each egg white, depending on how sweet you want it to be. Two egg whites are sufficient for an 8-inch (20 centimeter) pie, three for a 9-inch (23 centimeter) one. In a medium-sized mixing bowl, using a wire whisk or electric beater, beat the egg whites until they are frothy. Gradually beat in the sugar and continue beating until the meringue mixture forms stiff peaks. Pile the meringue on top of the filling to cover it completely. For a soft meringue bake at 400°F (200°C), for 6-10 minutes, that is until just the peaks of the meringue are brown. For a crunchy meringue bake at 350°F (180°C) for 20-25 minutes, or until the meringue has set and is golden brown on top.

Chapter Seven

Preparing tasty food is the core of a good meal, but it is not the whole story. For dietary balance and attractive presentation are of almost equal importance. All meals, whether for single people, families, or guests, should contain variety in color, texture and nutrition.

Finishing touches are of three sorts, those that are built into the menu planning, those that are part of the table arrangement and general ambience, and those that garnish the food to enhance its attractiveness. Thus planning the finishing touches begins as soon as you think about a meal.

Meal planning

When planning your meal, remember color – if fish is served in white sauce, trim with parsley; ham should be accompanied by cauliflower and a green vegetable instead of carrots. Texture, too, should be important. Have contrasts within the same course and between courses. For example, crunchy raw vegetables with a smooth cheese quiche or a beef casserole followed by a crisp lettuce salad. Flavors should offer contrasts: a bland pudding after a spicy main course; a succulent roast followed by tangy citrus fruits.

By serving a variety of foods at a meal and in the course of a day, you ensure a balanced diet. But understanding the principles of nutrition is equally important.

Nutrition

As either menu planner or cook, you should know the basics of good nutrition, which should be observed in all meal planning. This will ensure good health and reduce the likelihood of obesity. It should also reduce your food budget, because the foods that are best for you are

often less expensive than those that provide little benefit.

Most foods contain three substances, carbohydrates, fats and proteins. Only a few foods are pure: sugar (100 percent carbohydrate); oil and lard (100 percent fat). Foods also contain minerals and vitamins, both of which are essential to good health, appearance and general well being.

Carbohydrates are the general name given to the starches and sugars in our diet. Virtually your entire intake is of vegetable origin, especially grains, with only traces found in meat, poultry and fish.

Fats are of both animal and plant origin, and everybody should have some of each kind daily. But since much of the fat in our diet is hidden, you should use a minimum of animal fats in cooking. It is important, however, to include some vegetable fats daily. Fats mainly of animal origin cause a build-up in the arteries of fatty substances called cholesterol, which can be dangerous to health (see p. 48). Thus as menu planner and cook you should work to keep total fat intake down, while ensuring an adequate intake of vegetable fats.

Your body uses carbohydrates to supply energy, and when the carbohydrates are used up it turns to the fats, converting them first to carbohydrates and then to energy. Conversely, excess carbohydrates are changed into fats for storage for future needs. Gaining weight means your food intake is greater than your energy needs, and your body is storing the rest as fat.

Proteins, which are of both animal and vegetable origin, form the building blocks for our bodies. They are made up of many different amino acids, of which eight are essential for adults and ten for children. Animal protein contains all the essential amino acids, whereas no vegetable protein contains all eight. Thus

vegetarians need to consume a wide range of protein foods to ensure adequate amounts of all the essential amino acids.

About 11 percent of an adult's food intake and 14 percent of a child's or adolescent's should be protein.

If your protein intake is greater than your body needs, the excess is converted into carbohydrates for energy (and from carbohydrates into fat for storage once energy needs are fulfilled).

Minerals are required for strong bones and teeth, for maintaining the correct composition of body fluids (blood, lymph), and for cell development.

The most important minerals are calcium, magnesium and phosphorus for teeth and bones; iron, phosphorus, potassium and sulphur for body cells, and sodium, chlorine and potassium for body fluids. Other minerals needed in minute amounts are usually supplied in a normal diet. In some inland parts of the world, however, iodine is lacking in the soil and hence is not found in vegetables. Goiter, the swelling and malfunctioning of the thyroid gland, can result from a complete lack of iodine in the diet. Eat salt-water fish or use iodized or sea salt if you have reason to believe your diet lacks sufficient iodine.

Vitamins are organic substances found in foods. They are also essential for maintaining a healthy body. If you follow a diet based on the seven food groups discussed below, you should get enough of all vitamins. Sometimes, however, your diet does become deficient, and in this case vitamin tablets are recommended.

Some vitamins, such as A, D and E, are often found in food with a high proportion of fat, whereas others, especially C and some of the B complex, are water soluble, which means they are lost when food is overcooked and decrease in amount when food is stored too long or exposed to air. A variety of diseases are caused by vitamin deficiency; most noteworthy is scurvy caused by a lack of vitamin C.

Calorie is the unit used to measure the energy output of food (in Europe soon to be replaced by a common unit called the *joule*). Pure protein and pure carbohydrate supply 116 calories per ounce (or 4 calories per gram), while pure fat supplies 263 calories per ounce (or 9 per gram). Calorie counts for foods differ greatly because few foods are pure.

Nutritionists recommend that adults obtain no more than 25 percent of their calorie intake from fats and the rest from carbohydrates and protein. The big problem for most people is to keep their fat consumption down. The cook can help here by frying fewer foods, draining fried food well on paper towels, and by using

less butter in cooking and on bread. And remember that those favorite snack foods chocolate, potato chips and nuts are extremely high in fats.

The number of calories needed depends on age, weight, height and amount of activity. Thus a 154-pound (70 kg) man requires 2600-2800 calories per day whereas a 126-pound (55 kg) woman needs 1850-2000. Children and adolescents require more calories in relation to their size, with a 56-pound (27 kg) child needing as much as an adult woman.

In order to fulfill all the nutritional needs described above, a variety of foods must be eaten daily. To help people choose these foods, some nutritionists have placed foods in seven categories and recommend the number of servings of each daily. Thus without counting

calories or proteins, minerals or vitamins you are able to achieve a daily balance. You will notice that alcoholic beverages and snack foods are not included; these supply calories without giving nutritive benefit.

Family Meal Planning

When you are planning meals, you must take into account foods eaten outside the home, both in terms of calories and of balanced diet. If foods from categories 1, 2, 5 and 7 predominate away from home, you should emphasize the other groups at breakfast and the evening meal.

Unless you are lucky or have only one to feed, you are going to have to balance the likes and dislikes of several people, while trying to maintain daily and weekly

Daily Nutritional requirements	
Category	**Minimum quantity daily**
1. Bread, cereals, flour	2 servings daily
2. Milk, milk products, including cheese	2 servings daily
3. Meat, poultry, fish, eggs, dried beans	1 or more servings daily
4. Leafy, green and yellow vegetables	2 servings daily
5. Potatoes, root and other vegetables not in 4, fruits	2 servings daily
6. Citrus fruits, tomatoes, strawberries, raw cabbage	1 or more servings daily
7. Butter, margarine, fats oils	2 tablespoons (25 grams) daily

variety. If you plan your menus in advance (see Buying Wisely in Chapter Two and the basic techniques discussed in Chapters Five and Six), obtaining variety will be easier. Try to include a new recipe weekly and introduce new foods occasionally.

When you are presented with the chance to broaden fussy eaters' habits, don't miss the opportunity. Being overly-solicitous at menu planning time only ensures limiting both your range as a cook and their overall appreciation of food. Be different, quietly serve the meal and see what happens. A grudging 'it was OK' means you should try it again next month. Even an outright 'no' may not mean 'never again'. Rely on your instincts as a gauge. If the food is good and well-prepared, enjoyment is sure to follow.

Try not to serve the same combinations every time – chicken and peas, steak and carrots – which can become tiresome and predictable. Also do not always serve the same meal on the same day of the week; every Monday should not be Sunday's leftovers, or every Wednesday hamburgers. In addition to your regular favorites, include things you enjoy less frequently or which are seasonal: beef tongue, scallops, game, asparagus, to name only a few.

A well-planned and calculated meal should not have small amounts of leftovers like a tablespoon of potato and a half piece of meat. But on special occasions you should plan to have enough leftovers for another meal, since large roasts are more economical and more succulent than smaller cuts. Also you save time and energy (both fuel and personal) in the cooking.

Above all keep the dinner atmosphere pleasant and relaxed. Meals should be the time for coming together for enjoyable, lively conversation and controversy and arguments should be avoided.

Cooking for guests

Party cooking should not differ greatly from family cooking, although you do have more details to think about. These comprise the menu, including perhaps wine, the table setting and your dress. What you prepare need not be complicated or expensive, though it should be carefully garnished and well presented. Smell, presentation and taste in that order determine the pleasure of the diners.

The success of a party is based on a combination of a well-planned menu, good cooking, and a relaxed host and/or hostess, who is with the guests most of the time. The last is more important than the food, because people have come to enjoy good talk and cameraderie, and the food is only an adjunct, albeit an important one, to this. A nervous, fussing host or hostess presenting an excellent meal will be less successful than one who can combine good food with a relaxed lively atmosphere.

In menu planning follow the same family-meal rules for achieving a balanced diet, choosing food from a larger number of categories. Additionally, control the number of calories by using rich additions sparingly. If you use cream in your main course sauce, avoid serving it with the dessert, no matter how customary.

You should also know the dietary needs of your guests (low calorie, low fat, allergic, diabetic, delicate digestion) and unobtrusively cater to it by serving diet-approved foods. (In serious cases consult with the person in advance to make sure.) The following menu would fit many diets: broiled stuffed mushroom or tomato, followed by baked fish, one or two vegetables, plain potatoes and a lightly dressed green salad, and ending with a fresh fruit salad with a meringue topping. It is festive, low in fat and calories, and filling. Those without special diets would be satisfied too.

The traditional menu calls for a first course which can be soup, fruit, meat, fish or vegetables. It should be relatively small, to whet the appetite not satisfy it, and contrast in color, texture and content with the main course. Often these initial courses can be served on individual plates – they can be put on the table before the guests come to it and will then form part of the table decor.

This course is followed by the main course which combines a protein dish (usually hot and meat, poultry or fish) with vegetables and probably a sauce. Everything should be served from warmed platters and dishes onto warmed plates. Garnishing, which need not be fancy, is important (see below), because appearance counts for a lot. Servings need not be large when you are offering many courses. A green or mixed salad could follow the main course using the same plates.

Next comes either the dessert or the cheese. Both are not necessary, but if you are serving both, keep the dessert light. Which you decide to have first is a matter of personal preference. When you are changing wines for the cheese course, it might, but does not have to, follow the dessert to give a break between the different wines.

Sometimes instead of, or in addition to cheese and dessert, a savory may be served, following the European custom. A savory is a small, highly seasoned dish generally hot, which is used to end a dinner. The original objective was to clear the palate before the port or liqueur.

Non-traditional dinners need not be divided so strictly into courses and, in fact, it is sometimes pleasant to serve a number of courses together, buffet style. The first course or appetizer can be healthy finger foods – raw vegetables, marinated mushrooms, shrimp and dip, to name only a few – to be eaten with pre-dinner drinks.

Organize preparations for a dinner party in the same way as for any other meal, though it is advisable to write out a full timetable (see methods of preparation, Chapters Five and Six). In addition to the food you must decide on how to set the table.

Table setting: When you are setting a table the rule is to place the cutlery you are going to use first at the outside. Knives and spoons go on the right, forks on the left. If your starter calls for a fork and knife put them farthest from the center; closer to the plate put the knife and fork for the main course. The dessert spoon is beside the plate or may be brought out with the dessert.

The wine glass (or glasses) go at the top right-hand corner of the setting with the glass you are using first on the right (outside). The bread and butter plate, possibly with a napkin on it, is placed to the left of the fork.

You serve from the left and clear from the right. At all but the most formal dinners it is acceptable to pass plates with food such as the meat, if the platter is too heavy or hot to handle .

At a dinner party you and your guests spend a large part of the evening sitting around the table, so how it looks is important. You can create a mood by the type of table you set. Crisp white linen or a lace cloth and napkins are perfect with sparkling glasses and fine china for a formal meal, solid-color or printed cotton sets off bright china or heavy earthenware to advantage.

Color is a mood maker too: for light summer meals plain pale colors or fresh floral cottons are attractive; in winter a richly colored cloth and napkins look both warm and welcoming. Have mats or trivets to put the hot serving dishes on; these can either match or contrast with the tablecloth.

Candles and flowers always make a table look festive, but remember that your guests would probably like to see one another without looking through or around the centerpiece. Even if a large centerpiece is on the table when the guests arrive, remove it before the meal is served, if possible, for everyone's comfort. A low centerpiece, perhaps with candles in it, may not interfere with the sight lines and can stay throughout the meal. Use non-drip candles, which are more expensive, but save your table and tablecloth from dripping wax.

Garnishes: Garnishes are any edible decorations that are added just before serving to improve the appearance of food. They are used with every part of the meal from appetizer to dessert, though not necessarily with every course. It would be unwise, for instance, to provide beautiful complex garnishes with several courses, because you would be overdressing the meal. One outstanding garnish, however, can be accompanied during a meal by several simple ones.

Simple garnishes frequently supply contrasts in color, texture or flavor. Hence the popularity of parsley, minced or as a sprig; and watercress with meats and non-green vegetables; and of whipped cream and flaked almonds on desserts. Other simple garnishes include diced or grated cheese, sliced or whole olives, onion rings (raw or marinated), minced fresh herbs, shirred hard-boiled eggs, toasted sesame seeds and shredded coconut. And remember aspic and colored gelatins. Citrus fruits, cut into slices or wedges, are used both for color and flavor.

Soup garnishes sometimes indicate what is being served. For example, asparagus tips are floated on a cream of asparagus soup or mushroom slices on a mushroom soup. At other times minced herbs or croûtons (small fried bread cubes) are used to supply contrasting flavor and texture.

Simple dessert garnishes include clustered fresh berries or glacéed fruits, chocolate shavings, tiny meringues and chopped nuts. On fresh fruit, shredded coconut or mint leaves may be used.

Garnishes can also be complex, requiring considerable cutting and combining or using an icing bag and nozzle. In most cases these decorations go better with canapés, appetizers, simple luncheon dishes and cold buffets rather than with a hot main dinner course. One exception is mashed potato piped around a serving platter or individual dishes with the main course, usually in a sauce piled in the center and reheated under the broiler. Cakes, too, can be magnificently decorated using an icing bag and the various nozzles available.

While garnishes are important for appearance, you must not use too many at once, for simplicity is always best. No food should be completely hidden by its garnish. In general, no more than two should be used at a time and, except for the dessert course, one of these should be green (parsley, fresh herbs, watercress). Thus, garnish a fish with lemon slices and finely minced parsley spread in a single line rather than randomly scattered, or chops with tomato wedges and watercress. For dessert, a pudding with whipped cream and a few chocolate curls is more appealing than one heaped with cream, chopped nuts and fruit.

Beverages

Beverages comprise all drinking liquids, including alcoholic ones. Coffee and tea are the most complex to deal with because of the wide range of choice and the numerous methods of brewing. Milk, which is a relatively simple beverage, is discussed elsewhere (see pages 52-54).

Tea

If tea were simple to make more people would drink a well-made cup. It is made from the leaves of the plant *Camellia sinensis*, which is widely cultivated in many tropical and sub-tropical regions of the world.

There are three principal classifications: Black, Green and Oolong.

Black Tea is the most common and still the most popular tea in the western world. Its leaves are fully fermented in the manufacturing process, which makes them black.

Green Tea is produced mainly in China and Japan, and for that reason is frequently referred to as China or Chinese tea. Its particular characteristic is that the leaf is dried immediately and does not undergo fermentation, which preserves the green color of the leaves. Green tea is more astringent in flavor than black tea and tends to be an acquired taste.

Oolong Tea is only partly fermented before drying and is manufactured in Taiwan and China. The leaves are brown in color and, when brewed, produce a pale brown tea with a characteristic aroma and flavor.

How to make tea

In order to make perfect tea every time follow this method:

Fill the kettle with water fresh from the cold tap and place over moderate heat. Just before the water boils, pour a little of it into the teapot to warm the pot and then discard the water. (This enables the tea to infuse better.) Place one teaspoon of tea per person and one 'for the pot' in the teapot. As soon as the water boils bring the teapot to the kettle and pour in the water. Place the lid on the pot and allow to stand for 3-5 minutes before using. Serve with milk, sugar or lemon to taste.

Iced tea, one of the great joys of life, especially when summer days are hot, can be a refreshing change anytime. Ideally, strong, freshly brewed tea is poured over many ice cubes that melt and cool the drink. But this method is extravagant and impractical when the supply of ice is limited. You can pour the leftover morning brew into a jar and chill it, or make a second strong pot to strain and refrigerate.

To serve, place three or four ice cubes in a tall glass, pour the tea over them slowly, and serve. Pass sugar and lemon separately. Sometimes a sprig of mint is added as well. Tea that is cloudy has been made with hard water; sometimes it clears when ice is added. Sugar will cloud it as well.

Tea leaves should be stored in airtight containers to retain freshness and full flavor. Also buy often and in small amounts. Experiment with unfamiliar teas and vary them with the time of day and occasion. So, you see, tea can be far more exciting than just a cup of hot water and a teabag.

Coffee

The flavor of coffee, like that of wine, depends greatly on where it has been grown, because climate, soil, elevation, aspect and age all affect the final product.

Most packaged coffee consists of a blend from several sources chosen to complement one another and to give a distinctive, uniform flavor. Some coffees, however, come from a single area. Most Brazilian coffee, for instance, is blended because it is somewhat harsh, but the finest quality is sold unblended as Brazilian. Other names found on special coffees are Colombia, Kenya, Blue Mountain (Jamaica) and moka (Yemen). Each has unique, subtle differences in flavor.

The different coffee-making methods discussed below require grinds of different degrees of fineness. Infused and percolated coffees call for a medium grind; the filtered and suction method for a fine grind.

How to make coffee

Some basic principles apply to coffee-making no matter what type of coffee you

144

make. The best coffee, for instance, is made from freshly roasted beans ground just before you make the coffee. Ideally, coffee should not be allowed to boil, and although 1-2 minutes of boiling is not detrimental to the taste and flavor of the finished coffee, continued boiling will certainly impair its quality.

Basically, western-style coffee-making consists of passing boiling water through coffee grounds, carrying with it the color and flavor but leaving the grounds behind, usually in a separate section of the coffee pot.

Infused coffee: Pour boiling water onto freshly ground coffee in a warmed container (about 1 tablespoon of coffee per person). Stir the coffee and leave the container in a warm place for about 10 minutes. Pour the coffee through a strainer into a heated coffee pot, or straight into coffee cups.

Percolated coffee: Methods vary widely according to the type of percolator used, and it is, therefore, wise to follow the instructions given with your percolator. The principle involved, however, is that the water circulates through the coffee grounds, extracting the flavor and color and then drips through a strainer, leaving the grounds behind.

Filtered coffee: This is a great favorite in France, and can be produced by placing a perforated filter over a cup or pot and filling the filter with about 1 tablespoon of coffee per person. Then pour boiling water through the filter, to extract flavor and color as it drips into the cup or pot below.

Suction method: First, fill the lower container with water and the upper with coffee grounds. On heating, the water is sucked up the funnel between the two containers, remaining there for about 3 minutes. When it is removed from the heat, the coffee filters down into the lower container, leaving the grounds in the upper section.

Espresso or Italian coffee: This is strong, dark, slightly bitter and made under pressure in a machine. It can also be made in a drip pot, or *napoletana*, the basket of the inner cylinder being filled with very finely ground coffee and the outer cylinder with water. The spouted vessel is then placed on top of the drip pot, with the spout facing downward. Over low heat, the water is brought to a boil. The *napoletana* is then reversed so that the spout points upward and lets

the water drip slowly through the grounds.

Arabic, Turkish or Greek coffee: This is more complicated – and more wasteful in terms of the amount of coffee grounds used. It is, nevertheless, a most attractive beverage and one that is becoming increasingly popular in western countries. To make Turkish coffee, boil water in a Turkish coffee-maker over moderate heat. Add sugar to taste (usually about 1 teaspoon per cup) and 2½ teaspoons of very finely pulverized coffee grounds to the pot, allowing the coffee grounds to remain on the surface of the water. Bring to the boil again, then remove from the heat to allow the froth to die down. Boil again, then remove from the heat. As the froth dies down, stir the coffee grounds into the liquid. Pour the coffee immediately into small demitasse cups, allowing 1-2 minutes before drinking to let the sediment sink to the bottom of the cup.

Instant coffee: Although not up to the standard of good freshly brewed coffee, instant coffee is used in most homes. And with a little care its quality can be improved. Most important, use enough powder. Next, instead of pouring boiling water directly onto the powder (which scorches and gives it a bitter taste), pour it into the bowl of a metal spoon and let it run into the cup or pot. This cools the water just enough to ensure maximum flavor.

Storage

Once roasted, coffee does not keep fresh for long. Therefore buy it in small amounts and keep it in airtight jars in a cool place.

Beer

Beer is a brewed and fermented beverage made from malted barley or other cereal grains. It is flavored with hops, the tiny blossoms of the hop vine. Since the making of beer dates back to the beginning of history, it is not surprising that many types of beer, with different flavors and consistencies, have developed. The two major divisions are light beer, the more popular in most of the western world, and dark beer. The differences depend on how the grain has been treated before fermentation and on the particular type of yeast used for the fermentation. I

Irish coffee and a plunger coffee pot.

general, beer contains about 3-7 percent alcohol, though a few types have a higher alcohol content.

In the western world, light beers are favored today, and lager has probably become the most widely popular. The famous beers of Denmark, Holland, and Germany are all lagers, and most countries have home-brewed lagers as well. In England, bitter, slightly darker and less carbonated than lager, is popular. The term ale encompasses all the light brews that are not lagers.

Stout and porter are in most places only known as names found in old books, but both remain popular in some areas. Ireland, for instance, is famed for its stout. Both these beers are dark, or black, made from roasted malt, sometimes with the addition of burned sugar.

Beer may be served at any time. Its characteristic sharp tang complements highly flavored or spicy dishes and such foods as hamburgers, steaks, pizza, corned beef and cabbage, stews, sausages, cold meats, all pork dishes and fried dishes. Almost all the sharper cheeses go well with beer or ale.

Wine

Wine is the fermented juice of grapes. One species of vine, *Vitis vinifera*, produces almost all the grapes used in wine-making (the only exception being some hardy vines native to the northeastern United States which are the species *Vitis labrusca*).

Wine is an alcoholic drink, ranging from about 7-13 percent alcoholic strength for table wines and around 20 percent for fortified wines. Wine can be red, white or rosé, still or sparkling, sweet or dry.

Wine is made wherever grapes are grown, that is, in most non-tropical areas without extremely harsh winters. Major producing areas lie along the northern shore of the Mediterranean from Cyprus and Greece to Spain and also in North Africa. Italy has the largest wine output, but arguably the greatest wines are produced in France, in areas north of the Mediterranean shore and in Germany, around the Rhine and Moselle valleys. Other superb wine areas include the one around Lake Balaton in Hungary and in the Balkans, particularly northern Yugoslavia. In the U.S., California is known for outstanding wines, and New York State has several excellent wines. Others

146

of good quality come from Australia, South Africa, Chile and Argentina. Frequently, wines from less well-known areas give good quality for less money.

Wine and Food

Wine is in the happy position of being inextricably bound up with the pleasant ritual of eating good food. Whether a simple cheese and bread snack or a full gourmet *haute cuisine* dinner, wine can and does add to its luster and enjoyment.

There are some general guidelines as to which wine best accompanies different foods, but they are all necessarily subjective and need not be followed slavishly – if you prefer a red wine with fish or a light white wine with a rich meat casserole, the choice is yours. The wine and food chart on page 148 is intended to serve as a guide for the inexperienced wine drinker who is uncertain about what to purchase and/or wishes to try something different. But, in addition, remember these general 'natural' rules – mainly based on common sense rather than on a refined palate!

1. National cuisines and wines (if the country produces wine) usually complement each other and whenever possible should be served together – a Château Lafite, beautiful though it is, will do relatively little for a rich Spaghetti Bolognese while a good rustic Chianti Classico will; and by the same token, that same Chianti will not enhance the delicate flavor of Beef Wellington in the same way as a Château Lafite.

2. If you are serving more than one wine with a meal, the general – and sensible – thing to do is to serve white before red, young wines before mature, dry before sweet.

Buying Wines

Most of us, most of the time, buy 'vin ordinaire' or ordinary, usually inexpensive wine. Some such wines can be awful, but many are surprisingly good. And the only way to discover which you like is by tasting. Make a point of remembering the name and the shipper of wines you have enjoyed. If you find you like several wines from the same source, it can be worth trying other wines distributed by the same company.

In stores, examine the labels, noting how specific the information is. Something called 'dry red table wine' can come from any source and is likely to be a blend of

wines from many different places, probably even from several different countries or regions. Look for California varietal wines — chablis, pinot noir — or areas — Napa Valley. California wines are noted for their uniform quality, and only the most expensive have detailed labels. Inexpensive wines are generally good value for money. They are blended with the name on the bottle indicating the predominant variety of grape. Expensive wines are winery bottled using grapes of one type from a local area; often they are dated, though quality varies less than in Europe.

At the expensive end of the market are the château-bottled wines of France, the village-named wines of the Rhine and Moselle. Many have specific and identifiable names, almost all will be subject to the *appellation controlée* laws of their region. They are almost always expensive, many should not be drunk until 8-12 years after the date on the bottle, and for a special occasion there is absolutely nothing to beat them.

Wine continues to grow and develop even after it is bottled, therefore, you are dealing with a living substance which must be handled gently. No wine should be bought and drunk on the same day. This is because it has been shaken up in transit, which makes it bitter and unpleasant. Even an inexpensive wine will improve by resting quietly for a few days; for expensive wines the resting period should be longer.

Red wines should be opened in advance. With fine wines the timing depends on age and variety; with more ordinary ones an hour or so is plenty. Decanting red wine helps to aerate it, bringing out its full flavor. With old, expensive wines, decanting is also done in order to leave any deposit behind. Pour gently and slowly in either case so as not to disturb the wine. A wine basket is unnecessary with young wines.

White wines and rosés are not normally uncorked in advance.

Red wines should be served at a cool room temperature of about 65°F (18°C). White wine, rosé and champagne are all served chilled. The sweeter the wine the colder it should be. Thus a dry wine should be refrigerated about 2 hours before serving, a sweet one up to 5 hours in advance. Wine that is too cold lacks full flavor.

Since wine loses its flavor soon after

opening, if you use only a small quantity from a bottle it is advisable to transfer the remaining wine into a smaller bottle and re-cork it. Ideally, the wine should be used within a week of opening the bottle.

The best all-purpose glass for most wines should be clear, to show the true colour of the wine, a tulip shape, so that the bouquet of the wine isn't lost and, most important, the right size. Glasses should never be filled more than half-full; therefore a general all-purpose glass for wine should be about 8-10 fluid ounces (250-300 milliliters) in size. Champagne should not be served in the old fashioned shallow shape since these allow the sparkling bubbles to evaporate too quickly.

Storing wine

Not everyone has or needs a wine cellar. All you need is a dark place with a relatively uniform temperature, preferably between 50°-60°F (10°-18°C), though uniformity is more important than cool temperature.

Bottles must rest on their sides; never stand upright, for the cork will dry out and let air in and air can ruin wine. Thus you will need either wine racks (bought or homemade) or a sturdy wine box or two. (Sherry cartons are often more durable than wine cartons.) Always remove the bottles gently to disturb them as little as possible.

Cooking with wine

The addition of wine to a recipe gives flavor to the blandest of stews, transforms the most ordinary dessert into an elegant one and adds zest to otherwise dull sauces.

Cooking with wine can actually save money on food, too. Think of the amount of money you can spend on special sauces, pickles and chutneys to liven up dull dishes; a stew or casserole dish cooked with wine never requires such additions at the table. And wine used in a marinade can tenderize even the cheapest cuts of meat.

Some final tips

Having done all the work, you face the question of what to wear. Naturally style is personal and clothing should suit the occasion, but beyond this give some thought to practical considerations. First wear clothes you can work in comfortably and easily. They should not be too tight

Moselle wine with grape name (reisling) and an AP (quality) number on the label.

or too warm. You are going to have to move around a lot as well as bend often. Wear comfortable shoes for the same reason. And for women, especially, watch out for your sleeves. Long or three-quarter length sleeves have a nasty way of scooping up gravy, catching cooking-spoon handles and knocking off frostings and meringues as you reach across to do something. The best advice is don't wear such sleeves; second best advice is to fold them up out of harm's way.

Wear a big coverall apron while transferring food to serving dishes and carving. If you do not have one, tuck one dish towel in at your neck and a second at your waist. Spots are annoying and difficult to get out of good clothes and cleaning bills are high.

Ultimately the recipe for any dinner or party boils down to plan ahead, cook ahead, do your best, stay flexible, and enjoy the meal, your family and your guests. Take occasional disaster as it comes, neither making a great fuss over it nor letting it cause complete depression. These things happen to everyone. If unexpected people turn up, add another vegetable or another course or even another type of meat. One successful party that increased from six to ten without warning was stretched out by serving a pound of sausages, each halved, along with the small roast. A simple savory of grilled cheese on small bread squares served with a good sprinkling of freshly ground pepper followed the dessert. Nobody left hungry and all enjoyed the evening including the host and hostess.

The label of a blended light Italian wine, with the Italian equivalent of appellation côntrolée.

A label with all the signs of a medium-quality white Brugundy, including 'mise en bouteilles'.

Wine and food chart

Hors d'oeuvre

Pâté, quiche, etc

Fairly strong dry white, such as Traminer, a Rhine wine such as Rüdesheimer, rosé such as Rosé d'Anjou or light red, such as Beaujolais

Salad or cold hors d'oeuvre

Dry white, such as Alsatian Sylvaner or Yugoslavian Zilavka or Riesling

Soups

Dry sherry or a light Madeira is served with consommés, otherwise wine is not usually served with soup

Fish

Broiled or lightly poached fish

Light wine, such as Chablis, Pouilly Fuissé or Moselle

Fish in rich cream sauce

Heavy white, such as white Burgundy (Meursault, Montrachet) or Rhine wine, such as Niersteiner

Shellfish

Light white (Chablis is traditional with oysters), Muscadet, Italian Soave or a slightly flinty Loire, such as Sancerre or Vouvray

Shellfish served as a risotto or with rich sauce

Rosé, such as Tavel, a white Loire wine, such as Pouilly Fumé or a white Burgundy, such as Puligny Montrachet

Smoked Fish

Heavy white, such as white Burgundy, Alsatian Traminer or a spicy Rhine spätlese wine

Dark meat

Beef, roasted or broiled

Bordeaux, such as Château Montrose or St. Emilion (Any good Bordeaux is perfect with a roast.)

Beef casseroles and stews

Sturdy red Burgundy, such as Beaune, a Rhône wine, such as Châteauneuf-du-Pape, a heavier Italian red, such as Barolo or a Hungarian Egri Bikaver

Steaks

Bordeaux, such as St. Estephe, a medium red Burgundy, such as Nuits St. Georges, or a Californian Cabernet Sauvignon

Lamb, roasted or broiled

Bordeaux, such as a Margaux, a light Burgundy, such as Beaujolais or Macon or a light Italian wine, such as Bardolino or Valpolicella or a Californian Cabernet Sauvignon

Lamb casseroles, stews and risottos

Bordeaux, such as a Medoc, Cabernet Sauvignon, an Italian wine such as Chianti or Valpolicella

Game (grouse, partridge, pheasant)

Bordeaux, such as St. Emilion or Château Haut-Brion

Hare, venison

Strong red, such as Côtes du Rhône or a heavy Burgundy, such as Chambertin

White meat

Pork

Medium-sweet white, such as Graves or Orvieto or a rosé, such as Côtes de Provence or Mateus

Veal

Strong white, such as Montrachet, Pinot Chardonnay or a light red, such as Valpolicella, Zinfandel or Beaujolais

Ham

Rosé, such as Tavel or Rosé d'Anjou or a light red, such as Macon

Poultry

Chicken, cooked simply

Heavier white, such as Hungarian Riesling or a white Burgundy

Chicken cooked with red wine or in a very rich vegetable-type stew

Light red, such as Beaujolais or Fleurie

Duck

Heavy white Burgundy, such as Meurseult or a rosé, such as Tavel

Goose

White, such as Rhine wine or an Alsatian or Hungarian Riesling

Turkey

Heavy white, such as Traminer, a Rhine wine or a rosé, such as Côtes de Provence

Cheese

Soft (Brie, Camembert, etc)

Medium red Burgundy, such as Beaune or a Bordeaux, such as St. Julien

Medium (Port-Salut, Cheddar, etc)

Light, fruity red, such as Fleurie or Beaujolais, or a spicy white, such as Alsatian Gewürtztraminer or a Tavel

Cream or Goat's

Medium white, such as Graves, an Alsatian Traminer or a Rhine wine

Blue cheese (Stilton, etc)

Light red such as Bardolino, a medium Burgundy such as Brouilly or a Cabernet Sauvignon

Desserts

Sauternes or Barsac are the traditional dessert wines, but any German wine marked spätlese or auslese would also be suitable. For an extra rich dessert, try a Hungarian Tokay.

After-dinner

Port, the heavier Madeiras or, for a change, a mature Hungarian Tokay or the 'queen of Sauternes', Château d'Yquem

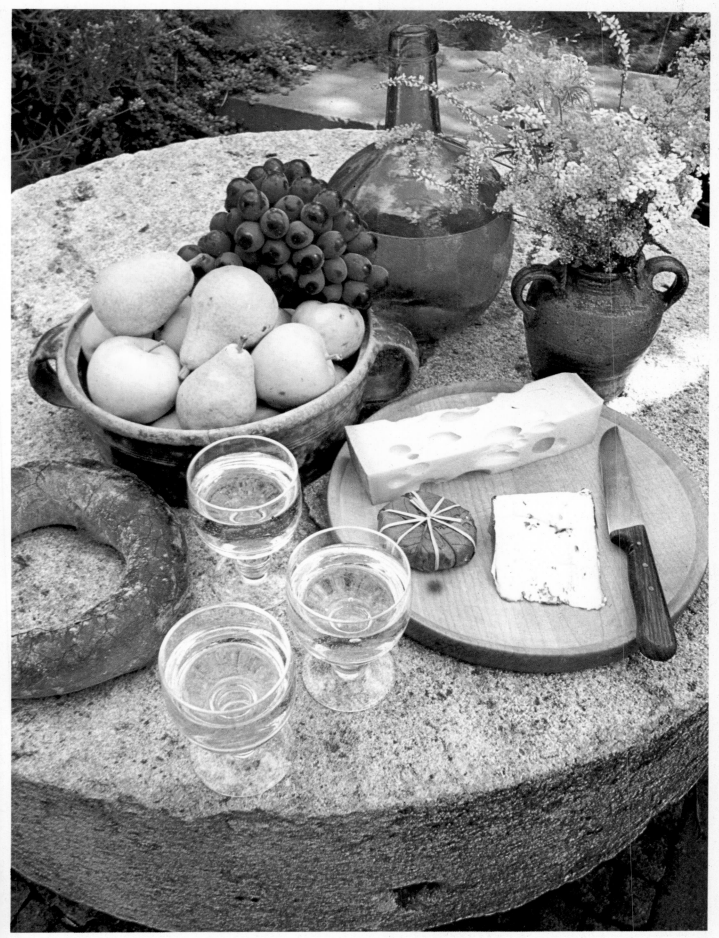

Index

Note: Numbers in italics refer to illustrations.

Picture Credits
Bryce Attwell 55;
Barnaby's Picture Library 22/3;
Camera Press/Photo by H. von Sterneck 149;
Alan Duns 4/5, 16, 47, 49, 53, 59, 65, 72, 84, 88, 93, 94, 120, 127, 128, 129, 131, 145;
Eddie Ely 30, 116t;
Melvin Grey 24;
Graeme Harris 62/3;
John Hovell 32, 36;
Courtesy of Hygena 2000 11;
Paul Kemp 13b, 109, 136, 137, 138;
Don Last 80;
David Levin 13t, 109, 137, 138;
David Meldrum 33, 90, 91, 119;
Roger Phillips 2/3, 12, 19, 27, 43, 45, 50/1, 57, 60, 77, 81, 82, 83, 86, 87, 113, 116b, 118, 123, 124, 125, 132, 139, 147;
Courtesy of Thorn Electrical Appliances 28;
Transworld Feature Syndicate 141;
Jerry Tubby 35;
Courtesy of W. F. Rational Kitchens 6.